A Primer on the Book of Revelation

A Primer on the Book of Revelation

TED NOEL

RESOURCE *Publications* • Eugene, Oregon

A PRIMER ON THE BOOK OF REVELATION

Copyright © 2010 Ted Noel. All rights reserved. Except for brief quotations in critical publications or reviews, no part of this book may be reproduced in any manner without prior written permission from the publisher. Write: Permissions, Wipf and Stock Publishers, 199 W. 8th Ave., Suite 3, Eugene, OR 97401.

Resource Publications
A Division of Wipf and Stock Publishers
199 W. 8th Ave., Suite 3
Eugene, OR 97401
www.wipfandstock.com

ISBN 13: 978-1-55635-532-5

Manufactured in the U.S.A.

Scripture taken from the NEW AMERICAN STANDARD BIBLE®, Copyright © 1960, 1962, 1963, 1971, 1972, 1973, 1975, 1977, 1995 by The Lockman Foundation. Used by permission.

Scripture taken from HOLY BIBLE, NEW INTERNATIONAL VERSION®. Copyright © 1973, 1978, 1984 by International Bible Society. Used by permission of Zondervan Publishing House.

Contents

Acknowledgments vii
Introduction ix

1. Patterns, Patterns, Patterns 1
2. Housekeeping (1:1–8) 11
3. Hello, Old Friend! (1:9–20) 17
4. "You Are Here" (2:1–4:1) 24
5. "Come on Up!" (4:2–11) 37
6. Coronation! (5:1–14) 43
7. I Hear Hoof Beats (6:1–17; 8:1, 3–5) 49
8. Twelve Thousand from Twelve Tribes (7:1–17) 63
9. Sound the Trumpet! (8:2, 6–9:21; 11:15a, 19) 69
10. When It's Over, It's *Over!* (10:1–11) 86
11. Measuring the Temple (11:1–14) 91
12. Bowls Full of Wrath (15:1—16:12; 16:17–17:2) 101
13. Armageddon! (16:13–16) 110
14. Once Over, Lightly 113
15. The Controversy over Worship, Part I (12:1–17) 119
16. The Controversy over Worship, Part II (13:1–18) 125
17. The Controversy over Worship, Part III (14:14–20) 135
18. Three Angels (14:1–13) 139

19 Millennium! (20:1–21:9) 145

20 The Harlot Rides the Beast (17:3–18) 154

21 One Called Faithful and True (19:11–21) 158

22 Two Choirs (18:1—19:10) 161

23 The New Jerusalem (21:10—22:5) 165

24 That's a Wrap! (22:6–21) 170

Appendix A—"666" in Perspective 173
Appendix B—The Year/Day Principle 187
Appendix C—The Structure of the Book of Revelation 192
Appendix D—The Fate of the Wicked 198

Acknowledgments

Where can I start to give thanks for all those who helped me in the preparation of this book? Obviously, the Lord who got my attention in 1993 is the First Cause and inspiration. He led me out of a dark hole into His gracious light, and set a fire for study in me.

Next, I must thank my late father for his devotion to critical thinking. In our home the clearest mind carried the day, whether in board games or debate. The value of this was driven home as Dad worked overtime on the team that got Apollo 13 home safely. He used that same clear careful logic to unravel the Gordian knot surrounding Revelation 17. Following his footsteps, I've tried to be as logical as possible as I listened to God's voice in the Apocalypse. I refused to accept any conclusion that didn't have clear logical support from scripture.

I can't leave out my wife Nancy. She has endured countless hours when I isolated myself in my study, reading commentaries, sorting out scriptural bits, and generally working away from her. When I slowed down, she encouraged me to keep going to complete the manuscript. She even sat through (and professed to enjoy) many hours of class discussion at Sabbath Grace Fellowship, where we used my first draft as a study guide. When I fell away from the task of completing the final text, she nudged me back into action.

Having mentioned SGF, I have to thank the class. We knocked things around pretty well when we went through Revelation. There were ideas and challenges from many angles. These led to many rewrites to include things the class thought was important. They also refined the way I said things. That made the final product more understandable and kept Christ front and center.

There are many professional theologians who, perhaps unwittingly, contributed to the book. Alan Bandy showed me the "in the Spirit" vision markers. Hans LaRondelle brought out the thematic organization of the Seals, Trumpets, and Bowls. Gregory Beale explored the Old Testament history of John's Greek grammar. There are many more, and I'm sure any list I might create would leave someone out or include someone else who might not prefer to be associated with me.

Very little of this book can properly be called "original." All of it builds on those who've gone before. None of it would be possible without their work. Perhaps John of Salisbury said it best, back in the twelfth century.

> We are like dwarves sitting on the shoulders of giants. We see more, and things that are more distant, than they did, not because our sight is superior or because we are taller than they, but because they raise us up, and by their great stature add to ours.

Ted Noel
Maitland, Florida
July, 2009

Introduction

Of making many books there is no end; and much study is a weariness of the flesh. Let us hear the conclusion of the whole matter: Fear God, and keep his commandments: for this is the whole duty of man.

(Eccl 12:12–13 KJV)

As I write these words, I'm teaching the book of Revelation to a class of beginning Christians. Why, you may ask, would I choose *that* book? After all, theologians of all persuasions for many centuries have said it was the most difficult book in the Bible. John Calvin refused to write a commentary on it and Martin Luther wished it wasn't even there.

When we look at proposed interpretations, the picture gets worse. Every possible flight of fancy has been published as the "last word." Some see literal monsters and unspeakable horrors. Others see figurative descriptions of past and future history. Most apply the visions to their own time, and think that John was seeing the evils that they saw in front of them. Some even take the book as a blow-by-blow description of coming events. With all this confusion and controversy, why would I subject beginners to such a book? Shouldn't I reserve it for an advanced seminary class?

We find the answer in its opening words.

> The Revelation of Jesus Christ, which God gave Him to show to His bond-servants, the things which must shortly take place; and He sent and communicated it by His angel to His bond-servant John, who bore witness to the word of God and to the testimony of Jesus Christ, even to all that he saw. (Rev 1:1–2 NAS)[1]

The book is about Jesus! The central issues of the gospel are there for us. They're a blessing for everyone who serves God (v. 3).

---

1. We'll be using the New American Standard Bible most of the time. Any place where we don't use it will be noted.

Revelation *does* require a bit of work, since it's written in symbolic language. God made sure that we'd see that by saying that it was "symbolized" to John.[2] This tells us that we should look for the biblical source for the unusual things in the visions.

John's original audience was familiar with Jewish traditions. Jews lived all through the Roman Empire, and they set up synagogues in many major cities. The apostles visited these synagogues, and Jewish converts were prominent members of early churches. This means that many of the images John recorded would have been obvious to them. But it's easy for us to forget that John was a *Jewish* disciple of a *Jewish* rabbi named Jesus.

The images John recorded *aren't* so obvious to us. We *aren't* Jewish. We didn't go to Hebrew school, read *Torah*, and celebrate the *Bar Mitzvah* at our twelfth birthday.[3] Few of us read biblical Hebrew. I hear you asking, "Why are you talking about Hebrew when John wrote in Greek?"

Scholars examining Revelation have noted two key features of the book. First, John used the Hebrew Scriptures a lot.[4] He learned his theology from Jesus, and He taught from the Old Testament.[5] John's thought patterns come from this foundation, which he uses over 800 times.[6] Sometimes he used exact phrasing or technical wording. Other times he used clearly recognizable Old Testament ideas. This means that we have to use John's Jewish thought pattern to understand Revelation.[7]

Sometimes John's Greek grammar is really bad.[8] Bishops of the early church didn't understand why John wrote that way, since they weren't as well founded in Old Testament Hebrew as John was. Now we know that John wasn't using bad grammar at all. Instead, he was quoting the Hebrew

---

2. The word translated "communicated" is *semaino*, and suggests communication by way of symbols.

3. To any Messianic Jews reading this, please accept my apologies. Most people who read this book won't be Jewish.

4. This is the Old Testament. Modern Jews call it the *TaNaKh*.

5. It would have been extraordinarily difficult for Jesus to teach from the New Testament, since its first book wasn't written until decades after he died.

6. Since there are only 404 verses in the book, it's fair to say that it's saturated with Old Testament material.

7. I often tell people that you can't understand the book without wearing a yarmulke.

8. Dionysius of Alexandria (died 264-265 AD) said that John's "use of the Greek language is not accurate, but he employs barbarous idioms, in some places committing downright solecisms." (from Eusebius, *Ecclesiastical History* 7.25.26-27)

Scriptures, which he translated word-for-word into Greek.[9] Because of differences between the two languages, the good grammar of Hebrew sometimes became bad grammar in Greek. John did this to point us back to his starting place to bring its meaning into the book.

This shows that we need to learn about the Old Testament. In particular, we need to study the temple, since it was the center of Hebrew identity. Its architecture and services are part of almost every part of Revelation.

There's another reason we need to know about the temple. It teaches us about Jesus. The incense burning on the golden altar was an acted-out prophecy of the prayers of the saints rising before God.[10] The mercy seat on the Ark of the Covenant was God's throne on earth (Lev 16:2), and pointed to his throne in heaven (Ps 11:4).

Each of these acted-out prophecies is called a "type." A type points forward from its small reality to a much larger truth called the "antitype."[11] For example, when John the Baptist said "Behold, the Lamb of God who takes away the sin of the world!" (John 1:29), he identified Jesus as the (large) antitype of the (small) sacrificial lamb type in the temple.

My beginners haven't had any trouble understanding typology because the types in the temple point forward to Jesus, who is the heart and soul of the gospel. Typology is another way of explaining the gospel, and the gospel is what brought them to Christ.

Almost every week I ask the class this key question: "What is the first rule of biblical interpretation?" They answer, "The Bible interprets itself." Now, I know that sounds like I'm telling you that you'll learn Greek by reading Greek, even if you don't know what the letters are. That's obviously nonsense, so let me explain what's going on.

When we have to figure out what a symbol means, we'll usually find the answer by searching through the Bible.[12] First we'll see how John used

---

9. Sometimes the quotes are from the Septuagint (abbreviated LXX), a translation of the Hebrew Scriptures into Greek done about 200 BC. Other times it appears that John directly translated the Hebrew into Greek himself.

10. This symbolic use of incense is explicit in Revelation 5:8 and 8:3–4.

11. It's easy in English to think that "anti" means "opposed to." It really means "in place of," so the "antitype" comes "in place of" the "type."

12. The infrequent exception to this rule comes from the occasional mention of a common item from John's day, such as the white stone in Revelation 2:17.

the term other places in Revelation. Often that will solve the riddle.[13] If that isn't enough, we'll look at other passages that use the same language. Most of the time, the symbol will mean the same thing in both places.

> But know this first of all, that no prophecy of Scripture is a matter of one's own interpretation, for no prophecy was ever made by an act of human will, but men moved by the Holy Spirit spoke from God. (2 Pet 1:20–21)

Peter says that we aren't supposed to interpret prophecy by ourselves. God always reveals the proper interpretation. He told the prophets what message to write. He also told his servants how to explain His prophecies. So if we want to understand the prophets, we need to listen to them.

The book of Revelation isn't about strange beasts or plagues. Those bits of the story are symbols that help us understand how the gospel will play out in history. They come from things John learned in Hebrew school. If we learn about those things, we'll understand them, too.

This book is written for the everyday Christian who's willing to open his Bible. Because John's literary source is the Old Testament, we'll go there a lot. My class enjoys this, since it helps them see the gospel in every part of the Bible. Sometimes the process of discovery will make us dig deep. This can make my comments seem stiff. I'll avoid that like the plague, but please forgive me if I get a bit academic once in a while.

Next, there will be a lot of text citations in parentheses. Texts from Revelation will be just numbers—chapter and verse. After all, that's the book we're exploring. Citations from outside Revelation will include the book name, using standard abbreviations. A citation after a scripture quote tells where that scripture was found. Other citations will tell where to find texts that support the point I'm making. Sometimes a citation will begin with "cf." That's the abbreviation for the Latin word *confer*, meaning "compare." Texts beginning with "cf." are there to give you a broader comparison to the text I'm using to make my point. Occasionally I'll use "ff." after a citation. That means I'm giving you the starting text. If you read on, you'll get the full picture of what I'm talking about.

As you've already noticed, there will be footnotes. Most of the time, a note will say something that might be distracting if it was in the main text.

---

13. One good example is the term "the great city" used in Revelation 11:8. In this text it's a bit unclear, but in the seven other places John uses it, it always means Babylon. That means that it means Babylon in 11:8 as well.

You've already seen a few of those. Other times the note will be a reference citation. We need them since this book has to respect standards of good scholarship, even if it's written in a relaxed style. Some books put the notes at the end of the chapter or even at the end of the book. I think that's rude because it makes you search for information that should literally be right under your thumb at the bottom of the page.

Sometimes a picture explains things better than words can. I'll put that picture on the page. Sometimes there will be really important ideas that deserve extra emphasis. I'll put those in highlight boxes.

Unfortunately, we can't study the Bible properly without spending some time with original languages. Most modern translations are pretty good, but there are some places where they miss the flavor of the original Hebrew or Greek. Once in a while they even get it wrong.[14] When those problems affect our understanding, we'll tackle the original Greek and Hebrew. For example, there are two kinds of crowns—the laurel wreath of victory (*stephanos* in Greek) and the king's crown (*diadema* in Greek). They're both normally translated "crown." The difference is important, but I'll try to keep discussions like that as non-technical as I can.

There are lots of commentaries on Revelation. Each one has something to offer, even this one! But each one was written by somebody other than God, including this one. That means you need to be careful to cross-check everything I say against what God says in the Bible.

As the teacher says, "My son, be warned: the writing of many books is endless, and excessive devotion *to books* is wearying to the body" (Eccl 12:12). To include every good point would make this book incredibly wearying. To paraphrase John 21:25, "The world could not contain the book." I can't do that to you. You want to strengthen your mind and your heart, not your muscles.

I'll try to include enough details to cover the essential parts of the subject. But I'll also try to avoid boring you with them. There are enough sermons that put you to sleep. Revelation should be interesting. Maybe I can help you to be as excited about the book as I am.

Before you dig deep into Revelation, you may want to read this book's companion volume, *A Primer on the Book of Daniel*.[15] Since Revelation

---

14. Please don't think I'm saying I'm a better translator than the people on the Bible translation teams. I'm not! But all translations have theological biases, and once in a while those biases force a translation away from the original intention.

15. *A Primer on the Book of Daniel* is also available from Resource Publications (2009).

uses Daniel more than any other Old Testament book, a good foundation in Daniel will make it easier to understand Revelation.

God gave us Revelation to encourage us. Let's walk together through the book that reveals more of Christ than any other single book in the Bible.

1

Patterns, Patterns, Patterns

On my first day in medical school, Dr. Roberts addressed the eighty would-be doctors in my class. "When Dr. Taylor and I instruct you in anatomy, we will first tell you what we're going to tell you. Then we will tell you what we said we said we were going to tell you. And when we are done, we will tell you what we've told you."[1]

This is what the book of Revelation does. First, it tells us where we're going. John's been imprisoned because he won't stop spreading the gospel (1:9). Along the way, he tells the gospel story a number of different ways. He ends in the New Jerusalem, which is so wonderful that words can't adequately describe it (chapters 21–22).

God didn't give John a script for future history. He showed him important features of His plan of salvation from a number of different angles. For example, the Seals and Trumpets (chapters 6–11) generally cover the same periods in salvation history.[2] The Seals focus on God's call of grace, while the Trumpets warn of troubles ahead if we reject Him. The two witnesses of chapter 11 give us one view of the church in times of trouble, while the woman fleeing into the wilderness (chapter 12) shows another.

DON'T THROW THIS BOOK AWAY!

Right here let me say one very important thing. The paragraph you just read may not agree with what you've heard before. It's easy to say, "This guy is crazy!" and close the book.[3] Please don't do that. We agree that the Bible is the word of God. It's understandable for anyone willing to

---

1. My wife Nancy says this is as confusing as the book of Revelation. Hopefully, by the time we're done, you'll understand Revelation better than most scholars.
2. All the things I'm introducing here will be discussed later in the book.
3. One caller on a radio show recently said exactly that about me.

study and allow God to lead. So open *your* Bible. Gather whatever tools and helps you can find and read what God said.[4] Write down questions. Compare passage with passage, and allow Scripture to interpret itself.[5] Don't accept anyone's ideas as truth until they've been fully investigated, *not even what I say in this book*. And never take your eyes off of Christ. If you'll do that, I think you'll find that the things I have to say agree with Scripture. By the way, don't always read just the verse I list. Read the verses before and after it. Those verses will give you a better feel for what I'm saying. Then you'll see why the verse I picked is important.

BACK TO REVELATION . . .

God didn't just tell the story once and then move on. Inside the Seals, Trumpets, and Bowls are "interludes." These are "picture-in-picture" sections that tell us more about the story. And some of these "telescope" inside each other. When we're done, it will almost seem like a set of those Russian matryoshka dolls where each doll has another one inside.

The book of Revelation gives theologians lots to play with, since the book has lots of unique features. There are so many "sevens" that they're almost impossible to count.[6] Some scholars say it was written in the form of a "chiasm," with many smaller chiasms inside it.[7] Unfortunately, scholars tend to disagree on the places where the main chiasm is divided, leaving us to wonder if they really know what they're talking about. We could go on for a while listing details that entertain "experts," but most of us would go to sleep. So let's focus on key patterns that will help *us* understand what's going on.

---

4. "Helps" is a general term for books such as Bible dictionaries, concordances, lexicons, and commentaries. Each contains things that help us understand the Bible.

5. Some people think the idea that Scripture interprets itself is nonsense. When we're done, I think you'll agree that the Bible *does* give us the tools to interpret itself.

6. Some that come to mind are candlesticks, churches, Spirits of God, seals, trumpets, and bowls. Theologians have listed as many as forty or fifty, depending on how they count.

7. A chiasm is a literary form where parallel thoughts are presented forward in the first half, then reversed in order in the second. When diagrammed, it looks like the left half of the Greek letter Chi (X). The middle item is the most important.

OLD TESTAMENT SOURCES

The first part of the book gives us one key. John sees Jesus walking among seven candlesticks (1:12–13). This is in the outer apartment of the temple. But the original tabernacle only had one lampstand (Exod 25:31), and Solomon's temple had ten (2 Chron 4:7). Nebuchadnezzar destroyed the temple in 587 BC and when the Jews returned to Jerusalem from Babylon they built another one. We don't know how many candlesticks it had. All we know is that the "utensils for the service of the house of your God" were returned (Ezra 7:19). Chances are no temple ever seven lampstands. So what's going on?

This vision takes a common Old Testament image and re-molds it.[8] In chapter 12 there's a beast with seven heads and ten horns. It comes from Daniel 7 by way of re-molding. Daniel saw a winged lion, a bear, a leopard with four heads, and a strange beast with ten horns. If we put these all together, we get seven heads and ten horns. In the fifth and sixth trumpets there are more strange demonic beasts. These monsters are also combinations of other Hebrew images. When we see Revelation combine symbols, we have a key that lets us unlock their new use.

The seven lampstands in chapter 1 tell us what the scene's about. "Seven" symbolizes perfection, holiness, and completion. We're looking at a perfect temple, with a perfect priest who's tending the candlesticks (2:5). This tells us that God wants us to see the daily temple ministry here. This temple pattern runs all through the book. We'll see it move in sequence from the daily ministry through Passover, Pentecost and the rest of the festival calendar. Some scenes are set in the heavenly temple. Other times small items will remind us of the temple. Almost every part of the book depends on the Old Testament temple pattern.

CATCH PHRASES

Another pattern is John's use of key words or phrases. The righteous **live in heaven** (13:6) while the wicked **live on the earth** (13:8). Sometimes it's **those who dwell on the earth** (3:10; 6:10, etc.), **the kings of the earth**

---

8. Most theologians will say, "John took the Old Testament images and recast them" or something to that general effect. But John did no such thing! John's reporting the vision God gave him. God took the original imagery and enhanced it to add meaning. I'll try to avoid saying that "John did" this or that. Credit must be given to the One True God who reveals Himself in the book.

(1:5; 6:15, etc.), and **the whole earth** (13:3). This geographic metaphor tells us who God's talking about.

Another key phrase is **that great city** (11:8; 16:19, etc.). It's another name for **Babylon** (14:8; 17:5, etc.), and **Babylon** is another name for the **Harlot** (17:1, 5, etc.). In the Old Testament, when God's people started worshiping idols, they were "playing the harlot" (cf. Judg 2:17). Any time we see any one of these names, we know that it's referring to apostate religion. And this shows us another pattern.

PARODY

Revelation plays opposites against each other. **Babylon** is a corrupt city. Its opposite is the **New Jerusalem**, the pure **bride** of Christ (21:2). We know from 19:7-8 that the saints are the **bride**. So if the saints are **Jerusalem**, then the wicked are **Babylon**. The contrast doesn't stop here. In 17:1-6, Babylon is described as a **woman, the great harlot**. This woman stands opposite to the pure **woman** of 12:1-6 who is persecuted by the **red dragon** (12:3-6). The pure woman represents the true followers of Christ, while the **harlot** represents the Satan's people. This pattern is called "parody."

Parody happens when a picture is *almost* right. When we look carefully, we see that it's really bogus. In 17:4 there's a woman **clothed in purple and scarlet, and adorned with gold and precious stones and pearls, having in her hand a gold cup**. This whore is a pitiful imitation of the true bride of Christ who's described in chapter 21:9-10 as the New Jerusalem. The bride also has gold (golden streets), precious stones (foundations), and pearls (gates). This parody is more direct in its contrast of names—**Babylon** vs. **Jerusalem**. Each time a parody pops up, the good and righteous is real, while the parody is a sick impersonation.

We've just confirmed something I said earlier from another angle. Good Bible study shows us the same thing again and again, as the Bible interprets itself from many angles. And this set of examples shows us *another* pattern.

SYMBOLISM

1:1 says that the revelation was given to John "by way of symbols." The Greek word *semaino* used here comes from *sema*, which means "a sign or symbol." **Babylon** is symbolic. It isn't a physical city any more than the **New Jerusalem** is a physical city. Some argue that identifying all those symbols in Revelation is "allegorizing." That is, we're taking the "reality" out of the book. Actually, using symbols enriches our understanding of the book, and allows us to get a larger picture of the real issues being discussed. You'll see how it works as we go along.

The fact that something is used as a symbol doesn't mean that it doesn't have any physical reality. A symbol is a real, physical image that points to something real, but bigger than the symbol itself. And the Bible isn't the only book that uses them. Augustine of Hippo used the imagery of **Babylon** and **Jerusalem** in his classic works *The City of Man* and *The City of God*, just without the names.

The way God tells the story shows us another pattern. In chapter 5, John's told that he'll see the **Lion of the tribe of Judah** (5:5). But instead of a lion, he sees a **lamb standing as if slain** (5:6). Both symbols are important ways of seeing the same thing. This pattern repeats in the **sealing of the saints** (chapter 7) and the **New Jerusalem** (chapters 21–22). Other keys words or phrases will pop up from time to time. Because we know about patterns in the book, we'll have no trouble using them to help us figure out what a passage means.

GOD'S PROBLEM

There's a war on! Satan decided it was unfair that Yahweh was the only God.[9] He should be worshiped, too (Ezek 28:2, Isa 14:13–14). So he led a rebellion in heaven, and a third of the angels joined him (12:4, 9). At the Tree in Eden, he called God a liar. Later he accused God of running a protection racket (Job 1:9–11). The list goes on.

We could suggest that God should have destroyed Satan and his followers before man was created. Then there'd be no one to tempt Adam and Eve. But that wouldn't solve anything. Somebody else could come up with Satan's objections again. God would have to destroy that rebel, and the next, and the next . . . That's not going to get rid of sin.

The real problem is that God wants everyone to love him unconditionally. But to be able to love, we also have to be able to *not* love. Let me say this a different way. Love is a choice, and love can't exist unless we choose it. God could prevent sin by not giving us the ability to choose, but that would make us robots, and that prevent love, too. He had to find a different way.

9. Yahweh is the personal name of the one true God in Hebrew. In the Old Testament it's usually translated "LORD."

God can only remove sin from the universe permanently by letting the drama of sin play out to its end. Then, when everyone has made a final decision either for or against Him, He can end it. But this gives Him a new problem. We don't have all the facts and can't see things the way God does, so He has to open the books and show every living being that everyone got a fair chance to be saved (20:12). In other words, everyone has to be totally convinced that God did it right. He can't leave any doubt anywhere. This isn't a case of no reasonable doubt. There must be *absolutely no doubt*.

Once everyone's totally convinced that the wicked have to be destroyed, God can deal with them. He can't allow them to suffer forever. That would make Him a liar because he said, "the wages of sin is death" and burning forever in Hell is *not* death (Rom 6:23). As long as the wicked are burning, sin is still present. God must destroy them completely, leaving "neither root nor branch" (Mal 4:1). Also, a hell that burns forever makes Him a tyrant for imposing a penalty far out of proportion to the crime, and that would destroy His universe of love all over again.

Before the final judgment, God has to let the war to go on to its end. If He didn't, there would always be doubters. But if He lets the drama play out through the last act, then the sin question will reach final closure. This is the big picture.[10]

THE BIG (LITERARY) PICTURE

Revelation 1:1 says that the book is **the revealing of Jesus Christ**. Didn't Jesus get pretty well revealed during his ministry? Certainly the gospels tell a lot about Him, and on the Emmaus road Jesus told the disciples a lot more (Luke 24:27). But it looks like we need to know even more.

If you take the first three chapters and added a few verses from the end of the book (22:12–21), you'd have a pretty nice apostolic letter. It begins with **John to the seven churches that are in Asia: Grace to you and peace** (1:4). This is almost identical to the greeting used by Paul and Peter in their letters. It closes with **The grace of the LORD Jesus be with all. Amen.** (22:21). Paul closes with this blessing in most of his letters, and Peter uses it once. So if we didn't have all that symbolic stuff in the middle, the Revelation would be pretty simple.

---

10. The "big picture" is called a "cosmic metanarrative" by theologians. That means that all the little stories (narratives) in the Bible get assembled into one giant story. The big story leaves out a lot of details, but shows us why God lets sin continue.

A closer look at the epistle gives us some clues about happening. First, the actual letter starts in verse 10. There John says, "**I heard behind me a loud voice like *the sound* of a trumpet.**" He turns around and sees Jesus walking around the lampstands in the holy place of the temple. The voice like a trumpet was God's voice, and this is a very important clue. Trumpets called Israel to assemble.

Ancient Uses of Trumpets
They announced: • the beginning and end of all Temple services (Num 10:9–10). • a call to battle (Neh 4:20). • victory in battle (1 Sam 6:15). • the anointing of a king (1 Kgs 1:34, 39). • the anointing of the Temple (2 Chron. 29:26–28). • the restoration of the Ark to the Jews (2 Sam. 6:16).

The only other time that God's voice sounded like a trumpet was at Mount Sinai (Exod. 19:16–19). There God gave Israel His covenant, so we can call that event *The Covenant Delivered* (Exod. 19:5; 24:4–7). If the epistle in Revelation is related to the covenant, there may be a pattern developing.

After a few preliminaries, Jesus dictates the seven letters to the churches. Each one follows the same general covenant form and looks just like a modern contract. The parties present themselves. Each party tells why he's able to do the deal. If you do your side, you'll get the payoff. If you don't do your part, you'll be in breach and you'll suffer the penalties. Finally, witnesses authenticate the deal.

LETTER OUTLINE	
LETTER	**COVENANT FORMULA**
1. "I am God."	1. Preamble
2. "I know who you are and what you're doing." "I've done good things in the past "(implied)."	2. Historical Prologue
3. "Here's what you need to do."	3. Stipulations
4. "If you do well, you'll be rewarded. If you do badly you'll be cursed."	4. Blessings and Cursings
5. "He who has an ear, let him hear." "I am the faithful and true witness."	5. Witnesses

At Sinai we had *The Covenant Delivered*. Here the contracts are spelled out in legal covenant form, so we can call them *The Covenant Described*. The symbolic part of Revelation will complete the pattern.

Sinai began with a voice like a trumpet. The letter in Revelation began with a voice like a trumpet. The symbolic part of Revelation also begins with a voice like a trumpet.

> After these things I looked, and behold, a door *standing* open in heaven, and the first voice which I had heard, like *the sound of a trumpet* speaking with me, said, "Come up here, and I will show you what must take place after these things. (4:1)

This time I'll give the answer up front. The symbolic part of Revelation is *The Covenant Displayed*. It tells the story of how God carries out his side of the covenant. Let's look at the outline.

THE COVENANT DISPLAYED

Revelation 4–5 is in the heavenly throne room where Jesus is crowned as our heavenly king.[11] The book of the covenant is ready to be opened (5:1). Jesus is **worthy to open the book and break its seals** because He has **overcome** (5:2, 5). His death on the cross gives Him the right to make the covenant with us.

It's not good enough to say, "This is the covenant, keep it!" God has His part to do as well. First, He says that He will draw all men to Himself (John 12:31). This is the call of grace. Because some won't listen when God calls, He must warn them about the judgment that's coming (Mark 16:16). Finally, when everyone has made up his mind, God must claim His saints and pour out the covenant curses on the wicked (Matt 24:31, Heb 10:26–31). Then this sinful age will end. This story runs from chapter 6 through chapter 16.

We talked a bit ago about Satan's false accusations. In the millennium we'll get to look at the books. Every redeemed saint and every heavenly being who's heard Satan's charges will see what was in the heart of everyone who rejected God. When every case has been completely checked out, we'll be able to sing "**Hallelujah! Salvation and glory and power belong to our God; because His judgments are true and righteous**" (19:1–2).

---

11. You'll have to trust me for now. We'll go through this when we get to that scene.

It would be easy for God to declare victory, make the earth into a new Eden, and let us move in. But God doesn't do things that way. He has an orderly way of dealing with mankind. He won't destroy anyone without first showing them why, so He'll resurrect the wicked. As a final demonstration, He'll let Satan to organize them for a final attack against the saints. When God blocks the attack, every wicked person will see his own guilt. Then God will destroy them.

Notice that I didn't say, "throw them into hell." The conventional idea of hell is a place where the wicked are tormented forever. But that's not what the Bible says. The wicked will die the "second death" (20:14).[12] They'll be gone forever.

When sin is over, God can make the earth into a new Eden. We'll move into our wonderful new home, and Christ will live with us, just like he did with Adam and Eve in the original Garden of Eden. This is the final covenant blessing.

THE OUTLINE, ONCE MORE

The *Covenant Displayed* looks like this:

> A: The Inauguration of the Worthy King who wants us with him.
> B: The story of the covenant in this age.
> B′: The story of the covenant in the millennial age.
> A′: The Consummation of the Worthy King who has us with him.

Now that's an awfully short outline. The book has a lot more details to fill in. Just to keep us oriented as we go through all those details, let's set up a map.

The Covenant Displayed

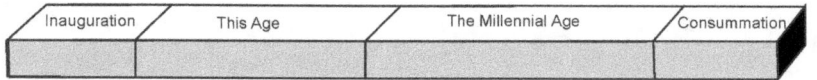

This graphic is our roadmap to the symbolic part of the book. As we explore a map, we'll look at an expanded section. That way you'll always know just where we are. You'll also see how everything fits together.

---

12. I'll discuss this in depth when we study the texts that deal with it. In particular, the Hebrew concept of "forever and ever" will be fun. You'll also want to read Appendix D.

Jesus wants us to be with Him. When He revealed Himself in Revelation, He began by outlining the covenant rules that let us walk with Him. They're in the letter in chapters 2–3. Then He showed how the story would play out. Every step is in good order with good reason. Nothing is arbitrary. All of it is designed to allow God to permanently remove sin from the universe. Then all of us will be blessed forever.

> **And he showed me a river of the water of life, clear as crystal, coming from the throne of God and of the Lamb, in the middle of its street. And on either side of the river was the tree of life, bearing twelve *kinds of* fruit, yielding its fruit every month; and the leaves of the tree were for the healing of the nations. And there shall no longer be any curse; and the throne of God and of the Lamb shall be in it, and His bond-servants shall serve Him; and they shall see His face, and His name *shall be* on their foreheads. And there shall no longer be *any* night; and they shall not have need of the light of a lamp nor the light of the sun, because the Lord God shall illumine them; and they shall reign forever and ever. (22:1–5)**

2

Housekeeping

Let all things be done properly and in an orderly manner.

1 COR 14:40

NO, THAT TEXT WASN'T originally intended to apply to the way a prophet wrote, but I thought it was too good to pass up. And John really did need to set things up properly for us to understand what he was writing about. He'd seen visions and knew this wasn't an ordinary message.

It's pretty clear that the Apostle Paul was trying to sort out some problems in the church in 1 Corinthians. The Apostle James wrote to encourage the church. But John's visions weren't anywhere near that obvious. They needed a much better introduction. So he began by telling us *what* was being written, *who* received it, *where* it was written, *to whom* it was written, and *why* it had to be written. Once all these things were taken care of, he could get on with the business of the visions.

WHAT?

What seems simple. It's **The Revelation of Jesus Christ**. Actually it's the revealing of the *Covenant* of Jesus Christ. He isn't just the Creator, the Son of God, and our redeeming sacrifice. All of these things make Him the maker of the Covenant that's defined in the letters to the churches (cf. Heb 8:6ff.). The rest of the book tells how it plays out in history. God's command to tell **the things which you have seen, and the things which are, and the things which shall take place after these things** echoes this (1:19).

Right now you're probably saying, "Wait a minute! The book is supposed to reveal Jesus, not the covenant." And in a way you're right. But in another way, Jesus *is* the covenant. He doesn't just make a deal with us and pay up when we get our part done. Instead, he created us (John 1:3). He saw that we would sin, so he prepared to pay the price for sin before he made us (Isa 53:5, 12, 1 Pet 1:20). Then, when the right time came, he died in our place (Heb 9:26). The covenant was meaningless until Jesus paid the price.[1] Then it was written in his blood (Matt 26:28, Heb 9:16-17). So in a very real way, Jesus *is* the covenant.

THROUGH WHOM?

Revelation was given to "John." Scholars spend a lot of energy debating who he was. Most say he was one of the twelve, "the disciple that Jesus loved" (John 19:26). Others argue that he was another John, maybe an early convert to the faith, possibly in Ephesus. When I read the arguments, it seems to me that some of them get their only exercise by jumping to conclusions.

The simplest answer is the one passed to us by tradition. The apostle John wrote the gospel, the three epistles, and the apocalypse. This fits with the message and setting. After all, of all God's messengers, which one would he be most likely to choose to deliver a special message? In this book, we'll assume that John is the apostle, not some other John.

WHERE?

John was a prisoner on the island of **Patmos** (1:9). This was one of several islands used by Roman Emperors for prisons. Conditions there would make Alcatraz look like Fantasy Island. On good days, prisoners got enough food to survive. They were literally worked to death.[2] Many were executed on a whim.

John's treatment wasn't any different from other Christians. Tradition says that Emperor Domitian had John boiled in oil, but he miraculously survived. All the other apostles were executed. Their followers were made into human torches, torn apart by wild animals in the coliseum, and worse (cf. Matt 10:16–22). Even today, many thousands die each year for their faith in Christ.

---

1. Scholars debate the meaning of Jesus' sacrifice on the Cross. Several views have scriptural support, and all are probably correct to some degree. That is, it has several aspects for us to study and wonder at. "Paid the price" is just one of them.

2. In the opening scene of the movie *Spartacus*, Kirk Douglas (Spartacus) is a Roman prisoner breaking rocks to be used in road-building. While generally correct, this scene is very generous to the Roman authorities. Most prisoners would have been in tattered clothes, physically wasted, and unable to assault a guard the way Spartacus does.

TO WHOM?

"John to the seven churches that are in Asia" (1:4). We know they weren't the only ones in Asia. Iconium, Lystra, and Derbe are left out (Acts 14:1, 6) and the church in Greece is ignored. But an apostolic letter to the seven churches would have been immediately copied and sent out. It wouldn't be long before churches everywhere had copies. John knew this, and **"He who has an ear, let him hear what the Spirit says to the churches"** at the end of each one emphasizes it. Jesus used this "hearing formula" several times to point out that everyone should carefully listen to what he had to say (Matt 11:15, etc.). It echoes the *Shema*, the very heart of Jewish faith.

> Hear, O Israel! The LORD is our God, the LORD is one!
> (Deut 6:4)

Every Jewish child learned this passage at a young age. When the Jews were dispersed across Asia and Europe, they carried this message with them. The pagan peoples where they moved had many gods, and this declaration reminded them of the one true God, the God of Israel.

The dispersed Jews founded synagogues wherever they went, and the apostles went to these synagogues on their journeys (Acts 13:14; 14:1; 17:1, etc.). Converts from these synagogues formed the core of the new churches, so they would have been very familiar with the *Shema*. When they heard **"He who has an ear, let him hear"** in Revelation, they knew that the message was for all of true Israel, the Israel of God (Gal 6:16).

WHY?

When the prophet Daniel interpreted Nebuchadnezzar's dream around 600 BC, God showed what would happen "in the latter days" (Dan 2:27–45). At Pentecost Peter declared that the latter days had begun (Acts 2:17 ff.). A few years later, John was shown **the things that must shortly take place**. The cosmic war was closer to its end, and this shortened perspective reminded John that sin can't go on forever. Today we're even closer to God's ultimate victory than John was.

It would be easy to say that the vision showed the future history of the world. God's in control of things, and has decreed certain things "must happen." But that doesn't tell us *why* God said they must happen. It just says, "He said it!" That isn't just unsatisfying, it's completely unhelpful. We're players in a cosmic battle. We need help to understand our role.

The covenant pattern in chapter 1 answers the "Why" question for us. Every part of the book is tied to the covenant. The messages to the churches spell out its particulars. Then the story in the rest of the book "puts flesh on its bones."

The covenant is what *must* happen. God is trustworthy. He *must* reward the saints who rely on him. This is why He can say, "**Blessed is he who keeps the words of the prophecy in this book**" (22:7 NIV, cf. 1:3). No one can "keep" a prophecy if it's just a set of predictions! God takes care of making the prophecy come true. All we do is watch. But if a prophecy includes divine instruction, then there's something vitally important we have to do. We have to follow (keep) those instructions.

The flip side of rewarding the saints is punishing the wicked. If the covenant has meaning, God *must* take care of that job as well. And when He's dealt with wicked people, He must take care of the source. Satan and his evil angels have to be destroyed. That's when all sin will be removed from the universe. Everyone will be immunized against sin.

OTHER BITS AND PIECES

We can translate verse 1 "the revealing of Jesus" or "the revealing by Jesus." In the messages to the churches, Jesus is the narrator. You can't get any closer to ultimate authority than that. Next John **bears witness to the word of God and to the testimony of Christ** directly from God Almighty (1:2). Nothing can be more important. Nothing can be truer. Further, he says that Christ testifies to it. Jesus **the faithful and true witness** (1:5).

Since John and Jesus are *both* witnesses, we have the first glimpse of another pattern. Revelation is full of "two witness theology." The covenant says, "on the evidence of two or three witnesses a matter shall be confirmed" (Deut 19:15). This legal language is very important, and we'll see it again. Since the covenant is a legal contract, witnesses to it (and its violation) are essential, and we'll see witnesses several places, always in a legal context.

Verses 5 and 6 introduce a new theme that we'll cover later. Jesus is the first-born of the dead, and the ruler of the kings of the earth. He's worthy to rule because He loves us, and released us from our sins by His blood (cf. 5:2–5). As a result of His worthiness to rule, He has made us to be a kingdom, priests to His God and Father (cf. 5:10). Jesus carried out the key part of the covenant on the cross. Because He died for us, He's able to elevate us to a royal position as priests.

	We Will be a Kingdom of Priests
	Exodus 19:5–6 God promises Israel they'll be a kingdom of priests if they will keep the covenant. **Isaiah 61:1–7** God promises Israel to reverse their bad fortunes after the Lord pours out his wrath on their wicked enemies. They will become a kingdom of priests. **Revelation 20:4–6** The saints *are* the kingdom of priests.
	*The key issue is Israel's commitment to the covenant. They are chosen to be *holy*. **See also Deut 33:2–4, Rom 12:1, 1 Pet 2:5–10. The New Testament applies the promises to faithful Israel to the church.

John pauses here for a moment to praise his Lord. To Him be the glory and the dominion forever and ever. Amen (1:6). Biblical Greek doesn't have exclamation marks, but I hear one every time I read this. John's excited! His Lord *is* the victor and king of the universe. There will be "no end to the increase of *His* government or of peace" (Isa 9:7, cf. Luke 1:33). He'll keep His promises! It doesn't matter that troubles are coming, because the glorious coming kingdom will make everything worth it. It will be wonderful beyond anything we can imagine (Isa 64:4). And just to put a finishing touch on this wonderful guarantee, John finishes the sentence with Amen.

"Amen" isn't a Greek word. It's a Hebrew word that means "truly." John took the Hebrew and wrote it with Greek letters to bring an emphatic "Yes!" to the end of the statement. In the first two verses he used legal language to emphasize that the story was true. This time he celebrates the truth. God is sovereign! The victory is certain! Amen!

Behold, He is coming with the clouds. John saw Jesus ascend in the clouds when He left the earth (Acts 1:9). He went to heaven, where he received his kingdom (Dan 7:13–14, Phil 2:9–11). Every eye will see Him. There won't be anything secret about it. For the saints, it will be the happiest time. They're leaving this cursed world for eternity with their

Redeemer. But for the wicked, it's trouble. All the tribes of the earth will mourn over Him.

Here's another pattern. The tribes of the earth aren't the saints. They're the wicked. When God promised Abraham that all the tribes of the earth would be blessed through him, He was talking about Abraham's wicked neighbors (Gen 12:3). Jesus used the same language when He said that "all of the tribes of the earth will mourn" when He comes back (Matt 24:30). In the sixth seal, we'll see them calling for the rocks to fall on them to hide them (6:15–17). The wicked aren't just sad, they're *terrified*.

And John celebrates again! Only this time, he finishes with Even so. Amen. This time he combines the Greek affirmative *nai* with *amen* to make it a double "Yes!" It's wonderful that God's coming for his saints. It's doubly wonderful that He'll defeat the enemies of His people.

If John had stopped here, he'd have given the whole message of the book in short form. But that wouldn't let us see what made him so excited. We wouldn't know why he could be so certain that everything would turn out the way it was promised. John's not about to leave us in the dark. He wanted us to see what he saw so we can be as sure of the victory is he was.

"I am the Alpha and the Omega," says the Lord God, "who is and who was and who is to come, the Almighty." The victory is won because God is who He is. He is the only one and there is no other. To emphasize this, Jesus uses the first and last letters of the Greek alphabet as His identity. Pagan Greek religions had used these letters to indicate the beginning and end of creation.[3] Christ, the true Creator, uses them in defiance of false gods to say that He alone is God. It also emphasizes that He is *everything*.[4] Nothing exists without him.

The one true God is truly the I AM. He has no beginning and will have no end. The pagan gods had beginnings in the rebellion of Satan, and will end with him in the lake of fire.

---

3. David Fideler, *Jesus Christ, Sun of God: Ancient Cosmology and Early Christian Symbolism* (Wheaton: Quest, 1993), 272–73.

4. Gregory Beale, *The Book of Revelation* (Grand Rapids: Eerdmans, 1999), 199. The combination of polar opposites "is a figure of speech called a *merism*." It is used "to highlight everything between the opposites."

3

Hello, Old Friend!

No longer do I call you slaves, for the slave does not know what his master is doing; but I have called you friends, for all things that I have heard from My Father I have made known to you.

(John 15:15)

Jesus chose his best friend among the disciples to be his messenger to the church (John 19:26). But John's always God's humble servant. He introduces himself as a **fellow partaker in the tribulation**. This almost sounds like he's sitting down to dinner. He sees his troubles on **Patmos** as quite ordinary, and certainly no more than any other Christian suffers.[1] He **perseveres** with his fellows, even while he's in prison.

When John sees his old friend, he falls to the ground in worship **as a dead man** (1:17). This attitude runs through the book. John has the greatest privilege a sinful man can have, a view into heaven, but he never focuses on himself. Every part of the book is about Jesus.

APOKALUPSIS ON "THE LORD'S DAY"

The book is **The Revelation of Jesus** (1:1). So many writers have gotten lost in its details that they've made it "The *Concealing* of Jesus." But John understood that his job was to report in a way that reveals just who Christ is. The word *apokalupsis* (revelation) that gives the book its title literally means "to make *fully* known." John is to tell *all* **the things he has seen** (1:19). Most of it was shown to him "through symbols." And he did his best to make sure

---

1. I just can't get this into my head. After all, tradition says that Domitian boiled John in oil! I can't even imagine how awful that has to be.

that we'd understand the symbols he saw. He saw the Old Testament context of the vision, and used familiar Old Testament language.

The story begins **on the Lord's Day**. John knew what this unusual phrase meant, and he expected his readers would too, or he wouldn't have used it. Unfortunately, it's not so clear to us, so it's time to do a little detective work.

The Greek word *kuriakeé* ("Lord's") shows up only one other place in the Bible (1 Cor 11:20). Paul uses it there when he talks about the Lord's Supper. He doesn't tell us when they held the Lord's Supper, but we know it was on Passover. The oldest "church manual" we know about, the *Didaché*,[2] calls that day "the Lord's Day."[3]

> **DIDACHÉ CHAPTER 14**
> Translated by Kirsopp Lake
>
> On the Lord's Day of the Lord come together, break bread and hold Eucharist, after confessing your transgressions that your offering may be pure; but let none who has a quarrel with his fellow join in your meeting until they be reconciled, that your sacrifice be not defiled.

The first Passover came in Egypt (Exod 12:1–14), and gave the Israelites freedom from Egyptian slavery. Christ died on Passover to free us from slavery to sin (1 Cor 5:7). His death on the cross is what makes him worthy to be our king (Rev 5). His covenant guarantees our salvation, but it was worthless until He died (Heb 9:17). This makes the Passover the most important day celebrating the God's eternal covenant of redemption. It's the day Jesus sealed the covenant with His blood. And that is why Paul tells us to Celebrate! the Lord's death (cf. 1 Cor 11:17–32). Passover is the birthday of our redemption.

---

2. The *Didache'* is roughly contemporary with the book of Revelation. While not part of scripture, it generally reflects the practices of the early church, and we should expect that John would be familiar with those practices, even if by chance he hadn't seen the book itself.

3. Scholars debate about when several ancient documents were written. There are questions about who wrote them. For example, chapter 67 of Justin Martyr's *First Apology* and the three attached letters are almost certainly forged. Translation issues get debated. For our purposes, we will accept only those documents that have been clearly shown to be legitimate. It's particularly important that the term "Lord's Day" was not clearly identified with the first day of the week until late in the second century. Any argument that tries to make John's use of the term mean the first day of the week is improper because it is using the term outside of its contemporary (to John) meaning.

When John uses **the Lord's Day** in the very first verse of the actual revelation, he's pointing us to the covenant. He wants us to see what he saw. God made a covenant with man. He did what He had to do to make the covenant valid.

With this introduction, John begins another pattern. The Passover started the exodus from Egypt. God uses the exodus motif as a *type* to tell the story of how the covenant plays out in history. It was a physical event where physical Israel was freed from physical captivity. Revelation tells the story of our release from spiritual captivity in language from the exodus, making salvation the *antitype*. The first reality is Old Testament history, while the larger reality is eternal salvation and freedom from sin. When language from the exodus appears in the book, God's using that story as a way to tell the story of redemption.

TYPOLOGY

. . . is a theological term that describes "acted-out prophecies." A **type** is a person, place, or event the Bible uses as a pattern. It always points to something bigger and more important in salvation history called the **antitype**. For example, when John the Baptist called Jesus "the lamb . . . that takes away the sin of the world" (John 1:29), he was using the sacrificial lamb in the temple (**type**—Lev 16:7–9, 15) to explain Jesus' place in the plan of salvation (**antitype**).

THE VOICE!

John was **in the Spirit** to see the first of four visions in the book. Immediately he heard **a loud voice like a trumpet**. No Hebrew could forget that voice. When the Israelites camped at Mount Sinai, God spoke from the mountain with a voice like a trumpet (Exod 19:9, 16). He gave the covenant to Moses so he could deliver it to the people (Exod 19:5; 24:7–8).

Before John could turn to see who was speaking, Jesus commissioned him to **write in a book what you see and send it to the seven churches**. Because there were more than seven churches in Asia, the number seven has to be symbolic, referring to perfection and holiness. The message would be God's perfect and holy covenant message to the church.

When John **turned**, he **saw seven golden lampstands**. He was in the outer apartment of the Temple where common priests served every day. His old friend Jesus was **in the middle of the lampstands**. He's the high priest, tending the lamps like priests did every day (cf. 2:1, 5). But Jesus couldn't be an ordinary priest, since He was from the tribe of Judah, and all the priests were Levites (Heb 7:14).

The **seven golden lampstands** show that this is the heavenly temple, the more perfect one, where Jesus is our High Priest *forever* (cf. Heb 9:11).[4] The Levitical priesthood was abolished when He died on the cross (Heb 7:11–12, Matt 27:51). Jesus now ministers for us and will be our only priest until the drama of sin is completed (Heb 7:25).

JESUS!

When John saw his old friend, the glorious view was almost more than he could describe. The **Son of Man** was dressed **in a robe reaching to the feet and girded across His breast with a golden girdle** like a high priest. **His head and His hair were white like white wool, like snow; and His eyes were like a flame of fire; and His feet *were* like burnished bronze**. This appearance wasn't new to John. He had "seen" all of the parts of this description as he'd studied the sacred writings, the Old Testament. But seeing in his mind's eye couldn't compare with the reality of being in God's presence. Even seeing **His face shining like the sun in its strength** at the Mount of Transfiguration couldn't prepare John for Jesus' glory here (Matt 17:2).

Old Testament Sources for Jesus' Appearance
• High priestly garments: Exodus 28
• Hair like white wool: Daniel 7:9
• Belt of gold, eyes like fire, feet of bronze: Daniel 10:5–6
• Related imagery: Ezekiel 1

---

4. Hebrews 7 emphasizes Jesus' permanent priesthood by using "forever" five times (vv. 17, 21, 24, 25, and 28), "permanently" (v. 24), and "always" (v. 25). The Levitical priesthood was not able to bring perfection (v. 11), but Christ does. His perfect priesthood is based on his "indestructible life" (v. 16). The Levitical structure was "useless" and had to be replaced (v. 18). God made the change, swore it with an oath, and will not change his mind (v. 21). It's hard to imagine a more emphatic argument that Jesus is the last priest. Since He ministers in the heavenly temple, there will never be another earthly temple in God's plan. There won't be another Levitical priest, either.

John fell at His feet as a dead man. Jesus' glory and holiness was more than any sinful man could handle. Even the High Priest on the Day of Atonement had to shield himself with a cloud of incense or he'd die (Lev 16:12–13). So until Jesus laid his hand upon him, John didn't have the strength to look at him or stand.

Jesus in the Temple
• High Priest: Long robe, golden girdle.
• God: "Son of Man," face shining like the sun.
• Judge: White hair, eyes like flames, feet of burnished bronze.
• King: Sword from his mouth.
• Protector: Stars in His hand.

We should take a moment to appreciate just how much God packed into this picture. Jesus is our high priest. He's also fully God (cf. Col 2:9). He protects the stars in His right hand, which are the "angels" of the seven churches, while he cares for the seven lampstands which are the seven churches. He's the presiding judge who then brings wrath on the wicked by the sharp two-edged sword that comes out of His mouth. This brings to mind Psalm 33:9.

> For He spoke, and it was done; He commanded, and it stood fast.

All God has to do is speak and His words become reality. Our awesome God could stamp out evil with a look, but He lets this world go on until every person has had a chance to accept salvation (2 Pet 3:9). But we must never forget that when everyone has had the chance to accept Christ, probation will close, and God will pour out his wrath in judgment on the wicked.[5]

Jesus says, "**Don't be afraid, I am the first and the last, and the living One; and I was dead, and behold, I am alive forevermore.**" With "**the first and the last**," Jesus identifies himself as the one true God.[6]

---

5. Probation is a term that describes a period where man has a chance to "straighten up and fly right." In God's plan of redemption, it's the time when it's possible to repent. After probation closes, no one will be able to accept Christ. As we'll see later, probation won't close till everyone has locked in his final answer. At that point the wicked won't *want* to accept Him.

6. The phrase "the first and the last" is a *merism*. This is a figure of speech that combines extremes to imply everything in between. So when Jesus says that He is "the first and the last," He's actually saying that He's everything to everyone in every age. It is by its very nature a claim of divinity, even without the quotation from God in Isaiah.

> "Thus says the LORD, the King of Israel And his Redeemer, the LORD of hosts: 'I am the first and I am the last, And there is no God besides Me. (Isa 44:6)

John doesn't need to be afraid, because this really is his old friend. The prophetic message to God's people is authentic, because Jesus is authentic. *They* are **the seven churches** and *they* are **the temple of God** (3:12, 11:1). Jesus cares for His church by trimming the lamps in the temple, removing those that don't shine (2:5, cf. Matt 5:14–16). God thoroughly blends Jewish and Christian imagery because He has only one chosen people throughout history. They were the church in the wilderness (Acts 7:38) and the church of the apostles (Matt 16:19). They were delivered from physical Egypt and will be delivered from spiritual Egypt (11:18). Old and New Testament images are so completely mixed that it's impossible to separate them.

This shouldn't surprise us. God's people have always walked with Him by faith (Mic 6:8, Hab 2:4, Heb 11). In the end times, they will continue to walk by faith (Rom 11:16–26). They will persevere to the end (2:2; 14:12). Then the One who has **the keys of death and Hades** will give them eternal life. Of course, if they neglect this great salvation (Heb 2:3), they will suffer the second death (2:11; 20:6, 14; 21:8).

A WAR CORRESPONDENT

Even before John looked, he was told to **write what you see**. Now Jesus gets specific. John's supposed to **write** down *three* things:

1. **the things you have seen,**
2. **the things which are, and**
3. **the things which shall take place after these things.**

The things he's seen is the vision. That seems pretty plain, unless you're a theologian.[7] Next come the things which are. Obviously, this describes the current state of things. Those may include the their historical background. Finally, he's supposed to tell about things that haven't happened yet.

---

[7] I don't mean to be hard on theologians, but sometimes it seems appropriate. While they're good at finding details in the Greek or connections between one text and another, a lot of the time they get wound up in little things and miss the big picture. Theologians have written a LOT about this passage trying to figure out a very simple statement.

The NetBible translates this as **write what you saw, what is, and what will be**.[8] This makes it a bit plainer. **What is, and what will be** are what John **saw** in vision. God showed him ultimate reality. But we have to remember that the focus is Jesus and His covenant with us. It's *not* about politics. It *is* about the way God deals with mankind as He calls us to repentance and obedience. It *is* about how Satan tries to defeat God and win our allegiance away from Him. There are political bits here and there, but those are landmarks to help us see the progress of the war between Christ and Satan. They are *not* there as the main point of the prophecy.

I know that right now many of you are ready to throw this book away. You've heard sermons about how Revelation is a detailed prediction of future events involving "the Antichrist" and "the Jews." Or you've read books that make the same kind of claim. Before you quit reading, remember how Jesus has already blended the church and ancient Israel in this one temple scene. We'll see this pattern again and again as we read through the book. Let's let Jesus reveal Himself. After all, this is the **Revelation of Jesus Christ**, not the revelation of Antichrist and the Jews.

---

8. If you're interested in technical language, this translation takes the Greek conjunction *kai* as "epexegetical." That means the text says, ". . . the things you see, *that is*, the things that are, and the things that are to come."

4

"You Are Here"

—SEEN IN PUBLIC BUILDINGS

You're in a large building when an alarm suddenly sounds. Your nose begins to twitch. Moments later, black smoke curls from the air-conditioning vents and your eyes begin to burn. If you stay where you are, the fire will trap and kill you. You have to get out, NOW! So you look at a poster on the wall with a map of the building. It has a red arrow with the words, "You Are Here." From the tip of the arrow a bold line shows your way out of this deathtrap. Then the smoke gets so thick that you can't see.

Just then a fireman arrives. You know he's a fireman, because he's wearing a fireman's outfit. He has the protective coat and hat and a bottle of breathing air. His radio keeps him in touch with help outside. He'll lead you to safety. It's a good thing, too, since you wouldn't be able to get out by yourself, anyway.

John has the same problem. In a manner of speaking, this world's on fire with sin. It threatens everyone's life. But the big threat isn't immediate physical death. John's facing that along with many of his friends (1:9). This threat is the **second death** in the **lake of fire** (20:14). The only way out is to read God's sign on the wall and follow His directions.

Jesus is going to give John a set of directions to lead the church out of the flames. It reads like seven messages to **seven churches**, but it's really *one* message to *the church*. God picked seven churches because they fit the way He explains His plan. Each one was a real church. Each one had a personality John's readers recognized. And almost every characteristic Jesus talks about can be found in almost every church anywhere in history. God chose *seven* because seven symbolizes perfection, telling us that this is His perfect message to His church.

SIGNS

Right here we're going to begin a series of signs like the "YOU ARE HERE" signs in that building. They will be maps that show us where we are in the book of Revelation. Theologians who say that Revelation is complicated aren't wrong. But they haven't had maps like this. Each map will have one of those "YOU ARE HERE" arrows, and each map will magnify the area we're looking at to make it easier to understand. As we go through the book, you'll become so familiar with its outline that it will be as simple to you as it was to John.

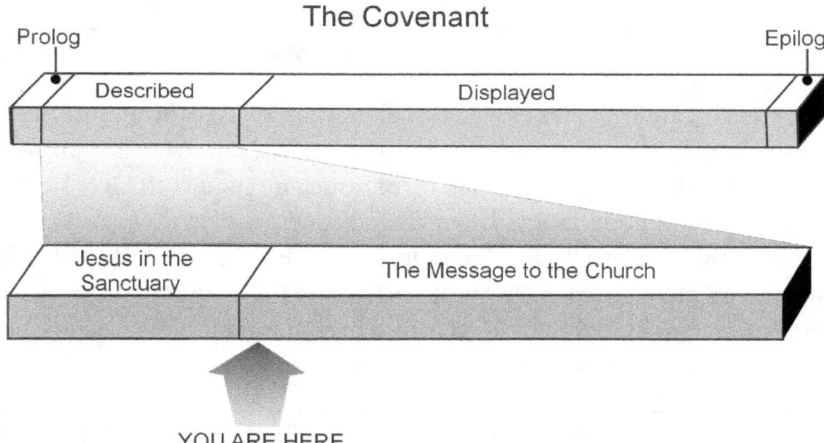

THE FIREMAN

This world is so full of the smoke from evil that nobody can find the way out. Every time we try, our own wicked nature trips us up. And things are getting worse, not better. We know our fireman is Jesus since we see his divine "clothing"—the **white hair, fiery eyes, golden girdle**, and so on. As we saw in the last chapter, each item calls to mind an Old Testament picture of God. These features point out His redemptive acts. Let's look at one of them.

Jesus is wearing **a golden girdle and a robe reaching to His feet** like the high priest wore during the Day of Atonement service (Exod 28, Lev 16). He's our high priest now (Heb 7). His death on the Cross is the sacrifice that cleanses our sins (Heb 9:26). His intercession for us is possible because He did all of the things that prophecy said the Messiah needed to do (Heb 7:25, Luke 24:26–27). And this brings us to a technical point. The message to the church is a divine covenant. It has all the required elements in standard legal order.[1]

Covenant Outline	
Preamble	God identifies himself.
Historical prolog	God tells how He's done His part of the covenant.
Stipulations	The terms of the covenant.
Blessings and Cursings	Rewards for fulfilling the covenant and penalties for failure.
Witnesses	Formalize the deal.

Jesus' "uniform" tells us who's speaking. Each part of the uniform tells us something about how He's done His part of the covenant. In contract law this is called *bona fides*, which literally means "good faith." It basically says, "I've done good things for you before, and I *will* do them again. My record speaks for itself." For Ephesus, Jesus tends the candlesticks (2:5), something done by ordinary priests every day. This emphasizes His daily ministry for us (Heb 7:25). Jesus is totally committed to our needs, and does all He can to be sure that we're prepared for salvation.

Jesus' "Fireman's Uniform"	
Ephesus	Holding seven stars, walking among the golden lampstands. 2:1, cf. 1:12–13, 16, 20.
Smyrna	The first and last, was dead, is alive. 2:8, cf. 1:17–18.
Pergamum	Has the sharp, two-edged sword. 2:12, cf. 1:16.
Thyatira	Eyes like fire, feet like bronze. 2:18, cf. 1:14–15.
Sardis	Seven spirits of God and the seven stars. 3:1, cf. 1:16, 20, cf. Exod 15:6.
Philadelphia	Holy and True, has Key of David, opens and shuts. 3:7, cf. 1:5, 18.
Laodicea	Faithful and true witness, author of creation. 3:14, cf. 1:5, John 1:1–3, Gen 1:1.

To Ephesus, Jesus' "uniform" tells about His care for His people throughout the ages. To Smyrna, it tells of His death on the cross for us.

---

1. Some scholars also point out that Jesus' "If you don't fix your problems, I'll act against you" is covenant lawsuit language. We'll talk about covenant lawsuits later.

Pergamum is reminded of God's judgments against the enemies of His people. Thyatira hears that God is sovereign over the universe, triumphant over all opposition. Sardis recalls that Jesus protects the church with a strong right hand. To Philadelphia the Key of David shouts out the marvelous message of His triumph over death. And finally, to Laodicea comes the author of creation, sovereign over men. He is a faithful witness, and has not hesitated to tell the truth about the works of any who rebelled against him.

We should be comforted by these pictures of Jesus. We're never out of God's love. As always, when His suffering people call, God will answer. And we'll see later that when this sinful age moves to its close, God will protect his people from the plagues that come on the wicked.

The fact that a particular problem only shows up in one church here doesn't mean it can't be found in other churches. God used local situations to highlight our common troubles. Any of them might apply to any of us. But let's not get ahead of ourselves. Let's see what was going on.

"YOU ARE HERE"

When you look at the poster, it shows exactly where you are in the building. The fireman comes to get you out safely. Usually he'll find you as his team sweeps the building, looking for anyone in trouble. But in the fire of sin, God comes right to you. You don't even have to tell Him where you are, because He already knows. All you have to do is ask to be rescued.

In the messages to the churches, God tells each one that He's been watching. He knows what their problems are. Ephesus is first.

> **I know your deeds and your toil and perseverance, and that you cannot endure evil men, and you put to the test those who call themselves apostles, and they are not, and you found them *to be* false; and you have perseverance and have endured for My name's sake, and have not grown weary. But I have *this* against you, that you have left your first love. Remember therefore from where you have fallen, and repent and do the deeds you did at first; or else I am coming to you, and will remove your lampstand out of its place—unless you repent. Yet this you do have, that you hate the deeds of the Nicolaitans, which I also hate. He who has an ear, let him hear what the Spirit says to the churches. To him who overcomes, I will grant to eat of the tree of life, which is in the Paradise of God. (2:2–8)**

God **knows their deeds**. They've been pretty good, refusing to **tolerate evil men**, like **false apostles**[2] and **the Nicolaitans**.[3] They have **persevered and endured** without **growing weary**. That's pretty high praise. But this church has **left its first love**.

God's far less concerned with works than with love. It's possible for us to do good things even if we don't love Him. But when that happens, He'll separate us from his saints and cast us into eternal fire (Matt 23:31–41). If we truly love Him, we'll do the things that come from love (Gal 5:22–23). He'll be able to trim the lamp of the Holy Spirit in our lives and use us for His purposes. Our works will be rewarded.

The believers in **Smyrna** have had **tribulation and poverty** (2:9). This double hit made them unable to provide the material things to survive. A group of evil Jews has been making it hard to keep the faith because of their **blasphemous** accusations. But this **synagogue of Satan** is not the end. Things are about to get worse. The **devil is about to cast some into prison** so **that they might be tested** (2:10).[4]

As we go through the rest of the churches, we hear echoes from all ages. In **Pergamum**, the believers are **holding fast to God's name** and **faith** in the heartland of the opposition, **where Satan's throne is** (2:13). **Antipas**, a **faithful witness, was killed** for his faith.[5] But some hold to the

---

2. You will notice that this isn't an exact quote from the verse. I put it in bold anyway, because it's what the verse says, although the word "false" is transposed from another part of the verse. ("False apostles" is substituted for "those who call themselves apostles, and they are not, and you found them *to be* false.") In other places words will be changed in quotations to let the form fit the sentence without sounding awkward. Those changes will not be allowed to change the meaning of the verse.

3. We're not sure who these people were. There are several theories, but for our purposes all we need to know is that they're a group of wicked people who probably started out as Christians.

4. The text goes on to say that this will last "ten days." To take this as meaning exactly "ten ordinary days" is to stretch the text beyond its roots. "Ten" is used in Hebrew writings to mean "several" or "a few" (Gen 31:7, Lev 26:26, Dan 1:20). Further, "days" is frequently used interchangeably with "years" in the Hebrew scriptures (Job 10:5; 32:7; 36:11, Pss 77:5; 90:9–10, etc.). This seems to be saying that the tribulation will last a "short time." See Appendix B for a discussion of the year/day principle.

5. This passage leads to our modern word "martyr." The Greek word for witness is *marturion*. Since Antipas was a "*marturion* unto death," he became a "martyr." The name "Antipas" opens up the possibility of Hebrew wordplay (a favorite sport of biblical writers). It can be the name of a real person, since Antipas was a shortened form of the Greek name "Antipater," as in "Herod Antipas." But it's made up of two Greek elements. "Anti-" means "in place of" and "pas" means "all." Combining them could mean "in place of all."

teaching of the Nicolaitans while others **hold the teaching of Balaam**, who led the Israelites to worship **idols** and **commit acts of immorality** (2:14). This reminds us that sin hasn't changed over the centuries.

We don't have to get too deep into details because the message is clear. God has standards. While He's willing to accept anyone who repents, He's *not* willing to let wickedness continue in the company of the saints. When we tolerate sin, that sin finds its way into our behavior. And we know how that story ends.

I'm going to skip over the other churches. Your pastor will find a lot of good material there for sermons, and there are some wonderful images. But if I go into all of them, I'll bore you, and that's not good.

These churches have just about every variety of Christian in them. Some stuck with God in the worst of times. Others seem to be doing pretty well, but let their love for God grow cold through neglect. One group followed God's law pretty well, while another tries to be politically correct and inclusive, putting everyone in danger. And a few have gone so far as to try to include their old sinful ways in their new "Christian" lives.

Every one of these virtues and vices has been in the church at every time in history. God knows the hearts of men (Ps 44:21). He's done His part in the past, and as we're about to see, He has an answer for every situation we can be in.

THE WAY OUT

When the fireman finds you in the smoke, his job is to get you out. But he can't help you if you won't go. In legal language, the terms of the covenant are *stipulations*. You do your part, and God will do His, since He's faithful.

The church at Ephesus has to **remember therefore from where they have fallen, and repent and do the deeds they did at first** (2:5). If they meet this stipulation, they'll get *blessings*. Christ will continue to watch over them. But if they don't, they'll receive *cursings*. In this case, He'll **remove their lampstand** so they won't be His church any more. This makes us think about what God did with the northern kingdom called

---

Since Jesus is the faithful witness (1:5) who died "in place of all," Antipas might be a reference to Jesus, with Pergamum being a symbolic reference to Jerusalem (cf. 11:8). Extending the wordplay, since we are "crucified with Christ" (Gal 2:20), Pergamum can even be a reference to the church throughout history. Curiously, that seems to be the point I was making before . . .

Israel. They were so wicked for so long that God finally dispersed them and called them "*Lo-ammi*" ("not my people," Hos 1:9).[6] God spread them out so thoroughly that nobody knows who they are.

God meets us where we are, but won't let us stay there. When we **have fallen** away from His growth plan, He comes back with a call and a warning. It's time to come home. Nothing less will do. If we try to make it on our own, we'll be lost forever.

The need to follow Christ and obey His commands should never be confused for salvation by works. That's legalism, and says that the things we do earn us points that help us to be saved. But, as Paul points out, our works never do anything to help us be saved (Rom 3:20, Gal 2:16). On the other hand, if we love God, we *will* keep His commandments (John 14:15). Let me put this another way.

> I do not keep God's commandments *to be saved*. I keep them because *I am saved*.

Smyrna's task sounds simple. They have to **be faithful until death** (2:10). Of course, this is more complicated than it sounds. Their **suffering** is going to be bad. But it doesn't mean that everyone in Smyrna will die. It just means that they need to live as if they're dying. Only a living faith that continues to the end is able to guarantee eternal life through Jesus.

The church at Pergamum was involved in **idolatry**. Their task is simple. **Repent!** If they don't, Jesus will **come to them quickly and make war against them with the sword of His mouth** (2:16). If this happens, it will make the suffering of Smyrna look like child's play. After all,

> Anyone who has set aside the Law of Moses dies without mercy on *the testimony of* two or three witnesses. How much severer punishment do you think he will deserve who has trampled under foot the Son of God, and has regarded as unclean the blood of the covenant by which he was sanctified, and has insulted the Spirit of grace? For we know Him who said, "Vengeance is Mine, I will repay." And again, "The Lord will judge His people." **It is a terrifying thing to fall into the hands of the living God**. (Heb 10:28–31, emphasis added)

By now it should be clear that God wants His covenant people to walk in His covenant. Failure to follow Him will have dire consequences. But following Him isn't complicated. As the prophet Micah put it, "What

---

6. This expression literally means "not my bloodline."

does the LORD require of you but to do justice, to love kindness, and to walk humbly with your God?" (Mic 6:8). All the problems that Jesus has been pointing out come from walking away from God. For example, Smyrna's idolatry was direct rebellion, since worshiping idols is putting a false god above the One True God.

Again, there are more details in the other churches, but let's move on.

BLESSINGS

In Ephesus, those who **overcome** will **eat fruit from the tree of life, which is in the Paradise of God** (2:7, cf. 22:2). Our long struggle will lead to immortality if we stay in love with our Savior (Gen 3:22, 2 Tim 4:7, 1 Cor 15:53). No matter how bad things are in this life, the reward in the next is better. The overcomer in Smyrna **will not be hurt by the second death. A crown of life** is reserved for him (2:10).

This "crown" is a laurel wreath like that given to the victor in an athletic event. It emphasizes that the saints are **victorious** through Christ over sin (15:2). It repeats Paul's statement that, "I have fought the good fight, I have finished the course, I have kept the faith; in the future there is laid up for me the crown (*stephanos*) of righteousness" (2 Tim 4:7–8).

> ### KEY GREEK WORD
> The word for "crown" here is *stephanos*, the laurel wreath given to the winner in an athletic contest. The other word translated "crown" in Revelation is *diadema*, a king's crown.

Each overcomer in Pergamum **will receive the hidden manna, and I will give him a white stone, and a new name written on the stone which no one knows but he who receives it** (2:17). The Israelites ate manna from heaven on their way from Egypt to the Promised Land (Exod 16:14ff.). Jesus is the true manna for the saints (John 6:30–35). In a symbolic way, Jesus has promised to live among the saints after they are raised to eternal life (John 14:1–3, Rev 21:22).

This image brings us to one of the patterns we talked about in chapter 2. The entire book of Revelation is built around pictures from the exodus. God used that historical event as a "type." That is, the deliverance of physical Israel from physical Egypt is an acted-out prophecy of the deliverance of spiritual Israel from spiritual Egypt. As we go through the book, more images will come from this story. They build up the big picture of what God's doing for anyone who is willing to follow Him.

The **new name** is another expression that comes from this same history. Abram (exalted father), was renamed "Abraham" (father of a multitude) after God promised that he'd be the father of nations (Gen 17:5). Jacob (one who takes by the heel) was renamed "Israel" (God perseveres) after he wrestled with God. Each time, the new name has a special importance in God's view. Here it's another expression of the promise to the overcomer.

The **white stone** is probably a reference to a "not guilty" vote by a court. Jesus took away our guilty verdict on the cross (Col 2:14). A white stone was also a pass to enter an "invitation-only" event. The wicked won't make it to the marriage supper of the lamb (19:9).

A FINAL CAUTION

Sardis was told to "**Remember therefore what you have received and heard; and keep *it*, and repent**" (3:3). The gospel isn't just something you receive. It's to be remembered and obeyed (2 Thes 1:8, 1 Pet 4:17). But there's something more important hidden in the Greek here. The word "keep" is *tēreō*, and means "to watch over, or guard." God gave the church a mission. It must spread the gospel to a dying world (Matt 28:19–20). "**If therefore you will not wake up, I will come like a thief, and you will not know at what hour I will come upon you.**" A church that doesn't *spread* the gospel is no better off than one that doesn't know it in the first place! The penalty reserved for Sardis is the same disaster Jesus promised for the wicked when he returned. He's coming "like a thief in the night" (cf. Matt 24:42–44, Luke 12:35–40). There won't be any warning, and the result will be catastrophic.

AND A FINAL BLESSING

Philadelphia has done well enough that Jesus doesn't say anything bad about them. Even though they only have a **little power, they've kept God's word and haven't denied His name** (3:8). As we saw just a bit ago, that word "kept" means that this church was a missionary church, spreading God's word to the people around them. **Because you have kept the word of My perseverance, I also will keep you from the hour of testing, that *hour* which is about to come upon the whole world, to test**

those who dwell upon the earth (3:10). This is awesome! There will be a short period time when God "tests" the world. The Greek word *peirasmou* means "to test to prove the nature of" **the world**. And this brings us to a very important pattern in the book of Revelation.

You've heard me say that the Bible interprets itself. Let's unpack this verse to see how this works. Jesus said that **those who dwell upon the earth** would have their nature tested. Since the issue in the Bible is "Are we for God or against Him?" it's not hard to see that this process has something to do with sorting out the saints and the wicked. But there's a lot more.

When God chose Abraham, He said, "in you all the families of the earth shall be blessed" (Gen 12:3). Did you catch that? Abraham was God's chosen man, a faithful servant (Heb 11:8–10; 13–19). So "the families of the earth" were the other people who didn't know the One True God. In Genesis 18:18, the phrase becomes "the nations of the earth." "The nations" is a term for the enemies of Israel all through the Old Testament.[7] In Joshua 4:24, we see "the peoples of the earth," again speaking of Israel's enemies.

In Revelation, **those who dwell on the earth** are God's enemies. In 6:10, the martyred saints ask for **vengeance** against them. In 8:13 and 12:12 **woes** are pronounced against them. In 11:10, they celebrate the death of God's **two witnesses**. In 13:8, 12, and 14 they **worship the beast**. In 17:12 and 18 they're allied with **Babylon, the mother of harlots**. It's hard to be clearer. The people being **tested** aren't the saints. The wicked go through the process of testing. And this brings us to a key question.

Why does God need to test anyone to prove their allegiance? After all, we know God knows our hearts (Luke 16:15, Acts 15:8). If He already knows, why does He need to test? It's really quite simple. God isn't the one who needs to know. The gospel is "a spectacle to the world, both to angels and men" (1 Cor 4:9). This is part of the answer to God's problem that we discussed in chapter 2. God has to demonstrate to *everyone*, men, angels, and even residents of other worlds (assuming they exist, cf. Job 1:6) that He treated every person on this earth with absolute fairness.

---

7. "The nations" is a biblical "code word" for anybody other than Israel. Since Israel is another name for the saints, "the nations" are the wicked. I know that I haven't gone through this in detail. As we go on through Revelation, this will become very clear. If you're in a hurry, get my book *I Want to be Left Behind* (Maitland, FL: BibleOnly Press, 2002), and read chapter 2. Other good references are O. Palmer Robertson's *The Israel of God* (Philipsburg, NJ: P&R, 2001), and Hans LaRondelle's *The Israel of God in Prophecy* (Berrien Springs, MI: Andrews University Press, 1996).

The saints are saints because they've been **faithful until death**. If they had to, they would have died for the gospel. They don't need any more testing. But the wicked have to be given every possible chance to repent. When they don't, they'll prove their loyalty to Satan (9:20–21). And when the universe checks the records, God will be vindicated from Satan's false accusations.

What does this mean for Philadelphia? They don't go through the testing! Does it mean that they're taken out of the earth while this goes on? No. That would defeat God's purpose. God can't take them out, because that would say the outcome is pre-judged, and that's not God's method. Noah wasn't taken out of the earth during the flood; he was saved *through* the flood in the ark (Gen 6–9). Daniel's three friends weren't kept out of the furnace; they were saved *through* the furnace (Dan 3). And the disciples weren't kept out of temptations; they were saved *through* the temptations (John 17:15). In every case, God's servants were **kept** from harm. Just like those other times, the saints will be there when it happens, completely protected by God. As the psalmist says:

> You will not be afraid of the terror by night, or of the arrow that flies by day; Of the pestilence that stalks in darkness, Or of the destruction that lays waste at noon. A thousand may fall at your side, and ten thousand at your right hand; *but* it shall not approach you. You will only look on with your eyes, and see the recompense of the wicked. For you have made the LORD, my refuge, *Even* the Most High, your dwelling place. (Pss 91:5–9)[8]

What an awesome God! Even in the worst of times, He'll look out for us. No saint has anything to fear during the time of testing. But there's an even greater promise here. Because Philadelphia was doing what God required, He promised to make the **synagogue of Satan . . . come and bow down at your feet, and to know that I have loved you** (3:9). After the millennium, when the wicked have been shown their guilt, they will give homage to God and His saints before they're destroyed in the **lake of fire**.

HOLD ON!

I know this is different from what you have heard before. Please don't add this to your list of stupid things I've said and throw the book down in disgust. Hopefully by now you've seen that I carefully support each new

---

8. We'll discuss this more when we get to the fifth and sixth trumpets.

idea with scripture. I'll cover this, too. But we won't get to the millennium for a while. So hang on. Discovering God's word can challenge old ideas, but it's exciting, too.

SEALING THE DEAL

The fire metaphor can only take us so far. We have to look at one last legal issue. No contract is valid unless it's witnessed. I can ask someone to build a house. We can reach a deal where all of the specifics are set. And we can both sign the paper. But if there's any problem later, neither one of us can enforce the contract because there aren't any witnesses. It's my word against his.

God's eternal covenant is the same. It has to be witnessed. And every one of the seven messages ends with, **He who has an ear, let him hear what the Spirit says to the churches**. This is a call for witnesses. "On the evidence of two or three witnesses a matter shall be confirmed" (Deut 19:15). Since there are more than "two or three" witnesses listed, the covenant is valid. And this brings us to a technical point.

This is called "two-witness theology." In Revelation 1 we saw Jesus **the faithful witness**. In Pergamum, **Antipas** was **my faithful witness**. This idea of two or three witnesses comes up again later on when **two witnesses testify** in **the holy city** (11:3ff). We'll discuss it more there, but for now it's important to see that this legal concept is a major part of the message. Even more important, the "hearing formula" comes from the *Shema*, the most central statement of Jewish faith.

> Hear, O Israel! The LORD is God, the LORD is One! (Deut 6:4)

When a Jewish lawyer asked Jesus what the greatest commandment in the law was, He began His answer with the *Shema* (Mark 12:28–33). He used the variant form **He who has an ear, let him hear** in His teaching to emphasize the universal need to hear and obey His message (Matt 11:15, Mark 4:23, Luke 14:35, etc.). This shows that the message to the church is universal. The Israelites in the wilderness had to hear and obey. The Jews in Jesus' day had to hear and obey. And we have to hear and obey.

In essence, there's only one covenant. It applies to everyone, whether Jew or Gentile (Rom 10:12). In Christ, every promise is "Yes" (2 Cor 1:20). There's no separation based on heritage, because Jesus makes all men into one people of God (Eph 2:13–16). And everyone shares in the same promises. We won't fear **the second death**, because we'll **eat of the tree of life, which is in the Paradise of God** (2:7). If we wanted to go through all of the biblical sources, we'd discover that the covenant is neatly summarized in Micah 6:8.

> He has told you, O man, what is good. And what does the LORD require of you but to do justice, to love kindness, and to walk humbly with your God?

PUTTING IT TOGETHER

The fire of sin burns hot today. Its smoke blinds us unless we turn to God for help. Some in the church have never lost their love for Him. Others have fallen into a variety of ills. These include political correctness, where we tolerate public sins because we don't want to be "judgmental." Others were immoral, thinking that once they have "been saved," they can't lose their salvation. And the worst off of all are those who have become self-sufficient. They don't think that they need to renew and refresh their walk with God daily.

Every church Jesus addressed is with us today. Most of their troubles are found in every local church body. That's why this is really "The Message to the Church." Yes, Jesus spoke to seven real churches, but He chose seven to symbolize his perfect and holy message to *the church*. No sin mentioned in the message is new. They've all been cancers among God's people since the beginning. And all of them have to be renounced. We must return to **our first love**. All Jesus asks is that we humbly walk with Him in love, and He will lead us safely out of the flames. The map on the wall was drawn with His blood on the cross. He is the living way out (Heb 10:19–25).

WE'RE NOT DONE

If God had stopped here, we'd have a nice letter to seven churches. But God's not done. **After this, I looked and saw an open door in heaven. The voice like a trumpet said, "Come up here, and I will show you what must happen after these things** (4:1).

Just as it seems that John's gotten all the message he's supposed to get, God tells him, "Not so fast. There's more." This time, because God uses His trumpet voice, we know that the covenant scene is changing. The *Covenant Described* is done, and the *Covenant Displayed* is about to begin.

5

"Come on Up!"

JOHN'S FIRST VISION ENDED with a **door open in heaven** and an invitation for him to **Come up here!** because there was more to see (4:1). These words remind us of something very important. Hebrew writers were very visual and painted graphic word pictures so their readers could see what they had seen. Like them, we have to use our mind's eye to "see" what John saw.

To understand what the pictures mean, we need some rules to let John's writing speak for itself. Without them, John's visions will turn into psychedelic nonsense. These rules are generally called the "Historical-Grammatical Method." In essence, we must:

1. Base our study on historical, physical and cultural settings.
2. Pay real attention to the grammar and structure of each sentence and paragraph.
3. Identify figurative language and determine its intended literal meaning.
4. Examine the context: the passage as a whole; the book as a whole; the book within its literary type and biblical setting.
5. Compare each passage to others that use the same language or talk about the same subject. We start with the same author, but these passages can be anywhere in the Bible.

In this case, John's invitation into heaven isn't new. It happened in Isaiah 6, Ezekiel 1, and several intertestamental Jewish apocalypses.[1] Angels guide the seer through heaven where he sees symbolic visions

---

1. "Intertestamental" refers to books written in the four centuries between the writing of the last book of the Old Testament and the first book of the New Testament.

of beasts and battles. Eventually he returns with a message of hope for God's harassed people. Satan may be causing trouble now, but God will eventually win and rescue His saints. This pattern was so well known that John's audience would have felt right at home. In a general way, they knew what was coming. The story of the war between God and Satan was about to play out in front of them, live and in Technicolor.[2] Since Jewish apocalypses tell symbolic stories, the **trumpet voice** should tell us that this installment's the story of the covenant.

INTERTESTAMENTAL JEWISH APOCALYPSES WITH FEATURES SIMILAR TO REVELATION		
1 Enoch	2 Baruch	2 Esdras
2 Enoch	3 Baruch	The Apocalypse of Abraham

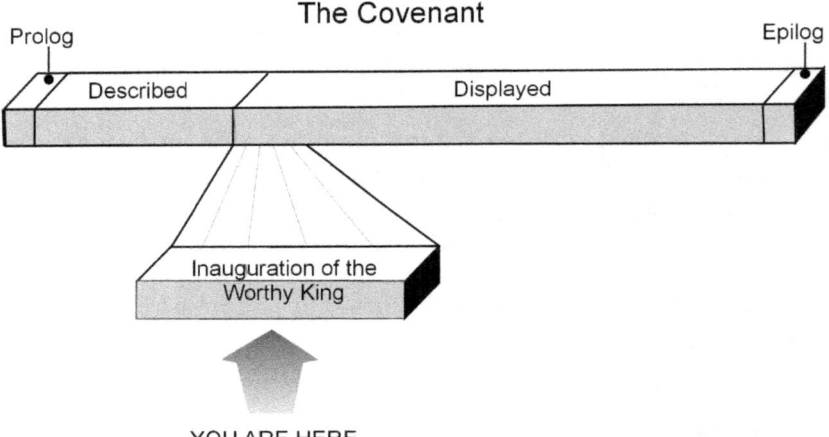

We're about to see the *Covenant Displayed*. The message to the church *described* the covenant. Now we get to see how it plays out. No, we're not going to get a detailed blow-by-blow future history ready for CNN or the New York Times. After all, that won't help us keep the words of the prophecy (1:3). We need information about the war between Christ and Satan. Battlefield intelligence will help us avoid the devil's ambushes.

John's immediately taken in the Spirit (4:2). These words mark the beginning of the second of four visions in the book. Each one moves the book to a new subject. And as we'll see, the last three deal with different eras.

---

2. To emphasize the need to think like John, I frequently tell my classes that they can't understand Revelation without their yarmulke (Jewish prayer cap).

"In the Spirit" Vision Markers in Revelation			
1:10	4:2	17:3	20:10
The Church	This Sinful Age	Millennium	New Earth

Like any good movie, the first step is to set the scene. John looks into the heavenly throne room and sees One sitting on the throne (4:2). No Jew would ever speak the name of Yahweh because it was just too sacred. So John found a respectful way to tell us that the Father is on the throne.

> **He who was sitting** *was* **like a jasper stone and a sardius in appearance; and** *there was* **a rainbow around the throne, like an emerald in appearance.** (4:3)

Jasper and **sardius** were the first and last stones listed in the breastplate of judgment that the high priest wore and emphasize that God is the judge of the universe (Exod 28:17-20 KJV). Ezekiel saw the **rainbow around the throne** as God prepared to pass judgment on apostate Israel (Ezek 1:27–28). It was also the sign God gave Noah as a guarantee of the covenant never to destroy the earth again with a flood (Gen 9:9–17).

> **From the throne proceed flashes of lightning and sounds and peals of thunder. And** *there were* **seven lamps of fire burning before the throne, which are the seven Spirits of God; and before the throne** *there was,* **as it were, a sea of glass like crystal.** (4:5-6)

Lightning, sounds, and peals of thunder take us back to Sinai, where God met with the Israelites to deliver the covenant (Exod 19:5–6; 16–19; 20:18; 34:28). The **sea of glass like crystal** recalls the laver in Solomon's temple, showing us that this scene is in God's temple in heaven (1 Kgs 7:23–25). The **seven lamps of fire** are the **seven golden lampstands** we saw in chapter 1. They are also the **seven Spirits of God**, and reflect off the **sea of glass** like a thousand diamonds, shining the glory of God everywhere for anyone who's willing to look. Jesus told the disciples that He couldn't be everywhere at once, but He'd send the Holy Spirit to do just that (John 16:7–11).[3]

To get the impact of the scene around the Father, imagine a double-wide throne like ancient kings used. The **elders** are in a circle around it, and in a larger circle are the **living creatures**.

---

3. By now you know that "seven" is just a way of emphasizing the holiness and perfection of the Holy Spirit, not a way of saying that there are seven holy spirits.

> And around the throne *were* twenty-four thrones; and upon the thrones *I saw* twenty-four elders sitting, clothed in white garments, and golden crowns on their heads.
>
> The twenty-four elders will fall down before Him who sits on the throne, and will worship Him who lives forever and ever, and will cast their crowns before the throne, saying, "Worthy art Thou, our Lord and our God, to receive glory and honor and power; for Thou didst create all things, and because of Thy will they existed, and were created." (4:4; 10–11)

Remember, this is symbolic and intended to tell a story. It's not intended to be physically exact.[4] Israel was called to be a "kingdom of priests" (Exod 19:6). The **elders** have the same number and function as priests.[5] They are overcomers and are called *presbuteroi*, a human job description. This means the **elders** are probably redeemed humans doing a priestly job. We can't tell whether they're the saints that Jesus took with him at His ascension or just part of the vision (Eph 4:8).

THE ELDERS
• There were 24 priestly courses (1 Chron 24:1–5).
• They present incense, a priestly act (5:8).
• They wear the victor's crown, the *stephanos*.
• They are *presbuteroi*, a title used for Jewish and church leaders (Matt 15:2; 26:3, Acts 2:17; 15:4, Titus 1:5, James 5:14).

The elders praise God as the Creator. This may seem odd, since John's gospel calls Jesus the Creator (John 1:2). But the two are "one" in essence, with a distinction that will let us see the way the covenant works (John 10:30). Shortly we'll see that Jesus' worthiness is based on the cross, not Creation.

The next part of the scene is around the throne. There we see

> ... four living creatures full of eyes in front and behind. And the first creature *was* like a lion, and the second creature like a calf, and the third creature had a face like that of a man, and the fourth creature *was* like a flying eagle. And the four living creatures, each one of them having six wings, are full of eyes

---

4. Requiring the scene to be physically exact is an error called "literalism." It makes it hard for us to hear God's message.

5. It's worth noting that the number 24 doesn't appear anywhere in scripture other than in the 24 priestly courses and the 24 elders.

around and within; and day and night they do not cease to say, "Holy, holy, holy, *is* the LORD God, the Almighty, who was and who is and who is to come." (4:6–8)

These **living creatures** are very similar to beings Ezekiel saw around God in the Temple (Ezek 1:4–12). They had human form and went wherever the Spirit went. This suggests that the living creatures represent people who follow God. Here they constantly praise God for his **holiness**, repeating his eternal nature.

The four have four different faces: **lion, calf, man,** and **eagle**. When the Israelites left Egypt, God instructed Moses to arrange the tribes in a specific way around the tabernacle (Num 2). The same four faces were on the flags of the four tribes that were closest to the tabernacle. Any person who went to the tabernacle had to pass one of the flags.

		ENSIGNS OF ISRAEL
Judah	East	**Lion** (Num 2:3, Gen 49:9)
Ephraim	West	**Ox** or **Calf** (Num 2:18, Deut 33:13–17)
Reuben	South	**Man** (Num 2:10, Gen 49:3)
Dan	North	**Eagle** (Num 2:25, Josephus, *Antiquities* book 12, chapter 4, section 12)[6]

God's presence was in the tabernacle in the wilderness (Lev 16:2). In a way these four tribes were the representatives of Israel guarding the approach to God. In the same way, the four living creatures have to be passed to approach the Almighty in the heavenly tabernacle. This confirms that the four living beings are symbolic representations of true Israel. Let's look at a picture of this.

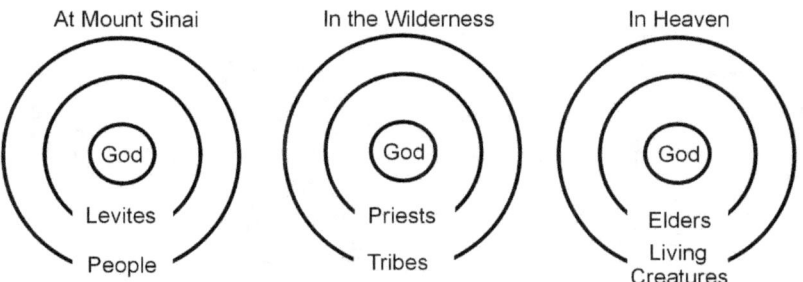

---

6. It's obvious that Josephus isn't a scripture reference. Genesis 49:17 calls Dan a snake. Tradition says that Ahiezer, one of the leaders of the tribe, didn't like the snake symbol and substituted an Eagle with the snake in its claws.

When John saw the picture on the right, it was a symbolic echo of the picture in the middle. God's in the center, with priests coming to minister in His presence in the tabernacle. The tribes formed the outer circle around the tabernacle. In turn, that picture's a reflection of the way things were arranged at Sinai (where the voice like a trumpet was first heard). God was at the top of the mountain. The Levites were allowed to be on the sides of the mountain (Exod 24:1–2), and the people had to stay away in a ring around the base (Exod 19:12). The physical arrangement in heaven repeats the story of Sinai and ancient Israel.

PUTTING THE SCENE TOGETHER

Revelation 4 shows us the throne room in the heavenly Temple. *El Shaddai*, the God of Israel, is seated on the throne, dressed as the Judge of the earth. Surrounding Him are the **Elders**, the priests of Israel. Every course is present, symbolically presenting all of Israel as a kingdom of priests. Since this imagery is applied to both physical Israel in the Old Testament (Exod 19:6) and the church in the New Testament (1 Pet 2:9), the saints of all ages are symbolically included.

The four **Living Creatures** are the next circle. They again represent Israel, this time as those who follow God wherever He leads. They praise God continually, crying **Holy, Holy, Holy**. When they praise, the elders **fall on their faces and cast their crowns** before God, showing that it is only through His marvelous gift of salvation that they are able to stand in His presence.

All this is glorious, but so far it doesn't tell us anything about why God showed this to John. That comes next.

6

Coronation!

AT THE **RIGHT HAND** of the Father sits a **scroll**. It has **writing inside and out**, and is **sealed with seven seals** (5:1). We've already seen that "seven" signifies perfection and completeness. But **who is worthy to open the scroll** (5:2)?

No one in heaven or on the earth or under the earth was able to open the scroll, or to look at it (5:3). Not one being in any part of the universe was **worthy**. The search went *everywhere*. Even the Father wasn't worthy![1] This made John **weep greatly** (5:4).[2] His crying shows us that John understood the scene and the importance of opening the scroll. This wasn't just a screenplay. It was important to him in a very personal way.

One of the elders told him, "Stop weeping. Behold, the Lion that is from the tribe of Judah, the Root of David, has overcome so as to open the book and its seven seals" (5:5). Jesus is worthy because **He was slain, and purchased for God with His blood** *men* **from every tribe and tongue and people and nation** (5:9). But why does the Cross make Him worthy to open the scroll when the Father isn't? After all, aren't both of them God?

Jesus is **the Lion of Judah** (Gen 49:9) and **the Root of David** (Isa 11:10; 53:1–2). Since Jesus **overcame**, John should expect to see a triumphant Jesus. But instead of a **Lion**, he sees a **lamb standing as if slain** (5:6). And this repeats a pattern. John was *told* one thing, but he *saw* something else. That happened in chapter 1 when he *heard* the **voice like a trumpet** but *saw* Jesus (1:10–12). But this time there's something else going on.

---

1. Before you get excited, remember that the Father's already in the scene, and the text says *nobody* could be found who was worthy. That *has* to include the Father!

2. The Greek word used here suggests the bitter wailing of mourners for the dead. John didn't just sob, he cried inconsolably.

Because a lamb could be a sin offering (Lev 4:32) or the Passover sacrifice (Lev 12:3–5), we have to play detective.

In the last chapter we identified the cast members. The **living creatures** and the **elders** both represented Israel. Since all twenty-four courses of priests (the elders) were present, this has to be one of the three feasts that all of the priests and men of Israel had to attend. Those are Passover, Pentecost, and Tabernacles (Deut 16:16). Passover was the only one with a sacrificial lamb.

The first Passover freed Israel from Egyptian slavery. Jesus' death as our Passover frees us from slavery to sin (1 Cor 5:7). This scene represents Passover. But there's more in this verse. The **lamb has seven horns and seven eyes, which are the seven Spirits of God, sent out into all the earth** (5:6). The Holy Spirit was sent into **all the earth** on Pentecost (Acts 1:8, 2:1–4). This scene also represents that festival. And this sets up another pattern.

The symbolic part of Revelation is built around the festival calendar. Passover and Pentecost were spring festivals, typologically fulfilled in Christ's first advent. Revelation presents them as completed. The fall festivals—Trumpets, Atonement, and Tabernacles—will be fulfilled as the story moves on. This calendar is the "backbone" of the symbolic part of the book.

Before we figure out what's in the scroll, let's listen to more of the scene.

> And when He had taken the book, the four living creatures and the twenty-four elders fell down before the Lamb, having each one a harp, and golden bowls full of incense, which are the prayers of the saints. And they sang a new song, saying, "Worthy art Thou to take the book, and to break its seals; for Thou wast slain, and didst purchase for God with Thy blood *men* from every tribe and tongue and people and nation. And Thou hast made them *to be* a kingdom and priests to our God; and they will reign upon the earth." (5:8–10)

When Jesus takes the scroll, the **living creatures** and **elders**—true Israel—God's kingdom of priests, bursts into praise. They present **incense—the prayers of the saints**—in a royal celebration of thanksgiving. They praise Jesus because he **purchased men from every tribe and tongue and people and nation with His blood**. You can't get any more universal than that. Nobody's left out. And this praise isn't just from "Jewish" voices.

In Exodus 19:5–6, God promised the Israelites they'd be His kingdom of priests *if* they'd "keep My covenant." Here **God has made** even Gentiles **to be priests to our God.** Since the elders are priests, the representatives of Israel before God, and some of them are Gentiles, "Israel" is now made up of believers from every ethnic group.³ God "broke down the barrier of the dividing wall" between Jews and Gentiles (Eph 2:14).

This uniquely "Jewish" scene is in the temple where Gentiles were forbidden.⁴ But a converted Gentile was "joined to the Lord," and could participate in Temple services (Isa 56:3). The Gentiles in this scene have received the promise to Israel and become part of the holiest tribe in Israel. They are true Jews in every way.⁵

The living creatures and elders continue praising (5:11). They're joined by **myriads and myriads and thousands of thousands of angels**. Using a **loud voice** they cry out, **Worthy is the Lamb that was slain to receive power and riches and wisdom and might and honor and glory and blessing**! (5:12). With seven-fold worthiness, Jesus receives the kingdom. And with this, **every created thing which is in heaven and on the earth and under the earth and on the sea, and all things in them** joins the chorus. Such a celebration is worth a moment of reflection.

> O Sing to the LORD a new song, for He has done wonderful things.
> His right hand and His holy arm have gained the victory for Him.
> The LORD has made known His salvation; He has revealed His
>   righteousness in the sight of the nations.
> He has remembered His lovingkindness and His faithfulness to
>   the house of Israel.
> All the ends of the earth have seen the salvation of our God.
> Shout joyfully to the LORD, all the earth; Break forth and sing for
>   joy and sing praises.

---

3. This is the point of Paul's argument in Romans 11:16–26. Unbelieving Jews are broken off from the olive tree named "Israel." Believing Gentiles are grafted into the olive tree. "In this manner" (Rom 11:26, literal translation) all the believers ("Israel") will be saved. This is discussed at length in chapter 2 of *I Want to be Left Behind* (Maitland, FL: BibleOnly Press, 2002).

4. There was death penalty for Gentiles who entered the Temple. In Acts 21:28, the Jews tried to kill Paul for supposedly bringing a Gentile into the Temple.

5. The rabbis point out that a Gentile who has fully converted to Judaism is a Jew in every way.

> Sing praises to the LORD with the lyre; with the lyre and the sound of melody.
> With trumpets and the sound of the horn shout joyfully before the King, the LORD.
> Let the sea roar and all it contains, the world and those who dwell in it.
> Let the rivers clap their hands;
> Let the mountains sing together for joy before the LORD; for He is coming to judge the earth;
> He will judge the world with righteousness, and the peoples with equity. (Psalm 98)

When man fell in Eden, nature was cursed (Gen 3:17–18), so even nature cries out for redemption. In the Psalm, man is called to sing "a new song" because the Lord "revealed" his righteousness to the entire world in the Messiah and the cross. The "sea and all it contains," "the world," "the rivers," and "the mountains" are to join in. As a result of the cross, Jesus will judge. In essence, this Psalm is a celebration of Jesus' enthronement. And because in many ways it's parallel to Revelation 4–5, it helps us see the nature of the ceremony there. But first, let's read the final line of the chapter.

> **"To Him who sits on the throne, and to the Lamb, *be* blessing and honor and glory and dominion forever and ever." And the four living creatures kept saying, "Amen." And the elders fell down and worshiped.** (5:13–14)

The key word here is **dominion**. The Greek word *kratos* signifies the power of a sovereign king. By picking up the **scroll**, Jesus completed the ceremony that gave him power to rule. We know when that happened.

> And Jesus came up and spoke to them, saying, "All authority has been given to Me in heaven and on earth" (Matt 28:18).

When Jesus ascended after the resurrection He was inaugurated as our King, an honor earned on the Cross (John 20:17, Php 2:8–11). The Cross is the reason Jesus is **worthy to open the scroll**. And this leaves us with a puzzle. What's the big deal with opening the scroll? To answer that, we have to look at the scene again.

First we saw representatives of Israel around the throne of the sovereign. Then we saw a scroll sitting on the throne to the Father's right. Jesus picked it up and rejoicing broke out. To a Jew, this scene would be very familiar. It's a coronation.

Steps in Crowning a New King	
1. The new king is anointed (1 Sam 16:13, 2 Kgs 9:6).	1. Jesus was anointed when He was baptized in the Jordan (Matt 3:17).
2. He is acclaimed by the people (1 Kgs 1:39).	2. He was acclaimed by the Holy Spirit.
3. He writes a copy of the Law in the presence of the priests (Deut 17:14–20).	3. He wrote the Law and delivered it at Sinai.
4. He receives the copy of the Law when he's crowned in the Temple (2 Kgs 11:9–12).	4. He received His copy of the Law from the position at the right hand of the father, where it was lying on the throne.
5. He's acclaimed by the people (2 Kgs 11:12).	5. All of true Israel celebrates His coronation.

This is the crowning of our great King. But what's the big deal with the scroll? Certainly the Father should be worthy to open the Torah scroll. After all, He and Jesus are both fully God. It's pretty hard to imagine a circumstance where they wouldn't be in full agreement on the Torah. They both already know what it says! There's got to be something more. Let's back up a bit.

The Torah was around long before the cross. Suppose Jesus hadn't lived a sinless life. Suppose He gave in to the temptation to simply do away with His tormentors and came down from the cross. The plan of salvation would have fallen apart. And it would have failed for a very specific reason.

Salvation is based on the covenant. It's a contract.[6] Its terms are spelled out in Torah. Basically, Jesus says that the wages for our sin is death (Rom 3:23). But He love us so much that He'll die for us. All we have to do is have faith in him.

---

6. Technically, it's an adhesion contract. Think about your driver's license. It's a privilege to drive, not a right. The state sets the terms, and there's no negotiation. You meet the terms or you don't drive. In the same way, the divine covenant offers us the privilege to live. We don't have to. But if we want to, we have to accept the covenant and meet its conditions. If we don't, God will eventually stop giving us life. We will die.

If Christ hadn't died on the Cross, He wouldn't have done His part. In legal terms, the Cross is His *bona fides*. He *has* to do His part. And that's why the cross makes Jesus worthy to open the scroll. Opening the scroll isn't designed to let Jesus read it. It lets Him *enforce* it to bless us with eternal life. Because He died for us on the cross, Jesus is able to say, "I did my part. Follow me and see what I can do for you."

Now we can understand what's happening. The Israel of God celebrates because Jesus **purchased them with His blood** (Gal 6:16). The angels celebrate because Hope has come. And John can stop crying because Israel has its King. Before the Cross, people kept the covenant in hopeful anticipation that it would be fulfilled. We follow it now because the Cross guarantees fulfillment.

This scene introduces the symbolic part of the book. When Jesus dictated the message to the church from the Temple, every part of that message had its roots in the introductory scene. The same is true here. Every part of the book from here on has its roots in Jesus' coronation as our covenant king. And the book of the covenant is the foundation of every vision to come. Now that Israel has its king, we're ready to see the *Covenant Displayed*.

7

I Hear Hoof Beats

JUST WHEN WE FIGURE out that the scroll is the covenant, the scene shifts. It looked like Jesus was going to read the terms of the covenant so nobody could get it wrong. Instead, we see the first of a group of scenes that make us wonder if someone put something in that bottle of spring water we've been drinking. Of course, it wouldn't make a lot of sense for Jesus to read the rules. After all, that's basically what He did in the message to the church. Each of its seven parts described the terms of the deal. He's got to do something different. We're about to see the next stage of the covenant drama.

The Covenant Displayed

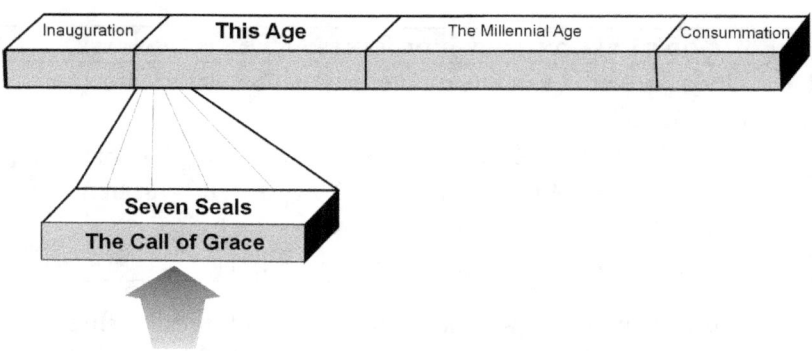

YOU ARE HERE

This scene begins with **and I saw** (6:1). This tells us there's a shift in focus, but this time it's not very dramatic. We're still in the temple. **The Lamb opens seals** and one-by-one the **four living creatures say, "Go."**[1]

---

1. Most translations say, "come," but that doesn't make a lot of sense here. The verb *erchomai* has a primary sense of motion and can mean "come" or "go." Here it's in the imperative or command form, instructing the riders to do something. In every case the

Each time, a **horse goes out** on a specific task (6:2, 3, 4, 8). Let's look at the big picture first.

The horses are different colors: white, red, black and pale. The imagery here comes from the prophet Zechariah. In chapters 1 and 6 he saw visions of different colored horses. Each time they "patrolled the earth." The four colors are different in Zechariah and John's visions, but that's not really important. What's important is that they went over the earth. Since this is the home of the earth dwellers, this represents God's interventions with the wicked (3:10, 6:10, etc.).

The horses bring war, strife, famine, and death. These are common Old Testament themes. Each one is a judgment God sends against His people when they run away from Him to join their wicked neighbors in rebellion. They're designed to get their attention.

We had a good example of this when Islamic terrorists destroyed the World Trade Center on 9/11. Churches were filled. People realized their mortality and their need for a savior. God used this evil act by wicked men to bring back people who had forgotten Him. His calamities come so that men will know that *He* is the only true God (Isa 45:6–8). That's why He sent the plagues on Egypt (Exod 7:5, 17). It's why He sent Nebuchadnezzar to destroy Jerusalem and take the Jews captive (Ezek 6–12). And that's what John sees.

God's Premonitory Judgments Against Apostasy
• "God's Arrows"—Famine, plague, destruction, wild beasts (Deut 32:23–25, 42).
• Sevenfold retribution—Sword, pestilence, famine (Lev 26:23–26).
• Sword, famine, pestilence (Jer 21:7–9, 24:10, 29:17–18, etc.).
• Famine, plague, wild beasts (Ezek 5:17).
• Sword, famine, plague, wild beasts (Ezek 14:21).

God's so anxious to save men that He doesn't just call them to come to Him (cf. 2 Pet 3:9). He intervenes in the world to get their attention. The "Four Horsemen of the Apocalypse" are "God's Arrows" to bring wayward people back to God. They represent the call of grace.

---

horse "goes" on its errand.

THE BIBLE INTERPRETS ITSELF

Let's stop for a moment. You may have heard that the book of Revelation is a detailed road map for coming events. Unfortunately, the teachers who said this forgot the key to understanding the Bible. The Bible *is* its own best interpreter. In the last few paragraphs, we didn't use the newspaper, cable news, or any ordinary man to tell us what the vision's about. Instead, we looked at what God told the prophets. We saw the language He used. Then we saw it matched the language of what He revealed to John. That's how we were able to let Jesus tell us what *He* meant. And that's the *only* way to properly understand the Bible.

If you simply can't accept what the Bible is saying, I pray that at some point God will get your attention the way He got mine. But please don't take this as saying that I know everything or that I don't make mistakes. Get out your Bible. Read the cross-references I give. Read what comes before and after them. See what God says there. See if it matches what I say here. If it doesn't, then go where God leads you. But if it does match, have the courage to listen to God as He speaks. Don't listen because I said it. Listen because God said it.

A WHITE HORSE

The four horsemen represent God's gracious call to men. This suggests another pattern. The seven Seals are based on a theme. They aren't designed to be a blow-by-blow future history. This suggests that the Trumpets and Bowls may also be designed around themes. We'll confirm that when we get there.

The first horseman **sat on a white** horse (6:2). This tells us a lot about him. Seventeen of the sixty five times "white" is used in the Bible are in Revelation, so that's where we should look. The saints are dressed in white (3:4–5; 4:4; 6:11; 7:9, 13–14; 19:14). It's the color of righteousness. No evil character ever gets to wear white.

A crown was given to him. This odd language deserves a comment. Theologians call it the "divine passive." We already saw that the name of God was too holy for any ordinary person to speak.[2] So when John wanted to say that God gave something to someone, he said that "it was given to him." Any Jewish reader here would automatically know that God was the one who gave the crown to the rider.

---

2. Many Jews get around this by calling God *ha Shem*, "the Name."

This is no ordinary crown. It's a *stephanos*, the laurel wreath of victory the saints in Smyrna and Philadelphia were promised if they were faithful (2:10; 3:11). This rider has been faithful and received his crown of victory. But notice that he goes out **overcoming, and to overcome**.[3] Saints who've received their crown don't go back to overcome anymore. But there is someone who overcame and continues to overcome. It's Jesus.

Before you get all worked up and complain that Jesus can't open the seal *and* ride the horse, let's back up a step. This is a *symbolic vision*. It doesn't have to follow the rules of physical reality. God can mix and match any way He wants to present His message. You've seen this in movies. In *Inspector General*, Danny Kaye has a conversation with three alter egos. He plays all of them, so there are four Danny Kaye's in the scene. It doesn't mean there were four of him in real life. It just means the scene needs four of him to tell the story. This means it's no big deal if Jesus both opens the first seal and is the rider on the white horse. It's the message that's important, and that message is in His **bow**.[4] In this case, the imagery comes from Isaiah.

> Who has aroused one from the east
> Whom He calls in righteousness to His feet?
> He delivers up nations before him,
> And subdues kings.
> He makes them like dust with his sword,
> As the wind-driven chaff with his bow." (Isa 41:2)

Here God speaks of His servant, a **king from the east** who does God's will by conquering His enemies with a bow (cf. 16:12).[5] Jesus overcame on the cross, and helps the saints to overcome by sending the Holy Spirit to dwell in them (John 16:7, Rom 8:9).

---

3. The Greek word *nikao* is usually translated "conquer" here. In the message to the church it's translated "overcome." The two English words mean roughly the same thing, but have a different impact. We're using "overcome" to show the connection to victory in righteousness instead of war.

4. We shouldn't think that is doesn't have any arrows because they aren't mentioned. The Old Testament talks about bows as weapons over forty times, but only mentions arrows sixteen times.

5. A bow is a particularly appropriate weapon to shoot God's arrows, don't you think?

A RED HORSE

> And when He broke the second seal, I heard the second living creature saying, "Come." And another, a red horse, went out; and to him who sat on it, it was granted to take peace from the earth, and that *men* should slay one another; and a great sword was given to him. (6:3-4)

Once again, God gives a weapon to the rider.[6] The *machairos* is a short **sword**, commonly used in battle. It can also be a dagger. It's hard to imagine a better image of the evil that men do to each other. Men often realize their need for God when facing death.[7]

It's tempting to try to figure out every detail, but sometimes we just can't be sure. The **red horse** is the color of blood (19:15). It's also the color of sin (Isa 1:18) and the color of the **red dragon**, a symbol of **Satan** (12:3). But it can also be the color of God's robe (Isa 63:1). Based on the rest of the imagery, it seems that the color of blood is the best choice, but we won't make it an article of faith.

A BLACK HORSE

> And when He broke the third seal, I heard the third living creature saying, "Come." And I looked, and behold, a black horse; and he who sat on it had a pair of scales in his hand. And I heard as it were a voice in the center of the four living creatures saying, "A quart of wheat for a denarius, and three quarts of barley for a denarius; and do not harm the oil and the wine." (6:5-6)

Let's tackle the simple parts first. A **denarius** was a day's wage in John's day. The **scales** allow the rider to weigh out a **quart of wheat** or **three quarts of barley** for that money. That little bit of food would be barely enough to keep a family from starving. When we add **oil and wine**, this looks like the picture of a famine. But it's more.

The golden lampstands in the temple represent the light each church sends to the world by the power of the Holy Spirit (Matt 5:14). This contrasts with the dark night that surrounds anyone who doesn't know Jesus (John 8:12). The lampstands in the temple burned olive oil, so the oil in this figure represents the Holy Spirit (Exod 27:20).

---

6. The divine passive again!
7. It's been said that there are no atheists in foxholes.

Wine can represent several things, depending on context. But one thing seems closest to Jesus. At the Last Supper it's, "My blood of the covenant, which is poured out for many for the forgiveness of sins" (Matt 26:27). When we drink the wine at the Lord's Supper (1 Cor 11:23–26), we proclaim the message of the cross.

When we put it all together, the **black horse** shows the darkness when we walk without God. The message of the cross is preserved through this spiritual famine. God will never allow the still, small voice of the Holy Spirit to be silenced (cf. 1 Kgs 19:12 KJV).

AN ASHEN HORSE

> And when He broke the fourth seal, I heard the voice of the fourth living creature saying, "Come." And I looked, and behold, an ashen horse; and he who sat on it had the name Death; and Hades was following with him. And authority was given to them over a fourth of the earth, to kill with sword and with famine and with pestilence and by the wild beasts of the earth. (6:7–8)

The word **ashen** just doesn't do justice to *chloros*. It's really a sickly pale green, like liquid Clorox bleach. The rider named **Death** has almost everything scary from a modern Halloween haunted house except the sickle. Even that might be there, since there's a **sickle** in the **harvest of the grapes of the earth** in 14:18–20. He **is given authority to kill with sword and with famine and with pestilence and by the wild beasts of the earth**.

This list should be familiar. It's an exact match for Ezekiel's list of God's judgments against apostasy. With a slight change, it's the list of "God's arrows" designed to make the apostate people come back. But death is limited to **a fourth of the earth**.

We have to be careful to avoid getting too literal here. This isn't as if God lines everybody up and kills every fourth person. "One fourth" is used several places in the Old Testament to mean a "small portion" (Num 23:10, 1 Sam 9:8, 2 Kgs 6:25). God allows part of the people who rebelled against Him to die as a warning to the rest.

THE HORSEMEN AS A GROUP

The **white horse and rider** present Christ's victory on the cross and His victory in His saints. The **red horse** represents the evil men do when separated from Christ. The **black horse** shows that even in the darkest times, the message of the gospel will never be stopped. And finally, the **ashen horse** gives a warning that rejecting God leads to death.

There isn't anything here that limits any part of this scene to any point in time. It's not a one-after-the-other sequence. The horses in Zechariah patrolled the earth at the same time. So do these.[8] But they're not physical horses. The message is very literal, but the horses are symbols. God never gives up. He will keep on calling to us until no one is left to answer.[9]

THE ALTAR

As the horses leave the scene, we can't forget that we're still in the Temple in heaven. Now our view changes to an altar. But which one? There are two . . .

> **And when He broke the fifth seal, I saw underneath the altar the souls of those who had been slain because of the word of God, and because of the testimony which they had maintained. (6:9)**

This is a picture of sacrificial death. There weren't any sacrifices at the golden altar of incense, so we're looking at the altar of sacrifice in the courtyard where the blood of sacrifices was poured (Lev 9:9). But John saw **souls**, not animal blood. What's going on?

Genesis 2:7 tells us that when God breathed the breath of life into Adam, he *became* a *living* soul.[10] Biblically, a soul is an entire person.[11] I know that may sound strange, but we're discovering what the Bible says, not what some preacher said. So what John saw was those who have died in the faith, pictured as sacrifices for sin.

They **were slain because of the word of God.** They're martyrs. We get the word "martyr" from the Greek word *marturion*, which means "witness." It was their witnessing for God that got them killed. This has been going on since Cain killed his brother Abel (Gen 4). And this brings us to a key question.

---

8. Remember, they are sent out into the earth, but are never recalled.

9. That's a part of the discussion of the Trumpets and Bowls, so I won't go into it here.

10. Genesis 1:20 and 24 call animals "souls" as well. Most modern translations call them "creatures," but the Hebrew word *nephesh* is used in both places.

11. We have to be careful here. The Bible sometimes uses words in a figurative sense. In The Song of Songs, Solomon's lover speaks of the one "her soul loves" (SS 3:2–4). This is poetic language, and must be interpreted in a non-literal way. On the other hand, John sees something physical in this scene, so we must interpret it on that basis.

WHEN DO THE HORSEMEN RIDE?

We didn't say *when* the four horses go out. All we figured out was *what* they represented. On the other hand, there have been souls under the altar since just after Eden. After all, they're martyrs, and those have been around since Cain killed Abel. In the same way, God's arrows, calamities designed to pull people back to God, have been around just as long. When God banished Cain, He cursed him so that he'd always be reminded of the God he left (Gen 4:10–12). Since then, God has used various misfortunes to prod people to come back. This means that the horsemen *and* the martyrs under the altar cover the entire history of sinful man. They don't come at any particular point in time. They represent all time.

I hear objections again! I've invented another crazy idea that doesn't match anything you've heard before. Those horsemen just *have to* represent specific time periods and events! But let me ask one thing. Have we looked at anything other than the Bible to help us understand these scenes? That should tell you what to believe.

THE MARTYRS' PLEA

> . . . and they cried out with a loud voice, saying, "How long, O Lord, holy and true, wilt Thou refrain from judging and avenging our blood on those who dwell on the earth?" (6:10)

As Christians, we aren't accustomed to hearing anyone plead for **revenge**. But this isn't as out of character as it seems. A number of Psalms are called "imprecatory." In them, the Psalmist pleads with God to get rid of his enemies.[12] It's not so much a cry for revenge as is it a plea for relief. It basically goes like this: "God, my enemies have been terrible. When are you going to stand up for me like you promised? When will things be good for *me*?"

This is really a covenant appeal. God promised to do good things for His people as part of the covenant. Those promises haven't been fulfilled. Saints die every day while God's enemies seem to be winning. But God can't come to their rescue yet. The drama of sin has to play out its final act so God can ring down the curtain on their suffering.

---

12. Psalm 69 is a good example.

THE ANSWER

And there was given to each of them a white robe; and they were told that they should rest for a little while longer, until those who were yet to be killed have been made perfect. (6:11)[13]

It will be **a little while longer** before the drama is done. With about 2,000 years since John wrote the book, it's easy to say that it's been a lot longer than that. But we should remember that God doesn't see time the way we do (2 Pet 3:8–9, cf. Ps 90:4). This sinful age will end "at the appointed time" (Dan 11:27, 35, Mark 13:33). God will continue to perfect His saints until the end. Satan's forces will kill a lot of them. But God guarantees their place in the kingdom by **giving each of them a white robe** (cf. 3:4–5, 18; 4:4, etc.). Their treasure is laid up in heaven, and can't be stolen or destroyed (Luke 12:33).

THE SIXTH SEAL

So far we've made a point of *not* putting the seals at any specific point in time. After all, martyrs and the call of grace have been part of every historical era. But the sixth seal is different. The events in it are a bit more than simple symbols. To the student of the Old Testament, they are *very* familiar.

When Jesus **breaks the seal**, there's **a great earthquake** (6:12). The **sun turns black** and **the moon becomes like blood**. This happens in a number of Old Testament prophecies at a very specific moment—The Day of the Lord. This is when the Lord rescues His people by "bringing destruction on the nations" (Ezek 32:9). "On that day," God "will make mortal man scarcer than pure gold" (Isa 13:12). The land will be "a desolation" (Hos 5:7). "Whoever calls on the name of the Lord will be delivered" (Joel 2:32).

---

13. The Greek of this verse is ambiguous. The translator has to choose how he'll translate it based on his view of the verse. This means you'll see several different versions of this in English. They may even seem to contradict each other. My translation may be different from what you're used to, but it's faithful to the original.

The Day of the Lord
• Sun Darkened   Job 2:10, 31; 3:15, Isa 5:30; 13:10; 24:23, Jer 4:28, Ezek 32:7; 30:13; Joel 2:2, 10; 3:15, Amos 5:18, 20; 8:9, Zeph 1:15
• Moon Darkened or Like Blood   Isa 13:10; 24:23, Ezek 32:7, Joel 2:10, 31; 3:15
• Earthquake   Isa 24:18–20; 29:6, Jer 4:24, Ezek 38:19, Amos 8:8, Hag 2:6, 21, Hab 3:10

Jesus told his disciples the same story with different words (Matt 24:36–42). When He returns for His saints, it will be "just like the days of Noah." Wicked people at the end of time will be destroyed just the way they were in the flood. Only the righteous will survive.

I can hear you saying, "There he goes again! That isn't what I was taught!" But I have to ask again, "Is this what the Bible says? Have I pulled this out of thin air, or have I stuck close to the Word of God to let it interpret itself?" Read the whole passage carefully. Notice how Jesus sets up two parallel scenes to make His point. Then decide.[14]

Let's back up a step. The Day of the Lord will end with all the saints in heaven (John 14:1–3). Since every wicked person will be killed, there won't be any live humans on earth.[15] But the Day of the Lord isn't over just yet. Let's look at the whole picture.

> And I looked when He broke the sixth seal, and there was a great earthquake; and the sun became black as sackcloth made of hair, and the whole moon became like blood; and the stars of the sky fell to the earth, as a fig tree casts its unripe figs when shaken by a great wind. And the sky was split apart like a scroll when it is rolled up; and every mountain and island were moved out of their places. (6:12–14)

This is a pretty amazing catastrophe. The **earthquake** is so big that **every mountain and island is moved out of its place**. Think about it. Mount Everest is in the middle of Hong Kong. Japan's next to California.[16]

---

14. Or see my discussion of Matthew 24:35–42 on pages 103–4, "Bowls Full of Wrath."

15. We'll talk about this more when we get to the millennium.

16. Please don't take this as literal. I'm just trying to get across how really big this earthquake is.

Ordinary earthquakes move the land a few feet and kill thousands. This is *miles* of movement. Nobody's likely to survive. Is it any wonder that:

> The kings of the earth and the great men and the commanders and the rich and the strong and every slave and free man, hid themselves in the caves and among the rocks of the mountains; and they said to the mountains and to the rocks, "Fall on us and hide us from the presence of Him who sits on the throne, and from the wrath of the Lamb; for the great day of their wrath has come; and who is able to stand? (6:15–17)

I know if an earthquake this bad came my way, *I'd* be scared. But the saints *aren't* scared. After all, this is **the wrath of the Lamb**, and the saints won't suffer from God's wrath (Rom 2:4–10; 5:9, Eph 5:6, 1 Thes 1:10; 5:9).

The wicked people ask a key question—**Who is able to stand?** The obvious answer is "the saints." After all, God's protecting them (Ps 91, esp. v. 8). But the vision includes a far more complete answer. We'll look at that after the seventh Seal.[17]

SILENCE IN HEAVEN

When He broke the seventh seal, there was silence in heaven for about half an hour (8:1). It would be a huge understatement to say that there's been a lot of speculation on this. But the Bible *does* provide the answer, if you know where to look.[18] Jumping forward a couple of verses, there's an **angel offering incense** (8:3–5). This means we're looking into the temple. Ordinarily there was constant music and a parade of animals being sacrificed.[19] But during the Day of Atonement service, the temple and the camp were silent. Scripture doesn't say this directly, so we have to be detectives.

The High Priest's robe had bells around its fringe. "It shall be on Aaron when he ministers; and its tinkling may be heard when he enters and leaves the holy place before the LORD, that he may not die" (Exod 28:35). Since the other priests could do everything except the Day of Atonement service, and they *didn't* need bells on their robes, this can only

---

17. My reason for skipping ahead will be clear when we get there.

18. "The key to the significance of the 'silence' must lie in the connotation that it has in the OT and in Jewish writings . . ." Beale, G. K., *The Book of Revelation* (Grand Rapids: Eerdmans, 1999), 445.

19. Edersheim, Alfred, *The Temple: Its Ministry and Services* (Peabody, MA: Hendrickson, 1995), 50–54.

be talking about the High Priest's work on the Day of Atonement. The bells were small and weren't very loud. This means they couldn't be heard very far, so the people had to be very quiet to hear them.

We have some other information that isn't in the Bible. Jewish rabbis preserved ancient teachings in the *Mishna*.[20] It confirms what we just figured out. During the Day of Atonement service, for about half an hour, the entire community gathered around the temple. Nobody could be in the Temple with the High Priest (Lev 16:17), so the only way they could know he hadn't been struck dead by God was when the bells on his robe tinkled after he came out of the room with the Ark of the Covenant.

> **An angel came and stood at the altar, holding a golden censer; and much incense was given to him, that he might add it to the prayers of all the saints upon the golden altar which was before the throne. And the smoke of the incense, with the prayers of the saints, went up before God out of the angel's hand. (8:3–4)**

On the Day of Atonement, the High Priest used two hands full of incense instead of the customary half *maneh* (Lev 16:12–13).[21] This **large amount of incense** confirms our conclusion that this scene is the Day of Atonement.

Every day, the Hebrew people brought sin sacrifices to the sanctuary. Through a complicated sequence of laying on of hands and manipulation of blood and flesh, the sin of the people was symbolically borne by the priests (Lev 10:17).[22] At the end of the year, all of the sin that had been borne by the priests was removed and placed on the scapegoat (Lev 16:21–22). The people were clean (Lev 16:30). This process was considered to be a great day of judgment. It's not the kind of judgment we usually think of where someone's on trial. Instead, it's a process where the Hebrews asked God for grace to forgive them. When the ceremony was complete, judgment had been made *in their favor*. Anyone who hadn't

---

20. This collection is also called the "oral Torah." It was teaching that filled in details not included in the books of Moses. That tradition says that many of the teachings were given by God but not written down. We may raise our eyebrows at that, but we can't question the Mishna's antiquity or its authentic presentation of Jewish practices.

21. Mishna Tractate *Yoma*, 4.4.IV.

22. I know this sounds strange, but ancient people looked at sin differently than we do. God worked in that arena to make an object lesson that would teach the people what Christ's mission was all about (Gal 3:24). We have to put ourselves into a Hebrew mindset to really understand what's being discussed.

confessed his sins by bringing them to the sanctuary was out of luck. He was "cut off from the camp" (Lev 23:29). Probation had closed for him.[23]

In the tabernacle on earth, the Day of Atonement was part of an annual cycle, so judgment came every year. But in heaven, the Day of Atonement is a one-time event (Heb 9:28). Judgment has been entered for the saints, and the wicked people who didn't repent have lost their chance to have their guilt removed. God can claim his saints and finish the Day of the Lord.

After finishing with the incense, **the angel took the censer; and he filled it with fire from the altar and threw it to the earth; and there followed peals of thunder and sounds and flashes of lightning and an earthquake** (8:5). By now all the incense has been burned. The last prayer has been offered. All that's left is a "fire that consumes the adversaries" (Heb 10:27).

The angel is in heaven, and he **throws the censer to the earth**. It has coals from the altar of sacrifice, so when it hits the earth it's a hail of fire. This brings back another Old Testament image: Sodom and Gomorrah. The Lord "rained brimstone and fire" on those wicked cities (Gen 19:15–25). It also recalls Ezekiel 10:2, where the prophet was told to scatter coals over wicked Jerusalem.

Hail as God's Weapon
• Plague against Egypt—Exod 9:18–30
• Against the Amorites—Josh 10:11
• Against David's enemies—Pss 18:12–13
• Against Ephraim—Isa 28:1–2
• Against Assyria—Isa 30:30
• Against liars—Isa 28:17
• Against false prophets—Ezek 13:11–13
• Against Gog—Ezek 38:22

---

23. We don't often run into the term "probation" to describe man's time on earth, but it's appropriate. Probation means a "proving" or "testing." Released prisoners often go through a period of "probation" so they can prove they've changed their ways. In the same way, everyone alive is "on probation," with angels of God as our probation officers (cf. Gen 22:12). Each person has the opportunity to choose salvation, but most will not. When God determines that the proper time has come, there won't be any more opportunity to be converted. Probation for mankind will have closed. At that time, every person who is righteous will "still be righteous," and whoever is filthy will "still be filthy" (22:11). This is the ultimate parallel to the yearly close of probation on the Day of Atonement.

This means that the seventh seal is more than the Day of Atonement. It's also the Day of the Lord. Hail is one description of how God will destroy the wicked. Since the Day of the Lord is the end of this age, nothing is left to happen on earth after this. God will have killed all the wicked people and taken the saints to heaven.

	7ᴛʜ Seal
Day of Atonement Language	• Silence in Heaven • Large amount of Incense
Day of the Lord Language	• Thunder • Lightning • Sounds • Earthquake • Coals hurled to earth

Wait a minute! There are fourteen chapters of the book to go![24] What can they be about if the end of earth's history is in the beginning of chapter eight? That's a good question. Remember that Revelation is an *Apocalypse*. The word has two meanings. In simple Greek, it means a "revealing." But it's also a common type of Jewish writing that tells the story of God's victory by looking at it from a number of different angles. This is called "recapitulation." Sports fans are familiar with this in post-game shows where the announcers "recap" the game by covering the highlights. A camera on the home team side shows one part, and a camera on the visitor's side shows another angle. End-zone cameras get a third. With all those angles, we get the best view of what's important.

In the same way, Revelation recaps the war between God and Satan. Each time Revelation recaps a section, we'll get a different view. And each new view reveals something important. Our first look at a major recap is next.

---

24. Actually, there are fifteen, since we skipped chapter 7 to get here.

8

Twelve Thousand from Twelve Tribes

Chapter 7 sits between the sixth and seventh Seals and is the first major recap. Its position suggests that it will give us a different perspective on the Seals.

The Seven Seals

Seals 1-6	The Sealing of the Saints	7th Seal
6:1-16	7:1-17	8:1, 3-5

YOU ARE HERE

When we skipped over this chapter, we left the wicked people crying out, **Who is able to stand?** (6:17). The answer came when **John saw four angels.** They were at **the four corners of the earth, holding back the four winds** (7:1). Now, the last time I checked, the world didn't have corners. And wind can come from more than four directions.

This is a place where you have to let yourself see with your mind's eye. Imagine the land spreading away from you as if it was flat. If you look far enough to the east, north, west, and south, you'll see the end. An angel stands there. His job is to protect the earth **so that no wind should blow on the earth or on the sea or on any tree.**

Again, we have to think visually. The only reason to hold back the wind is if it's destructive. These angels protect the earth from the nasty problems that will come along in the fifth and sixth Trumpets.[1] Those "winds of war" will be really bad news. And, because they come from beyond the earth, they're coming from an unearthly power—Satan.

---

1. By now you've figured out that I'm not really crazy. We'll talk about the Trumpets in the next chapter.

Another angel flies up **from the rising of the sun.**[2] This phrase is rich. It's used seven other times in the Bible,[3] and *every* time it tells of God's glory. The richest may be Malachi 4:2, where Jesus is prophesied to be "the sun of righteousness" who will rise from the east. This visual emphasizes that this angel comes from God's throne. In a way, we could say this angel is going ahead of Jesus as a messenger. The armies of God will be right behind.

In case you're wondering why I took so much time on a "trivial" item, it's not such a little thing. This direction shows up again in the sixth Bowl, and the work we just did will help us understand it there.

This angel **has the seal of the living God**, emphasizing the authority of the message. In ancient times, official documents were closed up and hot candle wax was dripped on the edge of the paper. Then the king would press his ring into the soft wax, leaving an impression. The seal showed that it was an official document.

The **angel** commands the **four angels not to harm the earth or the sea or the trees, until we have sealed the bond-servants of our God on their foreheads** (7:2-3). Does this mean that God will go around with hot wax and a ring to mark all His people? If we take Ezekiel 9:4 liter-al*istic*ally, the answer would be "Yes." But when we look at Exodus 13:9, we discover that eating unleavened bread for seven days is "a reminder on your forehead." That's not a visible mark. Instead, it's a way of saying that it's something you keep in mind. The symbolic visions of Ezekiel and Revelation use these figurative ways to say that these people belong to God. He knows who His people are (2 Tim 2:19).

God's been sealing people since the beginning of time (2 Cor 1:22, Eph 1:4; 4:30), so this isn't a sudden end-time event. Instead, it says that when the last saint has made his final decision for God, all of His people will have been sealed. Then all hell can break loose.[4]

John heard the number of those who were sealed (7:4). This is another one of those "I heard/I saw" patterns. John hears one set of details, and then sees something different. Let's listen in.

> And I heard the number of those who were sealed, one hundred and forty-four thousand sealed from every tribe of the sons of Israel: from the tribe of Judah . . . Reuben . . . Gad . . . Asher . . . Naphtali . . . Manasseh . . . Simeon . . . Levi . . . Issachar . . . Zebulun . . . Joseph . . . Benjamin. (7:4-8)

2. This is the east. Remember, this is *visual*, and the sun rises in the east.
3. Jdg 5:31, Pss 50:1; 133:3, Isa 41:25, 45:6, 59:9, and Mal 1:11.
4. But the saints don't need to worry. We'll talk about that later.

God's not saying that *exactly* twelve thousand are going to be saved from each physical tribe. That idea has a couple of really big problems. First, this list of tribes is different from every other list in the Bible. That suggests that the list is symbolic, and the **twelve thousand** from each **tribe** are **God's servants**. Next, twelve is often used as a number of completeness, so this refers to the complete number of the people Jesus saves.

Third, we know that the northern ten tribes were dispersed so completely that they can't be identified. God said they were so wicked that they weren't His bloodline any more (Hos 1:9).[5] Fourth, James addresses the church as "the twelve tribes" in his epistle (James 1:1). And of course, Paul makes it very clear that membership in Israel is determined by faith in Christ (Gal 3:29). Just like most of the rest of the book, this language is symbolic.

Name	Meaning
Judah	"Praise"—Israelites enter God's spiritual Jerusalem through gates called "Praise." (cf. Isa 60:18)
Reuben	"A Son" "Firstborn." (Gen 49:3, John 1:12, Rom 8:14–17, etc.)
Gad	"A Company"—of sons, redeemed. (Rev 7:9; 19:1, 6, etc.)
Asher	"Happy"—after. (John 13:17, etc.)
Naphtali	"Wrestling"—in prayer. (Gen 32:24–30, etc.)
Manasseh	"Forgetting"—self and the past. (Phil 3:13, Isa 65:17)
Simeon	"Hearing"—God's word. (1 Sam 3:10 "Speak, for Thy servant hears.")
Levi	"Joined"—to God. (John 15:1–7, Acts 2:47)
Issachar	"Servants" (Rom 6:16–22, etc.)
Zebulun	"Dwelling"—with God. (Ps 91:1, Isa 33:14, etc.)
Joseph	"Added"—joys and special blessings. (2 Pet 1:2, 5–11, etc.)
Benjamin	"Son of the right hand"—"In thy presence is fullness of joy; at Thy right hand there are pleasures for evermore." (Ps 16:11; Eph 2:6)[6]

---

5. The word there is *lo-ammi*. Most Bibles translate it "not my people." The word *am* implies "bloodline," so it really means "not my bloodline."

6. Modified slightly from Desmond Ford, *Crisis!* vol. 2 (Newcastle, CA: Desmond Ford Pub, 1982), 391.

A GREAT MULTITUDE

After this John looked and saw a great multitude which no one could count from every nation and tribe and people and tongue (7:9). This is the second half of the "I heard/I saw" pair. This uncountable mass of people is the 144,000. First John heard the number, then he saw the real thing. God's saved people aren't limited by nationality, language, or heritage. They are His bondservants. God doesn't care what your background is. All He wants is for you to follow Him (Rom 10:12, Gal 3:28–29, Col 3:11). And that's the message God wants us to hear.

When the wicked cry out, "Who is able to stand?" the answer comes loud and clear. On the last day, when God comes to claim His people, true Israel will stand tall, happy to see their redeemer (Gal 6:16). Because they're God's servants, they're counted as descendants of Abraham (Rom 9:8). They come from everywhere, and it doesn't matter whether they're "Jewish" or not.

The multitude **stands before the throne and before the Lamb**. They've been redeemed, and there's no way anyone's going to keep them away from their Redeemer! It's time for praise, and that's what they do. Dressed in **white robes**, they hold **palm branches**. They celebrate the King, just like the Jews did when Jesus entered Jerusalem as their Messiah (John 12:12–13, cf. Lev 23:40). They praise Him with **"Salvation to our God who sits on the throne, and to the Lamb" (7:10)**. The **angels, elders,** and **four living creatures** join in the chorus of praise (7:11–12).

One of the **elders** asks John if he knows who **these people clothed in white** are (7:13). John turns the question back to the elder, who answers,

> These are the ones who come out of the great tribulation, and they have washed their robes and made them white in the blood of the Lamb. For this reason, they are before the throne of God; and they serve Him day and night in His temple." (7:14–15)

Revelation doesn't tell us what **the great tribulation** is. Many interpreters suggest it's a period just before Jesus returns. But since the imagery of the fifth Seal goes all the way back to Cain and Abel, it seems more likely that it describes all the troubles caused by Satan's rebellion. The saints got through it by **washing their robes in the blood of the lamb**. This echoes the message to the church in Sardis (3:4–5). They are priests in **God's temple, serving Him day and night** (Exod 19:6, 1 Pet 2:9).

> He who sits on the throne shall spread His tabernacle over them. They shall hunger no more, neither thirst anymore; neither shall the sun beat down on them, nor any heat; for the Lamb in the center of the throne shall be their shepherd, and shall guide them to springs of the water of life; and God shall wipe every tear from their eyes. (7:15–17)

This is one of the most amazing promises in the Bible. But we have to walk into the picture to see it. It begins (literally) with **God will spread His *booth* over them**. This takes us back to the ancient Israel.

The Feast of Booths was a joyous memorial of God's protection for the Israelites in the wilderness (Lev 23:42). They celebrated by waving the *lulav*, often made of **palm branches** (7:9, cf. Lev 23:40). The people lived in **booths**—temporary shelters of saplings and branches – like the shelters they lived in during the exodus from bondage in Egypt (7:15). These **booths** didn't let the harsh desert **sun beat down on them** (7:16).[7] **God led them to springs of water** (7:17, cf. Isa 12:3, Exod 17:6). They **followed** the Lord in the pillar of fire at night and the pillar of smoke in the day (Exod 13:21–22).[8]

Right now, over 100,000 Christians are killed every year because they believe in Christ, so the protection in 7:15 isn't here yet. But when every person has made his final decision for or against Jesus, God will let Satan loose.[9] Then God will deliver His people (Jer 30:1–8). Horrible things will happen all around them, but it won't touch them (Ps 91).

At the end, **God will wipe every tear from their eyes**. This marvelous promise means that God will be with His people, *in person* (Pss 42:1–5, 116:6–9, Isa 25). This will happen in the New Jerusalem (21:4), when death has been swallowed up in victory (1 Cor 15:54). Bad things won't happen anymore. Sin will be wiped out forever, and we'll live with our Redeemer in the **new earth** (21:5).

---

7. The shade provided by the booth was a tremendous protection from the summer sun. As a result, "shade" became a symbol of divine protection, and is seen in a number of passages. Pss 17:8; 27:5; 31:20; 36:37; 57:1; 63:7; 91:1, Isa 4:6, Amos 9:11, Hos 14:7, etc.

8. It's possible to read 7:15 to say that God will spread His tent over them. This Middle Eastern image is a gracious host taking in guests. While they're in his tent, He will protect them as if they were his own family. Curiously, this is the same benefit as a booth.

9. We'll talk about this in the fifth and sixth Trumpets.

RECAP

The Seals tell the story of how God calls us to come to Him. The four horsemen are "God's Arrows," calamities that remind men that the only way out of this disaster called earth is to depend on God. The fifth Seal reminds us that faithful martyrs will be avenged in God's time. That vengeance arrives in the seventh Seal. While the saints celebrate the Day of Atonement, the wicked suffer in the Day of the Lord.

We've left two things out in this recap. First, the sealing of the saints (chapter 7) is an interlude. It answers the question in the sixth seal, but it does something else as well. It looks at the call of grace from a slightly different angle from the Seals.

The Seals show how God nudges mankind toward repentance. Calamities remind us of our need for a Redeemer. Sealed saints have answered the call. They're called "Israel," since they have the names of the twelve tribes. But they're really from every possible group of people. God doesn't care where you came from; He only cares where you're going. In the end, He will protect His own.

The second thing we left out was 8:2. The seventh Seal started in 8:1, then skipped to 8:3–5. The verse we skipped says that **angels were given seven trumpets**. This isn't part of the seals, but is a preview of coming attractions. Seven Trumpets are coming next. So the map of the Seals looks like this.

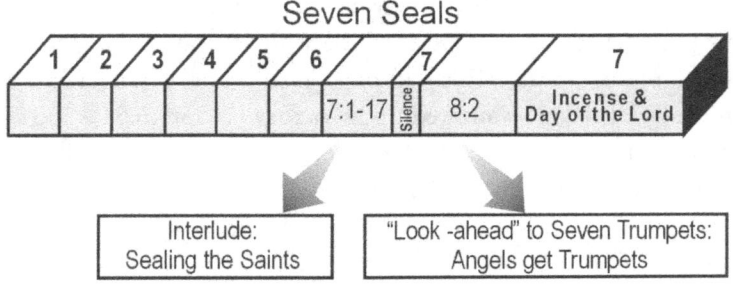

9

Sound the Trumpet!

Blow a trumpet in Zion, and sound an alarm on My holy mountain!
Let all the inhabitants of the land tremble,
for the day of the LORD is coming; Surely it is near.

(Joel 2:1)

It's amazing what we can find when we let the Bible interpret itself. The Seals didn't turn out to be detailed future history at all. They painted a symbolic picture of how God calls man to come to his gracious offer of salvation. Since they were built around a theme, it shouldn't surprise us if the Trumpets are organized around a theme, too. Let's start with the imagery.

Ancient Israel used trumpets on a number of occasions. Most of the time, they announced an assembly, usually at the temple. There was even an annual festival when trumpets were blown all day at the Temple (Lev 23:24).[1]

Trumpets in Ancient Israel
• Announced the approach of the Day of Atonement (Lev 23:24).
• Announced the beginning and end of all Temple services (Num 10:9–10).
• Called Israel to battle (Neh 4:20).
• Announced victory (1 Sam 6:15).
• Announced the anointing of a king (1 Kgs 1:34, 39).
• Announced the anointing of the Temple (2 Chron 29:26–28).
• Announced the restoration of the Ark to the Jews (2 Sam 6:16).
• Seven trumpets blew as the Israelites marched around Jericho (Josh 6).

---

1. In Hebrew, this is *Yom Teruah*, the Day of Blowing.

On the first day of the month of Tishri, ten days before the Day of Atonement, the priests blew trumpets to announce that the Day of Atonement was near. That Day was the "great day of judgment" in Hebrew thinking.[2] Everybody had to get ready for it. They had to confess every sin so they'd be clean when the service was over (Lev 16:30; 23:29).

The rabbis said that the Feast of Trumpets was "the little day of judgment" that prepared the people for the great Day of Judgment. It warned that you only had ten days to get right with God. This is the theme of the Trumpets. Jesus will come to judge soon. You need to be ready.

In the twenty-first century, judgment means a courtroom. If we're involved, it's a criminal trial where we'll end up in jail if we lose. But the Day of Atonement is the exact opposite. On "The Day," God's people call on Him to vindicate them from the accusations of Satan (12:10, cf. Jdg 11:27, Ps 35:24).[3] They cry out for relief from the opponent (cf. 1 Sam 24:15).[4] The final Day of Atonement will be judgment *in favor* of the saints (Dan 7:22, 27).

Of course, if you *haven't* gotten ready, you won't be on God's side. And you won't get any relief from the court. When judgment goes the saints' way, it will be against you, and "it is a terrifying thing to fall into the hands of the living God" (Heb 10:31).

The Covenant Displayed

| Inauguration | **This Age** | The Millennial Age | Consummation |

Seven Trumpets
Warning of Judgment

YOU ARE HERE

---

2. When the trumpets are blown at the Feast of Trumpets, ". . . the Rabbis hold that the blowing of the trumpets is intended . . . as a call to repentance—as it were, a blast to wake men from their sleep of sin" (Maimonides, *Moreh Nev.* iii. 43, in Alfred Edersheim, *The Temple* 236–237).

3. The Jews called the Day of Atonement "The Day." The section of the *Mishna* that talks about it is titled "*Yoma*," which literally means "The Day."

4. In Hebrew, the name *Satan* means "opponent."

The trumpets look like a series of calamities. There's hail and fire (8:7, cf. Exod 9:23), water turned to blood (8:8, cf. Exod 7:19–21), bitter water (8:11, cf. Exod 7:21), darkness (8:12, cf. Exod 10:21–22), locusts (9:3, cf. Exod 10:12–15), and death of a third of mankind (9:15, cf. Exod 12:29). This imagery comes straight from the plagues on Egypt. They served two purposes. First, God said, "I will lay My hand on Egypt, and bring out My hosts, My people the sons of Israel, from the land of Egypt by great judgments" (Exod 7:4). Second, the plagues against Egypt were intended to show that Yahweh was the one true God (Exod 7:5).

God delivered the Israelites from physical captivity in physical Egypt. Revelation takes this history and changes it into a picture of God's saints, true Israel, who are held captive in spiritual Egypt (11:8). The trumpet plagues show that God is sovereign, but wicked people generally ignore God just the way Pharaoh did. They miss the warning, and the result is **Woe!**

When one plague in Egypt was over, it was over. It didn't come back. Since the Trumpets are patterned after the plagues, they may be sequential. Our next clue comes after the fourth Trumpet:

> And I looked, and I heard an eagle flying in midheaven, saying with a loud voice, "Woe, woe, woe, to those who dwell on the earth, because of the remaining blasts of the trumpet of the three angels who are about to sound!" (8:13)

This marks a big difference between the first four Trumpets and the last three. **Woes** start with number five, making it a sequence marker. They only impact **those who dwell on the earth**. Since that's a code name for the wicked, the saints don't have to worry about those troubles. **Only those who *do not* have the seal of God can be harmed** (9:4). It's hard to make it any clearer. If you follow God, you'll be OK. If you don't, all hell breaks loose.[5]

Finally, the seventh Trumpet (the third Woe) is another view of the Day of Atonement and the Day of the Lord.[6] With all these clues, we're safe suggesting that the Trumpets are sequential. That doesn't mean they aren't related to a theme like the Seals. They warn about coming judgment. At the same time, they're different from the Seals by happening in a set order.

---

5. This may seem to be an odd expression for a biblical study, but when we examine the Woes in detail, you'll see that it's perfect.

6. We'll fill in the details when we get there.

THE FIRST TRUMPET

> And the first sounded, and there came hail and fire, mixed with blood, and they were thrown to the earth; and a third of the earth was burned up, and a third of the trees were burned up, and all the green grass was burned up. (8:7)

Hail in Israel's History
• Exod 9:18, 22–26—Plague against Egypt.
• Josh 10:11—God delivered Israel from the Amorites.
• Pss 18:12–14—God delivered David.
• Isa 28:1–2, 17, Ezek 13:11–13—God's weapon against apostate Israel and Judah.
• Job 38:22–23, Isa 30:30; 32:19, Ezek 38:22—God's weapon against the wicked on the Day of the Lord.

If we *see* the words instead of just *reading* them, this will make more sense. The **first angel sounds his trumpet**, and then there's a **hailstorm**. This should tip us off (again) that the Trumpets are aimed at God's enemies. By the way, some examples aren't literal. In Psalm 18 David's language is so far over the top that it has to be metaphorical. The language here doesn't have to be strictly literal, either.

This hail has **fire** in it. This combination makes us think of Sodom and Gomorrah (Gen 19:24–25), where God destroyed the cities with fire and brimstone. He did such a complete job that today nobody knows where they were. In a manner of speaking, we could say, "not one stone was left on another" (cf. Matt 24:2). And as we'll see in a minute, I didn't pick that quote out of the air.

Next, **a third of the earth was burned up, and a third of the trees were burned up, and all the green grass was burned up**. What's this about? Didn't I just say that hail was aimed at God's enemies? Trees and grass *aren't* God's enemies. Neither is the earth!

This is *symbolism*.[7] "Trees" and "grass" represent something else. Ezekiel describes God's judgment against Judah as a "sword against trees" (Ezek 21:10). He even speaks of "the fire of My wrath" (Ezek 21:31)! The prophet uses similar imagery other places (Ezek 17:1–24; 20:45–48; 31:3). "Grass" comes from Isaiah's famous statement that "The grass withers, the flower fades, but the word of our God stands forever" (Isa 40:6–8). The

---

7. Remember, Revelation 1:1 says that the message will be "symbolized" to John.

wicked people in Judah are the grass God will destroy when he comes in judgment.

Look at what's happened. We started out with a very strange prophecy. Nothing in it made any real sense. But when we looked at how the Old Testament prophets used imagery, the picture made sense. The original prophecy was directed against the wicked people of Jerusalem *before Nebuchadnezzar destroyed it in 587 BC*. God recorded the same imagery almost seven centuries later. What's going on?

God picked up a fulfilled prophecy and used it again to tell about another time Jerusalem would be destroyed. By using a well-known piece of history, He was able to paint a familiar picture. If we remember that Jews thought visually, then it makes sense. Trees are leaders, and grass is the rest of the (little) people. Specifically, they're opposed to Jesus, but live among His faithful people.

In AD 70, about a million Jews went to Jerusalem for Passover. When the Roman army destroyed the city, most of them were killed. "The grass" was burned up. This obviously didn't include the church, since Christians had left Jerusalem four years earlier. As for "a third" of the leaders, that number's not intended to be exact. We know some were able to surrender to the Romans.

God used the Roman army to destroy Jerusalem. This judgment was a warning to anyone who would rebel against Him and persecute His followers. Just like the plagues of Egypt, it showed that Yahweh is the one true God.[8] His vengeance began with the Jewish enemies of His kingdom.

THE SECOND TRUMPET

> And the second angel sounded, and something like a great mountain burning with fire was thrown into the sea; and a third of the sea became blood; and a third of the creatures, which were in the sea and had life, died; and a third of the ships were destroyed. (8:8–9)

Something like a great mountain burning with fire was thrown into the sea. This isn't a mountain. It's something like a mountain. This is one of those patterns we discussed. When an item is like something, it's not the real thing. It's a parody, a cheap imitation.

---

8. This is exactly what God says in Ezekiel 21:5.

Scripture uses "mountains" to represent kingdoms. The only true "great mountain" in the Bible is God's kingdom in Nebuchadnezzar's dream (Dan 2:35). "Something like a great mountain," has to be one of man's "great" kingdoms. Of course, it's really not so great. It's "Babylon," a "destroying mountain, who destroys the whole earth." borrowed from Jeremiah. God will make it into "a burnt out mountain" (Jer 51:25). When God throws it down this time, the carnage will be severe.

Of course, since this comes after AD 70, we aren't looking at ancient Babylon like Jeremiah was. When the Roman army leveled Jerusalem, both Jews and Christians thought of imperial Rome as a new Babylon, since it did the same thing to Jerusalem that Nebuchadnezzar had done centuries before.[9] Peter even signs his first letter from "Babylon" (1 Pet 5:13).[10]

The second Trumpet tells about imperial Rome and its fall. When we look at history, it's pretty clear that the disasters pictured in this prophecy came true. Yes, the language is a bit dramatic, but if we look at it with biblical glasses, we can see it. Later on John hears that the sea represents "peoples and multitudes, and nations and tongues" (17:15). Blood in the sea represents massive conflict that would easily kill a third of the population. Commerce (ships) would be affected the same way.

THE THIRD TRUMPET

And the third angel sounded, and a great star fell from heaven, burning like a torch, and it fell on a third of the rivers and on the springs of waters; and the name of the star is called Wormwood; and a third of the waters became wormwood; and many men died from the waters, because they were made bitter. (8:10–11)

A great star falls from heaven, burning like a torch. This can't be a physical star, since stars are a lot bigger than the earth. We have to go back to the Bible again to figure it out. God's servants are like stars in Daniel 12:3 and are stars in Revelation 12:1. But this star is named **Wormwood**, and that's not the name of any of God's friends.

Wormwood is bitter (Prov 5:4). Every time the Bible mentions it, it's linked with bad things. In Deuteronomy 29:18 and in Jeremiah 9:15 and

---

9. 4 Ezdras 3, 2 Baruch 10–11, 1 Enoch 18.

10. The New Living Translation interpretively renders this, "Your sister church here in Rome sends you greetings . . ."

23:15 it's poison that God will make His enemies drink. So Wormwood has to be Satan. To confirm this, let's look at the fifth Trumpet.

In 9:1 **the key of the bottomless pit was given to a star which had fallen to earth.** The divine passive means that God gave the key to this "star." That, of course, means that the star is really a person. When this person opens the bottomless pit, he releases a demonic horde. God's not about to let demons loose. But there will come a time when He'll let Satan do just that.

We have to be careful here, because we know that Satan was kicked out of heaven after the Cross (12:7-9). At the same time, the effect of his fall is the key element of the picture. It isn't labeled a "woe" here, but the results are bad enough that chapter 12 *does* call it a woe (12:12).

This image of a star falling on the **rivers and springs of waters** goes all the way back to Eden, where a single spring fed four rivers that watered the whole earth (Gen 2:10-14). In many ways, Eden was a temple.[11] The picture of a river flowing from the Temple to feed the earth is echoed in Ezekiel's vision (Ezek 47) and in the New Jerusalem (21:6, 22:1-2). When the star **makes the waters bitter,** it poisons the life-giving message of salvation that starts at the Temple of God, making **people die.**

Historically, the third Trumpet isn't hard to identify. It comes after the fall of pagan Rome, and distorts the gospel so much that people die. And it isn't just spiritual death. The Roman Church was *the* central civil power for over a thousand years. It banned Bible study on pain of death. It murdered reformers in the most brutal ways and persecuted simple Christians. It started bloody wars over minor theological disagreements. When it was done, over one hundred million people had been killed in the name of religion. We have no way to know how many are eternally lost because of its false teachings.[12]

THE FOURTH TRUMPET

And the fourth angel sounded, and a third of the sun and a third of the moon and a third of the stars were smitten, so that a third

---

11. It was built in seven days, and the tabernacle was built in seven stages. Its entrance was on the East, and Adam and Eve were banished through the gate on the East. An angel was stationed there, and the Hebrew word is the same word that describes the glory of God in the Temple. We could go on for several pages . . .

12. I'm not trying to be anti-Catholic. Because of its unbiblical teachings and persecution of opponents, the Reformers commonly saw the Roman Church as antichrist.

> of them might be darkened and the day might not shine for a third of it, and the night in the same way. (8:12)

By now we have a pretty good idea of the code God used in the Trumpets. When the evil star Wormwood poisoned the waters, it was a picture of Satan poisoning the water of life that flows from God. This time **a third of the stars are darkened**. That suggests that a number of God's people fall away from the truth. But what should we do with **a third of the sun and a third of the moon?**

The most obvious answer is that the Day of the Lord completely darkens the sun, moon and stars. Since this is **a third** as bad as the Day of the Lord, this must be a smaller calamity. But that's not all that helpful, since it doesn't give us any concrete help with the symbol itself.

Darkness is a "calamity" (Isa 45:7). The fourth Trumpet is a time when minds are darkened (Isa 8:20) and there are no prophets (Micah 3:6–7). Men lose sight of Jesus, the light of the world (John 8:12). Can there be a better description of the modern world?

Mankind has declared its independence from God. We have science, so we don't need Him. Man judges what's true and doesn't need God's laws. But this plague of rationalism can't completely blot out the true Light of the world. God still has dedicated servants. And just like a candle in the darkest cave, they reflect God's light into a world that serves darkness.

TRUMPETS 1—4 RECAP

Let's pause for a moment to reflect on the first four Trumpets. The first one destroyed the heart of Judaism—Jerusalem and the Temple—because the Jews rejected their missionary task and the Messiah. But it wasn't the end of everything. It was a warning of things to come if the rebellion continued. The second Trumpet destroyed Imperial Rome when it became hopelessly corrupt. The third Trumpet showed us the evils of Papal Rome in the Dark Ages. But these preliminary judgments have been ignored by a world that is blinded by its own ambition.

The fourth trumpet is sounding now. It's our last warning to repent before things get *really* bad. And, as we're about to see, when the fourth Trumpet stops blowing, no one else will ever choose to follow Christ. The "wars and rumors of wars" we see now are the direct result of man's refusal to follow God. Millions will die because they won't look to the one true Light.

> And I looked, and I heard an eagle flying in midheaven, saying with a loud voice, "Woe, woe, woe, to those who dwell on the earth, because of the remaining blasts of the trumpet of the three angels who are about to sound!" (8:13)

The last three Trumpets are **Woes**. Rebels bring these troubles on themselves (Num 21:29, Isa 3:8–11).

THE FIRST WOE

> And the fifth angel sounded, and I saw a star from heaven which had fallen to the earth; and the key of the bottomless pit was given to him. And he opened the bottomless pit; and smoke went up out of the pit, like the smoke of a great furnace; and the sun and the air were darkened by the smoke of the pit. And out of the smoke came forth locusts upon the earth; and power was given them, as the scorpions of the earth have power. And they were told that they should not hurt the grass of the earth, nor any green thing, nor any tree, but only the men who do not have the seal of God on their foreheads. And they were not permitted to kill anyone, but to torment for five months; and their torment was like the torment of a scorpion when it stings a man. And in those days men will seek death and will not find it; and they will long to die and death flees from them. And the appearance of the locusts was like horses prepared for battle; and on their heads, as it were, crowns like gold, and their faces were like the faces of men. And they had hair like the hair of women, and their teeth were like the teeth of lions. And they had breastplates like breastplates of iron; and the sound of their wings was like the sound of chariots, of many horses rushing to battle. And they have tails like scorpions, and stings; and in their tails is their power to hurt men for five months. They have as king over them, the angel of the abyss; his name in Hebrew is Abaddon, and in the Greek he has the name Apollyon. (9:1–11)

God gives the key of the bottomless pit to the fallen star named **Abaddon** or **Apollyon** (9:1, 11). This "Destroyer" is the angel of the bottomless pit (**abyss**). What's that?

About two hundred years before Christ Hebrew scholars translated the Hebrew Scriptures into Greek. This "Septuagint" became the ordinary Bible for the New Testament era.[13] Its main meaning for *abussos*—

---

13. We'll use the standard abbreviation LXX, the Roman numerals for 70, for the

bottomless pit—is the underworld where only demons live (Ps 35:7, Hab 3:10, cf. Luke 8:31). Satan is king over the demons.

Next, the locusts that come out of the abyss are not permitted to harm anyone who has the seal of God on their foreheads. So whatever happens during the woes can't hurt saints. This doesn't say that they aren't there. What it says is God will protect them. This echoes Psalm 91.

> A thousand may fall at your side, and ten thousand at your right hand; but it shall not approach you. You will only look on with your eyes, and see the recompense of the wicked. (Pss 91:7–8)

This should also take us back to 3:10, where God promises protection from **the hour of testing** that will come on those who **dwell on the earth**. The saints of Philadelphia will be protected from the fifth and sixth Trumpets.

Now that we've figured out the simple stuff, we come to one of those places where we really have to let scripture interpret itself. Scholarly commentaries on Revelation generally throw up their hands at the locusts. Many of them say they're "demonic beings"—as if we hadn't figured that out already. We can do better.

For a long time I was just as lost as the scholars. But when I finally decided to practice what I preach, something interesting happened. The weirdness of the picture didn't go away, but it did start to make sense. The first key is one of the patterns we talked about in the first chapter. Their **torment was *like* a scorpion sting**, they **looked *like* horses**, with **teeth *like* lions**, and **hair *like* women's hair**. There's more, but you get the picture.

These creatures *aren't* scorpions, or horses, or lions, or women. John's painting a caricature. These monsters are made out of fake parts. Our job is to figure out what each piece imitates. My favorites are the hair and crowns. They're the parts that made me see what John saw.

The locusts had **hair *like* the hair of women** (9:8). It's *not* a woman's hair. John wants us to see long flowing hair like a woman would have, just not on a woman (cf. 1 Cor 11:14–15). He could have pointed out long hair like Samson's, but that wouldn't be a parody (Jdg 13:7, 24).[14] Instead, John wanted us to see that this is a poor copy of the real thing. Samson was

---

Septuagint. This comes from a tradition that seventy scholars were involved in the translation.

14. Nazirites are the only scriptural example of men with long hair like women.

a Nazirite, and since Nazirites were the most devout of men in ancient Israel, this is a caricature of piety (Num 6:1–21).

Next, these locusts are wearing **as it were, crowns like gold** (9:7). "Crowns" here are *stephanoi*, the victor's crowns promised to those who overcome (2:10). But once again, *they aren't stephanoi*. They're phonies. They *aren't* made of gold; they're made of fool's gold. It's almost as if your twelve-year-old kid took a silk plant, wove it into a sort of wreath and spray-painted it gold. The message this image gives is that these locusts are counterfeit saints. They've got a bunch of parts that ought to be saintly, but when you get close, you can see the cardboard behind the paint.

I've listed all the body parts in the box. These complicated locusts are nothing more than an assembly of Old Testament images. Some represent faithfulness turned on its head. Others are pictures of God's enemies. The mix creates a picture of false religion masquerading as true faith. This is one example of what Jesus meant when He said "false Christs and false prophets will arise and will show great signs and wonders, so as to mislead, if possible, even the elect" (Matt 24:24).

"Locust" Body Parts
• **Horses prepared for battle**—God's enemies—Jer 6:23, 8:6, 50:42, Joel 2:4, Zech 10:5
• **Crowns like gold**—Phony saints—Exod 39:30, Psalm 21:3, Rev 2:10
• **Faces like men**—Wickedness—Dan 7:8, 20
• **Hair like women**—False piety—Num 6:5, 1 Cor 11:14–15
• **Teeth like lions**—Enemies of God—Ps 58:6, Joel 1:6
• **Breastplate of iron**—Parody of the breastplate of judgment worn by the high priest—Exod 28:15–30
• **Tails like scorpions**—Satan's power—Luke 10:19

The picture John saw replays the destruction of Jerusalem recorded by Joel (Joel 1–2). He saw unstoppable armies of locusts. They destroyed everything in their path. They turned a "Garden of Eden" into a "wilderness" (Joel 2:3). Joel prophesied a physical event, but John's presenting a spiritual event. To avoid confusion, let's explore this shift.

TYPOLOGY

We've already talked about typology. Types, like the destruction of Jerusalem in Joel, are acted-out prophecies that point to something bigger than themselves. In Joel, physical Jerusalem represents spiritual Jerusalem. Hebrews 12:18–24 shows us that physical Jerusalem isn't important anymore. God's replaced it with the church, which He calls "heavenly Jerusalem."

When we apply this using the background of Joel's story of the destruction of Jerusalem, we can see what John was seeing. This satanic cloud of "locusts" is really an overwhelming mass of false religion and piety. But it happens at a time when all of God's saints have been sealed. They can't be hurt! When we study the **two witnesses** of chapter 11, we'll discover that this is when they're "**killed**" (11:7).[15] That is, Christ's *true* witnesses will be silenced, only to be replaced by the *false* witnesses of Satan. But let's not get so far ahead of ourselves.

Like the Feast of Trumpets, the Seven Trumpets warn of coming judgment. Through the first four God calls mankind to accept His grace. Eventually everyone will have made up his mind, and God will stop calling. But He's not about to stop there because He's got a big problem to solve. Satan told the universe that his way is better than God's. So far, he hasn't really had a chance to prove his point, since God has really cramped his style. If God's going to prove His case, He has to let Satan loose.

But God isn't about to let Satan *completely* loose. First, He makes sure that His saints are protected (9:4). Next, Satan **isn't allowed to kill**. He can only **torment** (9:5). Finally, this can only last **five months**. This isn't necessarily a literal period of time. It's the length of locust season in the Middle East, so it probably represents the fact that God's still in ultimate control. And things are about to get even worse.

> The first woe is past; behold, two woes are still coming after these things. (9:12)

THE SECOND WOE

> And the sixth angel sounded, and I heard a voice from the four horns of the golden altar which is before God, one saying to the sixth angel who had the trumpet, "Release the four angels who

---

15. I know this sounds weird. How can you be "killed" but not hurt? Stay tuned . . .

> are bound at the great river Euphrates." And the four angels, who had been prepared for the hour and day and month and year, were released, so that they might kill a third of mankind. And the number of the armies of the horsemen was two hundred million; I heard the number of them. And this is how I saw in the vision the horses and those who sat on them: the riders had breastplates the color of fire and of hyacinth and of brimstone; and the heads of the horses are like the heads of lions; and out of their mouths proceed fire and smoke and brimstone. A third of mankind was killed by these three plagues, by the fire and the smoke and the brimstone, which proceeded out of their mouths. For the power of the horses is in their mouths and in their tails; for their tails are like serpents and have heads; and with them they do harm. (9:13–19)

We don't need to trace every part of the picture the way we did in the fifth trumpet. The Devil's army is huge (**200,000,000**). It has funky horses with the same **lion's heads** we saw before. **Fire and smoke and brimstone** are obviously violent ways to kill people.

A lot of modern interpreters see Apache helicopters, Hellfire missiles, and nuclear bombs in the sixth trumpet.[16] They get those ideas by matching John's visuals with the latest History Channel program on modern warfare. And they could be right! After all, this is a description of horrible violent death, something modern armies are very good at. But we have to be careful. John saw horses, not tanks. And most of the vision comes from Old Testament descriptions of armies that fought against ancient Israel. The real key is that this army belongs to Satan. And, since the saints are protected from the woes, the devastation falls on the wicked.

Even here, God's clearly in control. He issues the command **from the four horns of the golden altar of incense**. These horns were shaped like a ram's horn, the *shofar* blown at every call to worship or to war. This is the **voice like a trumpet** again. It's time to **"Release the four angels who are bound at the great river Euphrates."** These angels **had been prepared for the hour and day and month and year to kill a third of mankind**.[17]

God's angels wouldn't be bound, so these belong to Satan. He's been getting them ready for the moment when God will really let Him

---

16. If you read enough, you'll find just about every weapon in the modern armory in somebody's interpretation of this passage.

17. Some interpreters have used the KJV rendering—*an* hour, etc.—to say this verse is speaking about a *period* of time. They then use year-for-a-day math to figure it out. But the Greek is quite explicit that John's talking about a *point* in time.

loose. But even then, God's still in control. Satan can only kill a third of mankind.

The angels were **bound at the great river Euphrates**. This scene is part of one of those patterns we talked about. God's using the history of Israel again as prophecy. Because the Euphrates River went right through the city of Babylon it could survive any siege. The people could irrigate land inside the walls and grow enough food to outlast any army. It was truly a "River of Life" for Babylon (cf. 21:6; 22:1–3). Next, Babylon was Israel's enemy. It held the Jews captive for seventy years and destroyed the Temple, making the proper observance of God's ordinances impossible. These acted-out prophecies tell us what the sixth Trumpet means.

The Israel of God (Gal 6:16) has come out of spiritual Babylon (18:4) into the Jerusalem of God (Heb 12:22). The saints will all drink from the true River of Life in the New Jerusalem. On the other hand, the wicked are still part of Babylon. When the evil angels come out of the river, all Hell breaks loose as they go through Babylon. But even after all those people are killed, **the rest did not repent** (9:20–21).

WHAT'S THE POINT?

Let's back up for a moment. When the **Woes** start, God's saints are protected. This means that they've given themselves to Him fully. At the end of the woes, *nobody* else has repented. This points out two really important facts.

First, God revealed all of this to John just to get to a single punch line: **They did not repent**. The Trumpets are warnings designed to lead people to repentance. That is, they aren't about jets, tanks, and guns. They're not about politics and armies. They're about *salvation*. Any interpretation that misses this point is simply wrong.[18] This is the very same conclusion we reached when we studied the very first verse of the book. The book is about Jesus, and Jesus came for one purpose: to save us. Thus, the evil locusts in the woes aren't literal. They're symbolic. Second, at the end of the fourth trumpet, before the woes, every person in the world will have chosen for or against God. So why would God bother with the **Woes**?

---

18. Many "authorities" say that we shouldn't take such strong stands. But isn't God's call pretty strong? And isn't His warning even stronger? We'd be ignoring God's word if we didn't stand firmly for His message.

The first four trumpets blow while God is calling people to come out of sin into salvation. When they're done, everyone who will answer the call of grace will have answered. But God still has to prove to the universe that He's done everything possible to give mankind a chance to repent. So He changes gears. In effect He says, "You wouldn't come to My goodness when I called. Let's see if you'll run away from Satan's wickedness." And then all hell breaks loose.

God will give every person every possible chance to be saved. When the wicked decline the call of grace and then refuse to run away from evil, they've made it clear that there's no chance they'll ever go God's way. They choose their own fate. When the books are examined, there won't be any doubt that their fate is just and righteous (20:12–13).

Then the seventh Trumpet sounds. **Loud voices in Heaven say, "The kingdom of the world has become *the kingdom* of our Lord, and of His Christ; and He will reign forever and ever." The twenty-four elders fall on their faces and worship God. The time has come to reward God's bond-servants the prophets and the saints. The time has also come to destroy those who destroy the earth** (11:15, 16, 18).

This chorus of praise isn't actually part of the Trumpet, because it isn't a **woe** (11:14). Instead, it looks forward to the Bowls, just like 8:2 looked ahead to the Trumpets. But for a moment, let's go back to the seventh Seal.

The **half hour of silence** and **large amount of incense** were from the Day of Atonement. In the seventh Trumpet, **the Ark of the Covenant is seen in the Temple.** The only person who ever got to see the Ark was the High Priest, and the only time he ever got to see it was the Day of Atonement. So the seventh Seal and the seventh Trumpet are *both* pictures of the Day of Atonement.

Next, the seventh Seal had Day of the Lord language. There were thunder, lightning, sounds and an earthquake. We even saw hail, God's weapon against the wicked. When we look at the seventh Trumpet, all of the same things are there.

7ᵀᴴ Seal: 8:1–5	7ᵀᴴ Trumpet: 11:19
Day of Atonement Language • Silence in Heaven • Large amount of Incense	*Day of Atonement Language* • Ark Seen in Temple
Day of the Lord Language • Thunder • Lightning • Sounds • Earthquake • Coals hurled to earth	*Day of the Lord Language* • Thunder • Lightning • Sounds • Earthquake • Great hailstones

It's a basic principle of Bible interpretation that when two passages have a number of identical pieces, they're probably talking about the same thing.[19] Here they are almost completely identical. Their only real difference is what part of the Day of Atonement they describe. Since they are identical, the Seals and Trumpets are *not* a sequence of 14 events. They're parallel descriptions of God's plan.

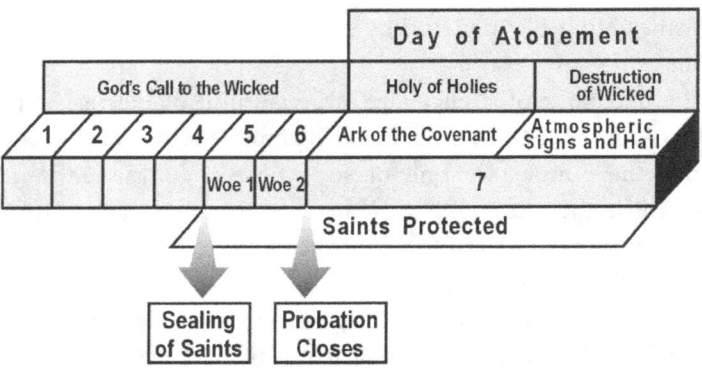

---

19. The professors call this "hermeneutics," from the Greek word *hermeneuō*, which means "to interpret." If you want to impress your friends, use "hermeneutics" instead of "interpretation."

God doesn't let His people wander on their own journey to destruction unmolested. He loves them too much to do that. So He prods them to come back. The Bible calls this "chastening" (Ps 94:10). He sends troubles to remind them that He's the source of all good things. This is the theme of the Seals. When gentle nudging isn't enough, God gets a bit stronger in His message. If you don't come back, things are going to get really bad. That's the theme of the Trumpets. And if you are so hardheaded that you won't listen, it's *OVER*. At least, that's what the next angel says . . .

10

When It's Over, It's *Over!*

WE SKIPPED TWO INTERLUDES when we jumped from the sixth Trumpet in chapter 9 to the seventh Trumpet at the end of chapter 11. These Trumpet interludes tell the story from different angles just the way the interlude in the Seals did.

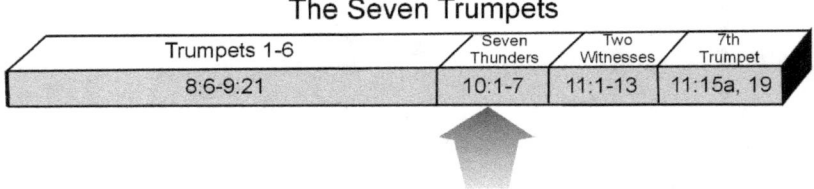

And I saw another strong angel coming down out of heaven, clothed with a cloud; and the rainbow was upon his head, and his face was like the sun, and his feet like pillars of fire. (10:1)

Scholars argue about who this angel is. He's got a **rainbow on his head**, something God has around His head in Ezekiel 1:28. His **face is like the sun**, like Jesus on the Mount of Transfiguration (Matt 17:2). God led the Israelites at night in the wilderness with **feet like pillars of fire** (Exod 13:21–22). His throne has fiery wheels in Daniel 7:9–10. Since every part of this description talks about God, this "angel" is God.[1]

It's important to notice that all these images of God have a common theme—deliverance. God gave Ezekiel a message of repentance that leads to deliverance if obeyed. Matthew previews the risen Lord who delivers us

---

1. Remember, this is a symbolic vision! The parts don't have to fit our modern sensibilities. The word *aggelos* (angel) means a "messenger," and this person is bringing a message. It *isn't* saying that God is a created being called an angel. This may sound odd, but in the Bible God appears as an angel (Exod 3:2ff. etc.). The word doesn't even have to mean a celestial being, since a man can be an angel (2 Sam 19:27).

from the curse of sin. In Exodus it's the God who delivered Israel "by great judgments" (Exod 7:4). And Daniel saw God presiding over the court that gives "judgment for the saints" (Dan 7:22). It's amazing. Even when God warns us about impending doom, He always reminds us that He'll redeem us if we let Him.[2]

He had in his hand a little book which was open. (10:2)

In chapter 5 the scroll was a *biblion* (**book**), but here it's a *biblaridion* (**little book**). Some interpreters suggest that these are two different books, but in verse 8, it's a *biblion* again, so there's really no reason to do that. And in this case, we'd have a real problem, since the only place the Bible uses *biblaridion* is here (verses 2, 9, & 10). The *biblion* is **in his hand** (v. 8). Finally, it's **open**. The whole point of taking the book in chapter 5 was to **open the book and its seven seals** (5:5). This is the book of the covenant.[3]

And he placed his right foot on the sea and his left on the land. (10:2)

Let's let this imagery soak in a bit. First, since Jesus has opened the book of the covenant, He's able to act with covenant authority. Next, by **placing His foot on the sea and the land** He shows ruling authority. When an ancient king won a victory, he put his foot on the defeated enemy's neck.[4]

The Trumpets warn that God *will* come to judge the wicked, so it's time to repent. Jesus is the conquering King who places the whole earth under His feet (cf. 1 Cor 15:25). What a promise! If you're on God's side, every enemy will be defeated. You don't need to be afraid.

He cried out with a loud voice, as when a lion roars. (10:3a)

Here's another Old Testament image—the voice of God (Hos 11:10).

> and when he had cried out, the seven peals of thunder uttered their voices. And when the seven peals of thunder had spoken, I was about to write; and I heard a voice from heaven saying, "Seal

---

2. This has been God's pattern from the beginning. In Genesis 3:15, as God kicks Adam and Eve out of Eden, He promises their ultimate redemption.

3. There's another important point here. In the Seals, the point of opening the scroll was to enforce the covenant in the sense of blessings for the saints. This time it's to enforce the covenant's other aspect—judgment on the wicked.

4. Josh 10:24–26, 2 Sam 22:38–39, cf. 1 Kgs 5:3, Pss 8:6; 18:38; 47:3; 110:1, Lam 3:34, Mal 4:3.

up the things which the seven peals of thunder have spoken, and do not write them." (10:3b–4)

This just invites interpreters to get crazy. If you read enough, you'll even find some who try to tell you what the **thunders said**, and that seems just a bit strange. After all, John was told *not* to write down what they said, and that tells us that the words aren't what's important. Instead, we need to know what "**thunders**" are. And if we let the Bible interpret itself, we find that whenever "thunder" is a **voice**, it's the voice of God (Exod 19:16, 19, 1 Sam 2:10, Ps 18:13). The picture just keeps getting richer.

First, the angel is Jesus, the Deliverer of Israel and Judge of the wicked. Then He speaks, but it's expressed symbolically as God's voice to emphasize that Jesus is God. Then the thunders—God's voice—are added to the chorus. We're deafened with divine emphasis. Whatever is about to be said isn't to be questioned. It comes straight from God. Then, as if we haven't gotten the picture, Jesus . . .

Swore by Him who lives forever and ever, who created heaven and the things in it, and the earth and the things in it, and the sea and the things in it. (10:6)

Progressive Emphasis
1. Appearance as "God the Deliverer/Judge"
2. God's voice—a lion's roar
3. God's voice—the seven thunders
4. Oath sworn on the Eternal God
5. Oath sworn on the Creator God

Just when it seems the picture is as clear as it can be, two *more* layers of emphasis are added. First, Jesus swears by Himself, the Almighty God. There's no higher authority to guarantee the oath (Ps 110:4, cf. Heb 7:21). But the oath isn't based just on God's sovereign power. It's based on his status as **Creator**, with full authority to command His creations (Neh 9:6, cf. Exod 20:11).[5]

---

5. It's worth spending a moment on this oath. 10:6 quotes Nehemiah 9:6. That text is an emphatically amplified quotation of Exodus 20:11. In Exodus, God's status as Creator gives Him universal authority. But it's more. It's the explicit reason why the weekly Sabbath day is holy to God. By importing this quotation into Revelation, God tells us that His seventh-day Sabbath remains important in the final days of earth's history.

By the time Jesus gets through the five steps of progressive emphasis here, there isn't any way He can add any more. He's used up His arsenal. It's almost as if He's saying, "I'm God. What I'm telling you is *TRUE*. But just in case you don't get the picture, I'm going to say it a different way. And if you're still having problems, I'll going to say it another way, then another and finally once more. If you don't get it by then, it's not My fault." And with that, we finally get to the bottom line.

> **There shall be delay no longer, but in the days of the voice of the seventh angel, when he is about to sound, then the mystery of God is finished, as He preached to His servants the prophets.** (10:6b–7)

When the last trumpet sounds, it's *OVER* (cf. 1 Cor 15:52). The **mystery of God**, the gospel, won't run on forever (Col 1:27; 4:3). The opportunity to repent will end at the seventh Trumpet.

This shouldn't surprise us. After all, the seventh Trumpet is the heavenly Day of Atonement. And, just like the Day of Atonement in ancient Israel, the beginning of the service closed the door to repentance. If you hadn't repented, you were lost (Lev 23:29). The same thing will happen at the end of the drama of sin. When it's over, *IT'S OVER*. There won't be any second chances. Just don't say you weren't warned.

ONCE MORE, WITH EMPHASIS

With the message complete, God's **voice from heaven** commands John to **"Go, take the book which is open in the hand of the angel who stands on the sea and on the land"** (10:8). Right about now, you've got to be wondering; "How can this be the voice of God? Isn't the angel Jesus, who is God? And didn't that voice belong to Jesus in 1:10?"

Think about the first Seal. Jesus was in two places at once in that vision. Because this is another vision, God isn't restrained by physical reality here either. There's a message to deliver, and God will tell it whatever way He needs to.

John **went to the angel, and told him to give him the little book. And he said, "Take it, and eat it; and it will make your stomach bitter, but in your mouth it will be sweet as honey"** (10:9). Talk about a strange lunch! Fortunately, the Old Testament tells us what's going on. The basic idea of **eating the word** is to internalize God's words so you fully understand them (Ps 119:103, Jer 15:16).

John **took the little book out of the angel's hand and ate it. In his mouth it was sweet as honey** (10:10a), just like it was for Ezekiel (Ezek 2:8–3:3). And why not? Covenant promises are sweet to everyone who accepts. But **when John had eaten it, his stomach was made bitter** (10:10b). This shouldn't be a surprise, either. The curses for covenant-breakers are harsh, but should be totally unnecessary. Everyone who will suffer those penalties has as much opportunity to be saved as anyone who enjoys its blessings. Jesus calls *all men* to Himself (John 12:32).

As soon as John ate the book, Jesus told him to **prophesy again concerning many peoples and nations and tongues and kings** (10:11). This time, one recap's not enough. God gave John the warning in the Trumpets. He repeated it in the **strong angel** scene. Now He's going to give it a *third* time. He's not going to give the wicked any excuses. If they reject salvation, it won't be because they didn't get a chance to accept.

11

Measuring The Temple

JOHN'S SECOND WARNING ISN'T as direct as the one in chapter 10. But that doesn't mean that we have to misunderstand it. We just have to remember that the Bible interprets itself.

The Seven Trumpets

Trumpets 1-6	Seven Thunders	Two Witnesses	7th Trumpet
8:6-9:21	10:1-7	11:1-13	11:15, 19

YOU ARE HERE

The angel gave John **a measuring rod like a staff** and told him to **measure the temple of God, and the altar, and those who worship in it** (11:1). This sounds pretty simple. Take the stick and see how big those things are. But John never actually measures anything. It would seem that he's not following directions very well, but that's because physical measuring isn't what God intended.

Before we go on, notice that there are *two* temples in this chapter. John's supposed to measure the first one. **The temple of God which is in heaven** is the second (11:19).[1] This means the first one's on earth.[2] In 3:12

---

1. It's also worth noticing that the temple of God in heaven isn't in the interlude, it's in the seventh Trumpet.
2. Let's not get this confused with the saints dwelling in heaven and the wicked dwelling on earth. Different language is used in different places to make different points. Also, the Temple discussion is where the debate over the date John wrote Revelation gets hot. Some say that this language means that Herod's temple was still standing, and thus John wrote before it was destroyed in AD 70. Others are sure that John wrote during the reign of Domitian in the AD 90's, 20+ years after the Temple was destroyed. This would mean that this interlude has to be symbolic. A third group also claims that John wrote in the AD 90s but this temple's on earth. That means the temple has to be rebuilt. Of course, the

the saints of Philadelphia are "**pillars in the temple of My God.**" They are **His tabernacle, those who dwell in heaven** (13:6). This is the closest context, and should be given great weight. But it's really only one witness, and we need two or three.

Paul declared that the church is the temple of God on earth (1 Cor 3:16–17; 6:19, Eph 2:19–22, Heb 12:12). Peter confirmed this in 1 Peter 2:4–8. But what are we supposed to do with the altar? The church is where spiritual sacrifices are offered to God (1 Pet 2:5). We offer the "sacrifice of praise" (Heb 13:15) instead of the bloody sacrifices of the Old Covenant. In a sense the church is an altar.

By now the final item in the list, **worshipers**, is a no-brainer. It's just another way of describing the church. So God uses the imagery of the physical temple to tell John to measure the saints. They are the **temple**, they are the **altar**, and they are the **worshipers**.[3] But what does "**measuring**" mean?

Once more, we look back to the Old Testament. "Measuring" can mean judgment (2 Sam 8:2, 2 Kgs 21:13), but the story in chapter 11 doesn't deal with the saints and judgment. It also means protection (Isa 28:16–17, Jer 31:38–40, Zech 1:16).

> **Leave out the court which is outside the temple and do not measure it, for it has been given to the nations; and they will tread under foot the holy city for forty-two months.** (11:2)

God's protection here doesn't reach unbelievers. The **courtyard** belongs to "**the nations.**"[4] These enemies of Israel **will tread under foot the holy city for forty-two months. Holy city** is another easy term to identify. It's Jerusalem. But it's *not* the capital of the nation of Judea or of the modern-day secular state called Israel.

When Jesus died, an angel tore the veil that separated the inner apartment from the rest of the temple (Matt 27:51). The sacred space that had been reserved for the high priest on the Day of Atonement was open

---

proper answer is to use the method we're following. The Bible identifies the temple for us, so it doesn't matter when the book was written!

3. This is just one more place where the imagery is used to describe someone or something in more than one way. The Greek says ". . . temple of God and (*kai*) the altar and (*kai*) those who worship . . ." When all three things are the same, translators say that it's "epexegetical." That means we can translate it as ". . . temple of God, *that is* the altar, *that is* those who worship . . ."

4. "The nations" is the generic Old Testament term for Israel's wicked neighbors.

for everyone to see. God's presence was gone. That temple had seen the last animal sacrifice in God's program. Its Levitical priesthood was out of a job. Jesus was the last sacrifice, and He became a new High Priest of the order of Melchizedek (Heb 7:14 ff). The saints are the new priesthood on earth (5:10), and the church is the heavenly Jerusalem (Heb 12:18–24).

Two problems pop up here. First, "How long is **forty-two months?**" Verse three calls it **twelve hundred and sixty days**. 12:6 has an identical period, and that can't be coincidence. In 12:14 it's called **a time and times and half a time**. Finally, **forty-two months** pops up again in 13:5. Since these passages all talk about the same period, an Old Testament source for any of these terms will tell us what they mean.

Time and times and half a time (12:14) is an exact quote of the LXX Greek of Daniel 12:7, which is a Hebrew quotation of Daniel 7:25, which was written in Aramaic. Daniel 7:25 is in the story of the little horn. That evil character is part of the fourth beast, the one that represents Rome. The little horn gets more space (nine verses) than the rest of the beasts combined. The saints "are given into his hand" for this period.

This raises a problem. If this is during Roman rule, 3½ years of oppression just doesn't fit.[5] The little horn showed up after the pagan empire broke up. Next, Daniel's prophecies focus on "the time of the end" (Dan 8:17). This strange period of time has to be a lot longer than 3½ literal years.

If we retrieve a method used widely during the Protestant Reformation, we find a more reasonable answer. The 1,260 "days" are really 1,260 years.[6] This oppression comes during the Dark Ages when the Roman Catholic Church forcibly suppressed "heresy." As the Reformation gained ground, the Catholic Church lost its ability to persecute non-conformists.

About this time, you're probably thinking, "This is crazy ... again! He's using strange methods to change simple time periods into something else. And this time period involves *two witnesses*—two people—not the whole church!" Once more I have to ask you to hang in there a bit longer. If you've

---

5. Preterists argue that this period is an exact match for Nero's persecution of Christians. But if we apply their methods, we'll find that it really doesn't match and the gematria used to identify Nero doesn't match, either. You'll have to look in Appendix A for the details. They're too long for a footnote.

6. The year/day principle is too involved to explore here. I'm using it because it's scriptural. For a full explanation, see Appendix B.

gotten this far, you've already been through this with me a couple of times. And each time you've seen me use the Bible to fill in the picture.

TWO WITNESSES

The second problem is the big one you've been wondering about. Who are these **two witnesses**? Like before, the Bible answers the question. We just have to let it speak.

> And I will grant *authority* to my two witnesses, and they will prophesy for twelve hundred and sixty days, clothed in sackcloth. (11:3)

Whoever the **witnesses** are, they **prophesy in sackcloth for twelve hundred and sixty days**. This isn't a trendy fashion statement. **Sackcloth and ashes** show total submission to God's sovereign authority. When a prophet dresses this way, it's his way of saying, "I am nothing; You are everything" to God (1 Chron 21:16, Ps 35:13, Dan 9:3). It fits with a situation where he's greatly oppressed like **the witnesses** (Ps 30:11, Lam 2:10).

Why are there *two* **witnesses**?[7] The book mentions three by name—John (1:2), Jesus (1:5; 3:14), and Antipas (2:13). Further, the martyrs in the fifth Seal were killed because of their truthful witnessing.[8] Jesus is truth (John 14:6). So these witnesses testify about Jesus. But this still doesn't help us with the number.

Under Hebrew law at least two witnesses are required in any legal proceeding (Deut 17:6; 19:15, Matt 18:16). The Sanhedrin couldn't convict Jesus because they couldn't get two witnesses to agree (Mark 14:56, 64). This principle is applied in "two-witness theology" where we need at least two texts to support our conclusions.

> These are the two olive trees and the two lampstands that stand before the Lord of the earth. (11:4)

---

7. Very few interpreters have bothered to ask why there are *two* witnesses. As a matter of fact, very few interpreters bother to ask, "Why?" about much of anything in scripture. Most are too involved in figuring out "what" the scripture is about. If they asked "Why?" they'd make their job a lot easier and get better answers.

8. The words here are interesting. We call people who have been killed for the faith "martyrs." This comes from the Greek word *marturion*, which means "witness." This use of the word may have been anticipated, since Antipas, one of the witnesses is identified as being killed because of his testimony (2:13).

Now we're getting somewhere. This is an explicit reference to a vision Zechariah saw of *one* lampstand and two olive trees before the Lord in the temple (Zech 4). The lampstands in the temple where Jesus was walking were the seven churches (1:20). Since they're in the apartment in front of God's throne, they **stand before the Lord of the earth**. God's "kingdom of priests" serves before the Lord forever (1 Pet 2:9). In other words, this is just another way to emphasize that the witnesses and the church are the same thing. Jesus told the disciples that they were His witnesses (Acts 1:8).

Because we've decoded a bunch of symbols, let's recap what we've discovered so we don't lose track. The **temple**, **altar**, and **worshipers** all describe the church. **Measuring** explains that God will protect them. The time that requires special protection will last about **1,260 years**. The church is totally submitted to God while it warns the world about God's coming judgment. They are the light of the world, **lampstands** filled with Holy Spirit oil (Matt 5:14).

> If anyone desires to harm them, fire proceeds out of their mouth and devours their enemies; and if anyone would desire to harm them, in this manner he must be killed. These have the power to shut up the sky, in order that rain may not fall during the days of their prophesying; and they have power over the waters to turn them into blood, and to smite the earth with every plague, as often as they desire. (11:5-6)

This is the part that makes people think the **two witnesses** are two specific people. After all, they seem to do very specific things that we haven't seen the church do. They **have the power to shut up the sky, in order that rain may not fall**. This recalls the three and a half years of drought during Elijah's time (Jam 5:17). Their **power over waters to turn them into blood** recalls the **plagues** of Egypt when Moses was alive (Exod 4:9).

Because this passage sounds so much like Moses and Elijah, some people even suggest that these two prophets will be reincarnated. But that's pretty far-fetched. After all, Moses and Elijah were taken to heaven (2 Kgs 2:11, Jude 9, Matt 17:3). It doesn't make a lot of sense for God to send them back, particularly since the witnesses **will be killed**, and Moses already died once.

Moses and Elijah were both teaching prophets. They gave God's message in times of great apostasy.[9] One story will illustrate what God wants us to see. Ahaziah, king of Samaria, sent soldiers to get Elijah (2 Kgs 1). Elijah, the "man of God," refused to come. With a word he destroyed the soldiers with fire from heaven. In a manner of speaking, **fire proceeded out of his mouth. In this manner he killed them.** But did Elijah kill the soldiers? No! God did it. We need to apply this symbolically (cf. 1:1).

Elijah, the "man of God," was able to call on God's power because he was in tune with God. Jesus, the very Son of God, completely in tune with the Father, declared, "the Son can do nothing of Himself, unless *it is* something He sees the Father doing; for whatever *the Father* does, these things the Son also does in like manner" (John 5:19). In other words, the **two witnesses**, figures of the men of God who preceded them, are in tune with God. That is, they are God's true church. When the saints call on God for help, whatever He sees as being of greatest benefit to His plan will be done (John 14:13–14).

We don't need to look for two people sometime in the future. There won't be a "Jerusalem Twosome" like in the *Left Behind*© novels. The imagery of the **witnesses** is designed to help us see the church faithfully spreading God's word of redemption and warning in an increasingly hostile world. They are the "7,000 in Israel who have not bowed the knee to Baal" (1 Kgs 19:18).

> **And when they have finished their testimony, the beast that comes up out of the abyss will make war with them, and overcome them and kill them. (11:7)**

When the witnesses finish their testimony, they will be killed. At first glance this seems to say that at the end of the 1,260 days every church member will be dead. And since that hasn't happened, it looks like I've led you down the garden path to a big mistake. Believe me, that's not what's going on. We just have to carefully examine the context and syntax. So hang on while we go deeper.[10]

---

9. The golden calf episode happened when Moses had been gone a few days (Exod 32), and Elijah lived during Ahab's reign (1 Kgs 17). It's hard to find greater moments of apostasy than those.

10. When I teach in church, I'm often accused of being "deep." What I'm really do-

In verse 3, the witnesses **testified in sackcloth and ashes for 1,260 days**. Is that the only time that the church testified? During the apostolic era, the church was an accepted part of the Roman Empire. There were difficulties, but by and large there wasn't any widespread organized persecution.[11] That came later, mostly during the Dark Ages. Then the Protestant Reformation led to worldwide evangelism that's still going on. So the witnesses are alive now.

The witnesses testify in sackcloth and ashes for the set period, but the text doesn't say anything about the rest of the time they testify. It just points out that they're in dire straits for that time. The church started witnessing at Pentecost and won't stop until **they've finished their testimony**. That job wasn't done at the end of the 1,260 days.

Let me say this a different way. In technical language, this passage has *disjunctive* syntax. That means the discussion has a break. The two parts—the time of sackcloth and ashes and the end of the witnessing—aren't connected. We don't have any information about how long the break is, but it's there. The same story is in Daniel 12.

> And one said to the man dressed in linen, who was above the waters of the river, "How long *will it be* until the end of *these* wonders?" And I heard the man dressed in linen, who was above the waters of the river, as he raised his right hand and his left toward heaven, and swore by Him who lives forever that it would be for a time, times, and half *a time*; and as soon as they finish shattering the power of the holy people, all these *events* will be completed. (Dan 12:6–7)

Daniel asks how long the drama of sin will last. The angel answers by pointing out the 1,260 days (time, times, and half a time). Then there's a semicolon. It's not in the Hebrew, but the Hebrew implies it. It's a *disjunctive* punctuation mark. What comes after it in the sentence doesn't come right after it in time. A period of time will pass *after* the end of the 1,260 days *before* the power of the holy people will be shattered. As Revelation says, ***after*** **the 1,260 days, when they have finished their testimony, the witnesses will be killed.**

These two prophecies are talking about the same thing. The church will warn the world that God will come to judge. During the 1,260 days

---

ing is being careful in dealing with details. I wish it wasn't necessary here, but so many interpreters have ignored the syntax that an error is commonly accepted as truth.

11. Nero was the first to systematically persecute Christians.

they spread the warning under extreme duress. A while after that, at an appointed time, the end will come (Dan 11:35). God doesn't tell us how much later, since we don't need to know (1 Thes 5:1).

Revelation fills in a detail Daniel didn't get. There's even a short period after the end of the witnessing.

> And when they have finished their testimony, the beast that comes up out of the abyss will make war with them, and overcome them and kill them. And their dead bodies *will lie* in the street of the great city which mystically is called Sodom and Egypt, where also their Lord was crucified. And those from the peoples and tribes and tongues and nations *will* look at their dead bodies for three and a half days, and will not permit their dead bodies to be laid in a tomb. And those who dwell on the earth *will* rejoice over them and make merry; and they will send gifts to one another, because these two prophets tormented those who dwell on the earth. (11:7–10)

After the saints finish their job, God will let **the beast from the abyss**—Satan!—shut them up. At least that's what it looks like. Actually the Holy Spirit tells them their work's over so they can sit tight and wait. When the church is silenced, to the wicked it will seem like the saints are dead. The fifth Trumpet sounds.

God took all of history trying to get sinful men to answer His call of grace. Once the last person comes to Him, there won't be any reason to keep warning the wicked. God could end things there, but He not going to. Satan slandered Him. Eventually the court will hear His suit. To provide every possible bit of evidence, He'll give the wicked another chance. They wouldn't answer His call of grace, so it's time to see if they'll run away from pure evil.

Of course, once the saints stop nagging the wicked about repentance, it's party time. The wicked **rejoice over the silenced church** because it looks like they've finally won (11:10). **The prophets** won't **torment** them anymore. Of course, they get to contend with all the problems Satan's reign brings, but we already know how that story turns out. **They don't repent** (9:20–21). God will end it all when there's enough evidence to prove the wicked won't ever run away from evil.

The victory party lasts for **three and a half days, while their bodies lie dead in the street** (11:8–9). Satan defeated his enemies, and nobody's available to bury them, a horrible disgrace (Deut 21:22–23). Killing the "false prophets" vindicates Satan (Jer 14:15–16). But his "victory" turns into crushing defeat when these true prophets are resurrected at the end of the three and a half days. Let's savor the imagery.

The breath of life from God came into them (11:11). This is how God brought Adam to life on the sixth day of Creation (Gen 2:7). Adam was created perfect and sinless, and we will be re-created perfect and sinless (1 Cor 15:51–53). Next, **they hear a great voice from heaven calling them home, and they go up in a cloud** (11:12, cf. 1 Thes 4:16–17). Just as Jesus rose after three days (Matt 27:63), then rose to heaven in a cloud (Acts 1:9), the saints will rise **after three and a half days,** to meet their Savior in the clouds.

God's enemies thought they'd won when the saints were silenced. But their party stopped just as quickly as it started. Christ's true victory strikes **great fear** into them when the church suddenly **stands on its feet** to be ready for its Savior. They call for the rocks to fall on them to hide them from Jesus' wrath (6:15–17).

Before we wrap this up, one more symbol just begs to be reviewed. When the witnesses are killed, **their bodies lie in the street of the great city which mystically is called Sodom and Egypt, where also their Lord was crucified**. If we take this at simple face value, this would be Jerusalem, since Jesus was crucified just outside Jerusalem. And we'd be wrong.

Identifying a single place on earth brings us back to literal*ism*. The only way it can work is if the two witnesses are exactly two people, and we've already figured out that they represent the entire church. Next, the "place" is identified as "the great city."

"The great city" is another name for **"Mystery, Babylon,"** the whore of 17:1–5 (18:10). This isn't a city at all. Ancient Babylon took Israel captive. Now it's a type for the apostasy that takes modern Israel captive.[12] **Sodom and Egypt** confirm this identification. **Sodom** was so wicked that God destroyed it with fire and brimstone (Gen 19:24, cf. Rev 8:7). In **Egypt**, Pharaoh held the ancient Israelites captive, refusing to recognize the One True God (Exod 5:2). The cross may have been near Jerusalem, but location wasn't the issue, wickedness was.

---

12. You may want to read Jeremiah 50–51 to see a larger example of how the Bible uses Babylon typologically.

Typological Use of Sodom and Egypt		
Sodom	Rulers of Jerusalem	Isa 1:10
	Wicked in Jerusalem	Isa 3:9, Ezek 16:46–56
	Wicked prophets	Jer 23:14
Egypt	Spiritual slavery	Isa 27:12
	God's opponent	Ezek 29–32, Zech 14:19
	"Jail" for idolaters	Hos 8:13
	Oppressor of saints	Zech 10:10–11

RECAP

Measuring the Temple symbolically shows how God protects the church as it warns the world about judgment. During the 42 months of sackcloth and ashes the church has a hard time, but things get better before the end. Saints keep on warning their neighbors until God tells them the job is done.

When the saints clam up, it looks to the world like their tormenters are dead, so they party hearty. Nobody repents and runs away from evil. This ends when God raises the saints to meet Him in the air. The wicked are terrified because they know the party's over and they're about to meet their doom.

This interlude's another way of telling the same story the Trumpets told. Now it's time to check out the last of the "sevens"—the seven Bowls.

12

Bowls Full of Wrath

And I saw another sign in heaven, great and marvelous, seven angels who had seven plagues, which are the last, because in them the wrath of God is finished.

(Rev 15:1)

WHERE ARE WE?

IF YOU'VE BEEN FOLLOWING closely, you've noticed that we just skipped three chapters. Later on you'll see another reason for this, but mainly we've been listening to this chorus in the middle of the seventh Trumpet.

> The time *came* for the dead to be judged, and *the time* to give their reward to Thy bond-servants the prophets and to the saints and to those who fear Thy name, the small and the great, and to destroy those who destroy the earth. (11:18)

This "look-ahead" is part of an important pattern. When we started the *Primer*, we noticed that Revelation is a Jewish apocalypse. That means it shows us the divine plan from one view, then backs up and shows another angle, and another, and so on. After the seventh Seal was opened (8:1), **the angels were given their Trumpets** (8:2), and then the seventh Seal was finished (8:3–5). It looked like this . . .

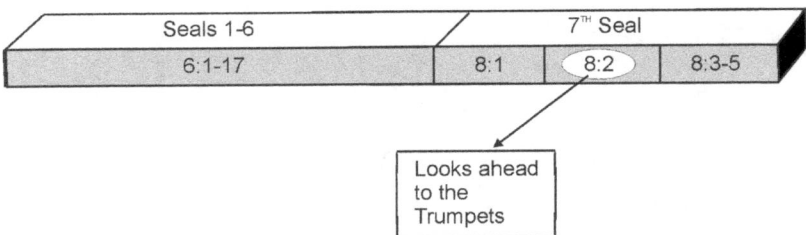

Because the seventh Trumpet also has this sort of "look-ahead," its map looks basically the same. But the seventh Bowl *doesn't* have a "look-ahead." That means that the Bowls finish this section of the book. The Seals, Trumpets, and Bowls make up a single unit. It looks like this . . .

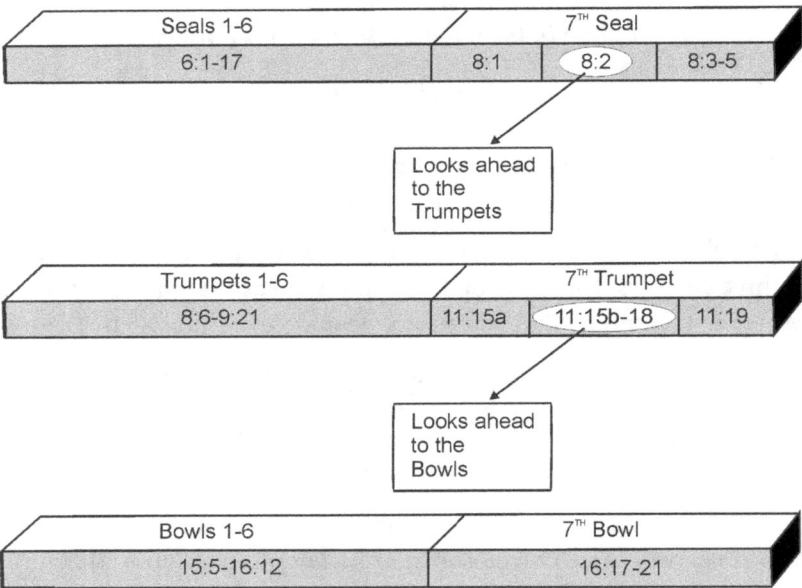

In a little while, we'll see that the seventh Bowl is essentially identical to the seventh Seal and seventh Trumpet. This means they're all the Day of Atonement. And since the Day of Atonement is also the Day of the Lord, this section of the book ends with Jesus coming to reward the saints and destroy the wicked. That's the end of the story of sin on this earth.

If you've been reading *really* carefully, you may think I've changed my story. After all, God's big problem is how to deal with sin in a way that prevents it from ever starting up again, and the Day of Atonement and Day of the Lord don't fix that problem. Guess what? You're right! But I *haven't* changed my story. We just haven't gotten to the final chapter yet. God will solve His problem . . . in *His* time.

You've also noticed I said the wicked will be destroyed when Jesus returns. This isn't preached very often, so let's listen to Jesus in Matthew 24:35–42. I've laid it out to make it easier to see.

INTRODUCTION	
Heaven and earth will pass away, but My words shall not pass away. But of that day and hour no one knows, not even the angels of heaven, nor the Son, but the Father alone. (35–36)	
A – INTRO	**B – INTRO**
For the coming of the Son of Man will be just like the days of Noah. (37)	so shall the coming of the Son of Man be. (39b)
A	**B**
For as in those days which were before the flood they were eating and drinking, they were marrying and giving in marriage, until the day that Noah entered the ark, and they did not understand until the flood came and took them all away; (38–39a)	Then there shall be two men in the field; one will be taken, and one will be left. Two women *will be* grinding at the mill; one will be taken, and one will be left. (40–41)
CONCLUSION	
Therefore be on the alert, for you do not know which day your Lord is coming. (42)	

Jesus bookends his message with, "You won't know when I'm coming . . . So be ready." In between He tells two parallel stories. First, all the unbelievers died in the Flood and "only Noah was left" (Gen 7:23).[1] Then Jesus says that at His return it's going to be just the same. One will be killed—like the wicked in Noah's day—and the other will remain—like Noah. Curiously, the word for "left" can be translated "forgiven," which allows us to translate verses 40 and 41 as "one will be taken, and one will be forgiven."[2] Put simply,

---

1. The Old Testament uses this idea dozens of times. Each time, if you're "taken," you're toast. If you're "left behind" you're one of God's faithful.
2. The word is *aphiemi*, which means "forgiven" in the Lord's Prayer (Matt 6:12).

Jesus told His disciples that when He came back He would rescue His saints and kill all the wicked. That's the Day of the Lord.

Now that we've wrapped up the preliminaries, let's dig into the Bowls. But let's remember to be careful. After all, they're still in the future and we can get ourselves in trouble if we're too definite about unfulfilled prophecy.[3] At the same time, if we use scripture to interpret scripture, we should be able to get a pretty good picture of what's coming.

THE BOWLS

John saw **another great sign in heaven, seven angels with the seven last plagues** (15:1). The plagues will **finish the wrath of God**, so they only affect the wicked. Like the Trumpets, they're modeled after the plagues of Egypt, another indication that they happen in order.

Before the angels can start, John sees something amazing. All the saints who were **victorious over the beast** are **standing on a sea of glass mixed with fire** (15:2). Now this isn't an ordinary "sea." It sits in front of the **temple of the tabernacle of the testimony in heaven** where the laver would normally be (15:5).[4]

Fire is red, so the saints are on a "Red Sea." They're singing the **Song of Moses and the Lamb**, an expanded version of the song ancient Israelites sang after God led them out of physical Egypt to freedom through the Red Sea (15:3, cf. Exod 14:31–15:2, 17–18). Jesus has completed the delivery of true Israel from spiritual Egypt.[5] It's time to celebrate! God's **righteous acts have been revealed** and **all the nations will worship God** (15:4).

When I read this, I have to take a deep breath as I see so many different ways God presents His message. It's fun to try to sort out the details, but most people really don't need to. With so many different versions of the End-Times Passover, everybody should be touched by one of them.[6] It might be the **Lord's Day** in 1:10, the imagery of the tabernacle in the wilderness, or the great multitude in heaven that no one can count. With every different description, God gives someone else a view of our deliver-

---

3. A lot of popular prophecy teachers have set dates for Christ's return. Hal Lindsay's book *The Late Great Planet Earth* predicted the "rapture" in 1988, with the beginning of the millennium in 1995. Lindsay was wrong.

4. The laver in Solomon's temple was called the "sea" (1 Kgs 7:23–26).

5. It would be easy to spiritualize all of this and remove any physical meaning. But this physical world is spiritual Egypt. Our deliverance will most definitely be physical.

6. Apologies to my friend Joe Ortiz, who recently published a book by that title.

ance from bondage in spiritual Egypt. Unfortunately, some won't accept His gift of grace.[7]

After this song **the tabernacle of the testimony which is in heaven was opened** (15:5). The seven angels with the seven plagues came out dressed in priestly **linen and golden girdles** (15:6, cf. Lev 16:3–4, Exod 28:2–8). **One of the four living creatures**, symbolic of Israel, **gave the angels bowls full of the wrath of God** (15:7).[8] One final time Israel calls on God to do what they can't do for themselves. The battle belongs to the Lord (1 Sam 17:47, 2 Chron 20:17). The Day of the Lord begins.

Before the angels can do anything, **the temple fills with smoke from the glory of God and from His power. No one was able to enter the temple until the seven plagues of the seven angels were finished** (15:8, cf. Exod 40:34–35, 1 Kgs 8:10). As the veil opens, the heavenly Day of Atonement service begins. God's glory fills the temple, ending the time for repentance (Lev 16:2, 13, 17; 23:29, 2 Thes 2:8 KJV). The wicked have condemned themselves because they won't ask for forgiveness (John 3:18). God announces the verdict from the tabernacle (16:17, cf. Num 16:19ff).

PLAGUES

The first four plagues are **poured out on the earth** (16:2), **the sea** (16:3), **the rivers** (16:4), and **the sun** (16:8). Every part of creation gets nailed. Adam was condemned to survive "by the sweat of his face," but that was only a shadow of what would eventually come (Gen 3:19). His death sentence was really a process of slow death (Gen 3:2–3, Rom 5:12). Now the curse is on steroids.

The first four Bowls echo plagues of Egypt. And just like in Egypt, **the wicked do not repent**, preferring to say, "Who is the Lord, that I should hear His voice?" (16:9, Exod 5:2). They suffer **horrible sores** like the Egyptians (16:2, Exod 9:9ff). The **sea turns into blood so that everything**

---

7. We can have a little fun here by letting our imagination run a bit. This "red" sea can be imagined as full of blood. The laver is used for washing—ceremonial cleansing. We're "washed in the blood of the Lamb." His blood "cleanses us from sin." This isn't really exegesis—drawing out what's in the text. Instead, it's hearing echoes in the atmosphere of the scene. A Jewish reader would probably feel this ambiance.

8. There's a bitter irony in this scene. These bowls are sacred vessels used for holy offerings in the tabernacle services (Num 7:13). Now they hold plagues that destroy the wicked.

dies the same way the Nile did (16:3, Exod 7:20-21). The **springs and rivers become blood** like the other water sources in Egypt (16:4, Exod 7:19).

What wonderful poetic justice! The harlot, **drunk with the blood of the saints** (17:6, 16:6), is forced to **drink blood by God's righteous judgments** (16:5-6). The tables are turned. The law of *lex talionis*—just retribution—finally finds its true mark. The principle of an eye for an eye comes full circle (Exod 21:23-24). God took His people out of physical Egypt by great judgments and He will bring them out of spiritual Egypt at the end of time by more great judgments (Exod 6:6; 7:4).

We have to ask if these plagues are literal and physical. My best guess is that they have a physical part, but we have to be careful. After all, they haven't happened yet, and they don't seem to have any obvious symbols in them. On the other hand, in the sixth seal the wicked cry out for relief from God's wrath (6:12-17). That sounds pretty physical.

The fourth plague **scorches men with fire from the sun** (6:8-9). This *isn't* a copy of one of the plagues of Egypt, but it does come from the exodus. The Israelites were sheltered in *sukkot* as they wandered in the wilderness.[9] The Seals interlude uses *sukkot* to symbolize God's protection during this very moment (7:14-17, cf. Ps 91).[10] The saints have nothing to fear while the wicked suffer.

The fifth plague is **darkness** (16:10-11). This was the last plague of Egypt before God delivered Israel at Passover (Exod 10:21-23). It has the same result here. The wicked **blaspheme the God of heaven and do not repent** (16:11, cf. Exod 9:35, etc.).[11]

God shows the wicked who He is, but they just get louder (cf. Exod 10:24). So the **sixth angel dries up the river Euphrates to make way for the kings from the east** (16:12). If we take this literal*istic*ally, we'd expect the physical river that runs through ancient Babylon to dry up so mechanized armies from India, China, and Japan can drive through. But literal*ism* doesn't look to the Bible for the answer. The real key is in ancient Babylon.

---

9. A *sukkah*, or booth, was a temporary shelter used during the wilderness wandering. God used this as the theme of the Feast of Booths (*Sukkot*).

10. Verse 15 can be literally translated, "He will erect a booth over them."

11. We could get technical here and say that they don't have a chance to repent since the Day of Atonement is underway. And that would be true. But the real importance of the comment is literary emphasis. The wicked people made an irrevocable choice against God a long time before. When the plagues come and they "do not repent," it just highlights the fact that they won't change their minds, no matter what. They belong to Satan, heart and soul.

Daniel 5 tells how Belshazzar, prince regent of Babylon, held the block party to end all block parties. Everybody who was anybody was there, and they all got stinking drunk. Even the army got wasted. God used Daniel to prosecute His covenant lawsuit against Belshazzar. God wrote the "Guilty!" verdict on the wall. Cyrus' army "**dried up the Euphrates**" by diverting it. They walked under the walls on the riverbed into Babylon. The Medo-Persian confederation executed the covenant verdict (Dan 5:30, cf. Isa 44:28–45:1).

Cyrus' army came from several kingdoms, including the Medes. They came from Persia—east of Babylon—so they were **kings from the east**. In Revelation God uses their conquest as a *type*. Physical Israel was captive in physical Babylon. Anyone who didn't worship the pagan gods risked his life (Dan 3). After seventy years of captivity, God got them home (Ezra 1).[12]

We are spiritual Israel, captive in spiritual Babylon.[13] Apostasy and false belief systems lead to confusion and sin, with horrible consequences. We can't go to our heavenly home (Heb 12:22–23, Rev 12:12) until Jesus comes to take us there (John 14:1–3, 1 Thes 4:13–17).

There's another parody in this typology. The River of Life runs through the New Jerusalem, our final home (22:1–2). Spiritual Babylon has its own "River of Life," the Euphrates. The real River of Life gives life to the saints (22:2). The river of Babylon leads to death for everyone who drinks from it.

When Cyrus dried up the Euphrates, he prepared the way for the kings from the east—Cyrus and his allies—to conquer Babylon and deliver the Jews. The sixth Bowl shows that Satan's forces won't be able to stand against Jesus' heavenly army (cf. Dan 10:13).

What literal event does the sixth Bowl represent? The Bible doesn't really help us. All we know is how it turns out. I know this isn't very satisfying, but God never promised us exhaustive information. He promised us *enough*. With Christ leading the armies of heaven, His followers have nothing to fear.

---

12. I can't leave this picture without looking back at Old Testament language. God calls Cyrus "my anointed" in Isaiah 45:1. *Mashiach* also means "Messiah." As the deliverer of Israel in Daniel 5, Cyrus is a type of the Messiah in the sixth Bowl.

13. You've probably noticed that I switched from "spiritual Egypt" to "spiritual Babylon." They're really the same. Both held Israel captive. Both time God delivered Israel by great judgments. And in the two witnesses interlude we saw that "mystical Egypt" (11:8) is also called "the great city" which is Babylon (17:5, 18). God uses them interchangeably to identify His people's captors.

THE SEVENTH BOWL

The seventh angel poured out his bowl upon the air; and a loud voice came out of the temple from the throne, saying, "It is done." The Day of Atonement is over. God's people are clean, and it's time to bring them home (Lev 16:30). Jesus' sacrifice on the cross has wiped away every one of their sins. God celebrates this with a thundering, **"It is done!"** The Greek verb here is in the "indicative active perfect" tense, emphasizing that this is the end. Temple work for God's people is *over*. As Paul says, this is when "we will be changed in an instant." We will put on immortality, and will never again suffer the corruption of sin (1 Cor 15:51–53). Victory is ours forever!

> And there were flashes of lightning and sounds and peals of thunder; and there was a great earthquake, such as there had not been since man came to be upon the earth, so great an earthquake *was it, and* so mighty. And the great city was split into three parts, and the cities of the nations fell. And Babylon the great was remembered before God, to give her the cup of the wine of His fierce wrath. And every island fled away, and the mountains were not found. And huge hailstones, about one hundred pounds each, came down from heaven upon men; and men blasphemed God because of the plague of the hail, because its plague was extremely severe. (16:18–21)

It's déjà vu from the seventh Seal and Trumpet. God brings in His Great and Terrible Day with a vengeance (Mal 4:5). He throws **hail** at His enemies and causes so much destruction with the **earthquake** that **every island flees away and the mountains are not found.** He returns the earth to the state it was before creation—unformed and unfilled.[14]

---

14. This is a literal translation of Genesis 1:2, where the earth is *tohu va bohu*, "unformed and unfilled."

7ᵀᴴ Seal: 8:1–5	7ᵀᴴ Trumpet: 11:19	7ᵀᴴ Bowl: 16:17–21
Day of Atonement Language • Silence in Heaven • Large amount of Incense	*Day of Atonement Language* • Ark Seen in Temple	*Day of Atonement Language* • Temple filled with God's glory • Voice from Throne, "It is done"
Day of the Lord Language • Thunder • Lightning • Sounds • Earthquake • Coals hurled to earth	*Day of the Lord Language* • Thunder • Lightning • Sounds • Earthquake • Great hailstones	*Day of the Lord Language* • Thunder • Lightning • Sounds • Earthquake • Huge hailstones

Earth as we know it is *done*. The drama of sin is *over*. Satan has had every chance to prove his allegations against God. Now God's people are with Him in heaven (John 14:1–3). All the wicked are dead on the desolate earth. But before we can see how God answers Satan's charges, we have to cover a couple of things we've skipped. First, there's the interlude in the Bowls. Next we'll examine the big interlude we skipped—the Controversy over Worship—in chapters 12–14. Then we can look at the Millennium.

13

Armageddon!

> And I saw *coming* out of the mouth of the dragon and out of the mouth of the beast and out of the mouth of the false prophet, three unclean spirits like frogs; for they are spirits of demons, performing signs, which go out to the kings of the whole world, to gather them together for the war of the great day of God, the Almighty. And they gathered them together to the place which in Hebrew is called Har-Magedon. (16:13–14, 16)

ARMAGEDDON PROBABLY GENERATES MORE sensational speculation than any part of Revelation.[1] Everyone's heard some impassioned preacher carrying on about how God **dries up the Euphrates River** so massive Indian, Chinese, and Japanese mechanized armies can drive to the Valley of Jezreel for a war with the Jews. Every kind of weapon is supposed to be on its way to the Mother of All Battles.[2]

There *isn't* any place on the map called "Armageddon," so we should almost expect this kind of wild ideas about it. And it *does* say that **the kings of the whole world were gathered together for war**. But before we start taking the symbols apart, let's remember just where we are.

The Seven Bowls

Bowls 1-6	Armageddon	7th Bowl
16:1-12	16:13-16	16:17-21

YOU ARE HERE

---

1. The Mark of the Beast is probably the only other thing that comes close.

2. Sorry, I couldn't resist using Saddam Hussein's line. But the armies are supposed to be going through Iraq . . .

This passage *isn't* part of the sixth Bowl. It's another interlude, a recap just like the interludes in the Seals and Trumpets. The Bowls echo the plagues of Egypt. Just like Pharaoh, the wicked get worked up against God. They "harden their hearts," and **refuse to repent** (16:11, cf. Exod 8:15, etc.).

The **Dragon** is Satan (12:9). The **Beast** represents human government.[3] The **False Prophet** is the voice of Satan through religious entities supported by human government. Like all false prophets, this **False Prophet** promotes idolatry. These three make up an evil trinity.

Just like Pharaoh, the false trinity fights to the bitter end against the true Trinity. When Moses and Aaron came to Pharaoh, they performed miracles to show they came from the one true God. Pharaoh's magicians duplicated some of the miracles, trying to show that Yahweh's claim was false. They turned their staffs into snakes (Exod 7:10–12), turned water into blood (Exod 7:20–22), and made **frogs** appear (Exod 8:6–7), refusing to recognize the One True God, but that was it. God wouldn't let them go any further.

Satan's people in end-times aren't any different. **Unclean spirits like frogs** symbolize their last desperate rebellion. They are **demons, performing miraculous signs. They gather the kings of the earth for the war of the great day of God, the Almighty**.

John's following a consistent pattern. God's people **dwell in heaven** (13:6), so they aren't **the kings of the earth**. They are the heavenly Jerusalem (Heb 12:22). Everyone else—the wicked—is an **earth-dweller** (6:10, 8:13, etc.).

Before we go any farther, we need to remember that Day of the Lord is the day God rescues His people by destroying His enemies. Why would any rational person want to be on God's bad side then? You'd have to be suicidal! Unfortunately, the bad guys have made up their minds. Facts don't matter. They're totally committed to Satan and hate Yahweh. They'd drive a chariot into the Red Sea even though they *know* they're going to drown. And right here I have to be careful with my metaphors.

I've been using physical language. But the battle *isn't* about land and armies. It's about *worship*. Satan wants to be worshiped, so he stirred up the revolt in Heaven. He got a lot of angels to follow him. And by the time of the end, he'll have a lot of humans worshiping him as well. But he can't stand losing anyone. His rebellion has to be *total*. And the final

---

3. We'll go through this in detail when we cover Revelation 13, since the Beast is the major player in that chapter. In brief, the Beast is a composite of Daniel 7's four beasts. Since they represent all human government from Daniel's time till Jesus returns, the beast represents human government.

showdown is at **the place which in Hebrew is known as Har-Magedon**. Like I said before, **Har-Magedon** isn't the name of a place on the map. It's a symbolic name that emphasizes the conflict between the worship of Yahweh and the worship of Satan.

Let's break the word down. The first part's simple. *Har* is the Hebrew word for a mountain. On the other hand, *Magedon* is used only once in scripture—Zechariah 12:11. The problem is that John's using transliteration—letters from one language to sound out another. We can't be quite sure if that's what John intended, but it's a good fit.

Magedon—Megiddo—is a city near Mount Carmel where the prophet Elijah had a showdown with Baal's prophets (1 Kgs 18:17–40).[4] After God showed His superiority, they still refused to worship Him, so Elijah killed them. That sounds a lot like Armageddon. God's enemies had a big confrontation with Yahweh and lost. His people were saved. It would be nice to stop here, but this isn't the only approach to *magedon*.

Because *magedon* sounds out Hebrew words using Greek letters, the word *mo'ed* ("assembly") may be the source.[5] The combined form would mean "the mountain of assembly," or the Temple mount (Isa 14:13). The *Jewish New Testament Commentary* adds *another* possibility. *Har-Magedon* may actually be *Har-Migdon*, "the mountain of His choice fruit," another name for Mount Zion.[6] Since God executes judgment from the sanctuary, this recalls what happened in the wilderness to Korah, Dathan, and Abiram (Num 16).

I hope you've noticed something here. *All three* options lead to the *same* conclusion! Armageddon isn't about physical war. It's about spiritual war. It's final decision time. Are you for or against God?

God's been trying to get us to come to Him all through the Seals, Trumpets, and Bowls. The Seals emphasize His grace. The Trumpets warns us that He won't wait forever. Finally, the Bowls show us the consequences for anyone who persists in rebellion. They'll get what they gave. We might suggest that the whole message can be summed up as:

> **Behold, I am coming like a thief. Blessed is the one who stays awake and keeps his garments, lest he walk about naked and men see his shame. (16:15)**

---

4. Mount Carmel could be called "the mountain of Megiddo," or *har magedon*.
5. It may not look right, but with properly pronounced Hebrew this works.
6. When the sanctuary finally got a permanent home, it was on Mount Zion. This is where Solomon's Temple and the second Temple were built.

14

Once Over, Lightly

We've spent so much time looking at details that I may have gotten you a little bit lost. So let's back up for a minute and refresh ourselves about where we've been.

God showed John the story of salvation from several different angles. In the Seals, He presented His call of grace. Just as that panorama was about to end, God paused and put another picture inside the first picture. He showed John **144,000 from every nation and tribe and people and tongue** (7:4; 9). These people had answered the call of grace. It looked like this:

The Seven Seals

Seals 1-6	The Sealing of the Saints	7th Seal
6:1-16	7:1-17	8:1, 3-5

|—— Interlude ——|

In the Trumpets, God did it again. Just as His warning of coming judgment was almost done, He stopped and showed John *two* recaps. It's almost as if He wanted everyone to know that this message was so important that it couldn't be repeated just once. The **Strong Angel** was blunt (8:1–8). His message was, **"When it's over, it's over!"** (10:7). The **two witnesses** (11:3ff) displayed how God's true church carries the warning to the wicked without regard for its own safety. The Trumpets look like this:

The Seven Trumpets

Trumpets 1-6	Seven Thunders	Two Witnesses	7th Trumpet
8:6-9:21	10:1-7	11:1-13	11:15a, 19

|—— Interlude ——|

Finally, God did it again in the Bowls. They told about God's punishment on the wicked as they continue to rebel against Him in the face of certain destruction (cf. 6:16–17; 16:11). And when this tableau was almost finished, God stopped one more time to show another picture of how Satan's slaves simply will not allow themselves to repent. Armageddon makes the Bowls look like this:

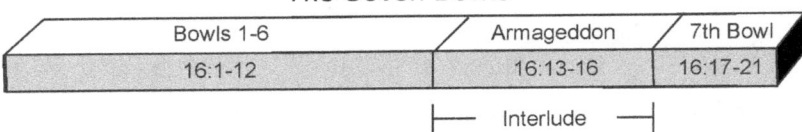

Together the three series tell the story of God's covenant in this sinful age. God first calls sinful mankind to repentance. He doesn't want anyone to be lost, so He takes His time and gives repeated warnings (2 Pet 3:8–9). He waits until nobody's left who'll answer His call. He even gives the wicked a chance to run away from evil. Then it's time for judgment. The Day of Atonement makes His people clean forever so they can rise to be with Him (1 Thes 4:13–17). The Day of the Lord destroys the wicked (1 Thes 5:1–3).

7ᵀᴴ Seal: 8:1–5	7ᵀᴴ Trumpet: 11:19	7ᵀᴴ Bowl: 16:17–21
Day of Atonement Language	*Day of Atonement Language*	*Day of Atonement Language*
• Silence in Heaven • Large amount of Incense	• Ark Seen in Temple	• Temple filled with God's glory • Voice from Throne, "It is done"
Day of the Lord Language	*Day of the Lord Language*	*Day of the Lord Language*
• Thunder • Lightning • Sounds • Earthquake • Coals hurled to earth	• Thunder • Lightning • Sounds • Earthquake • Great hailstones	• Thunder • Lightning • Sounds • Earthquake • Huge hailstones

Since all three series end in the Day of Atonement and the Day of the Lord, it's obvious that they overlap. If we check the various timing keys in them, we can see that they fit together like this:

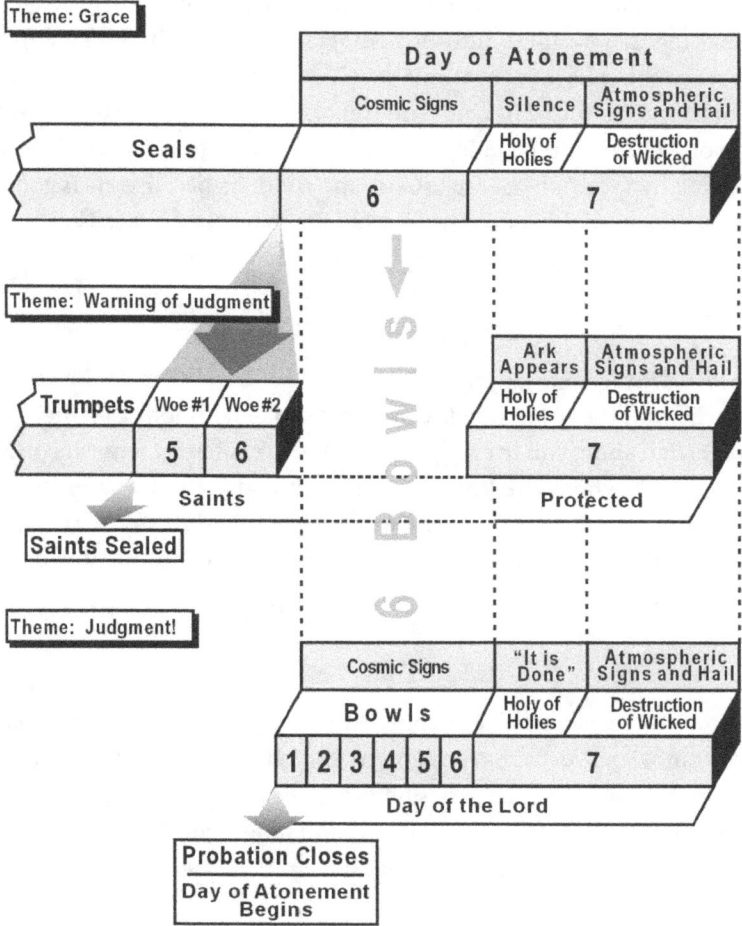

As I write this, I'm reminded that the call of grace isn't a threat. It's our Father calling to His lost children, inviting them to come home (cf. Hos 2:14). He holds out a promise of compassion because He doesn't want us to die (Hos 2:23).

Unfortunately, many just aren't listening. So God tailors His message for them. Maybe a stern warning will get through. "If you don't come to me, you'll seal your own fate (John 3:18). You've decided to go your own way, away from Me, the source of life. Eventually, you'll be so far away that you'll die."

Think about this for a minute. Because God loves us, He has to wait. He has to warn us. If He didn't love us, He could cut things off anytime He got bored, but His love for us makes God hold out to the last moment for that last soul to hear His call. And it makes Him sternly warn us. We just keep on getting into trouble, and He keeps trying to get us back. The bad stuff that happens isn't because God isn't good, it's because He *is* good. No, He doesn't cause the problems. But He lets them go on because He knows that somewhere along the line somebody else will hear His voice.

THERE'S MORE TO COME

Grace, warning, and judgment don't end the story! **One of the seven angels who had the seven bowls came and spoke with John, saying, "Come here, I shall show you the judgment of the great harlot who sits on many waters, with whom the kings of the earth committed** *acts of* **immorality, and those who dwell on the earth were made drunk with the wine of her immorality." (17:1-2)** There's a whole new drama ahead. In the meantime, we haven't finished the first story.

THE REST OF THIS STORY

By now you're asking what happened to chapters 12-14. Trust me, they haven't moved. We just haven't gotten to them because they're another interlude! We covered each series before going back to look at its interlude. The three series were Grace, Warning, and Judgment. Together they make another series, with another interlude.

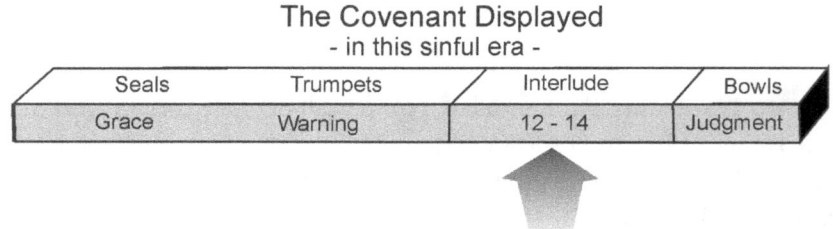

Because there are three parts to the message, there will be three parts to the interlude. Chapter 12 will recap the Seals, 13 the Trumpets, and 14 the Bowls. Please bear with me. I'm going to show this from the Bible, but it's just going to take some time. In fact, because these chapters have so much going on, it will take us *four* chapters. But the ride should be worth the wait.

There's one more thing. Chapters 12–14 have a special name—the *Controversy over Worship*. The reason will become obvious once we get into them. And since they're recaps of the Seals, Trumpets, and Bowls, this whole section of Revelation is the cosmic Controversy over Worship.

Let's go back to the beginning for a minute. In our first chapter we talked about God's problem. Satan was originally the highest angel. He rebelled, thinking that everyone should worship him instead of God. As Isaiah tells the story, Satan wanted to "raise (his) throne above the stars of God" and be "like the Most High" (Isa 12:13–14). We're right in the middle of this war about worship. God's actions to bring us back are the focus of chapters 6–16.

Just when you think I've sprung all the surprises I've got, there's one more. Chapter 14 has *another* interlude in it. It's the *Three Angels' Messages*. But by now, I think you've figured out that it's another recap covering chapters 12–14. But since those recap the Seals, Trumpets, and Bowls, the Three Angels recap the Seals, Trumpets, and Bowls, too. The whole thing looks like this:

118 A PRIMER ON THE BOOK OF REVELATION

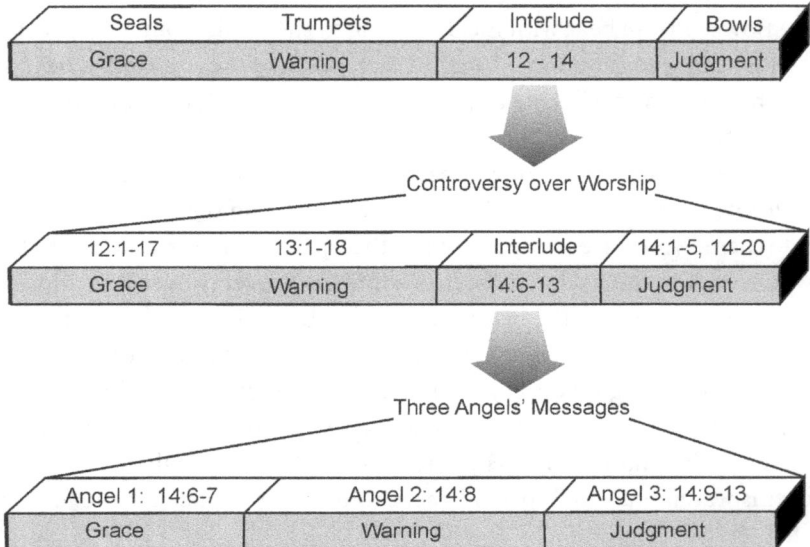

Now that you've figured out where we are in Revelation, take a break. Go to the kitchen and get a snack. Stretch your legs. Come back when you're ready to dig in again. I'll be here.

15

The Controversy over Worship, Part I

> *A great sign appeared in heaven: a woman clothed with the sun,*
> *and the moon under her feet, and on her head*
> *a crown of twelve stars (Rev 12:1)*

WITH THIS **GREAT SYMBOL**, God comes back to the story of grace. "**Great**" means that God really wants us to see that it's important. That means we need to spend enough time to understand it.

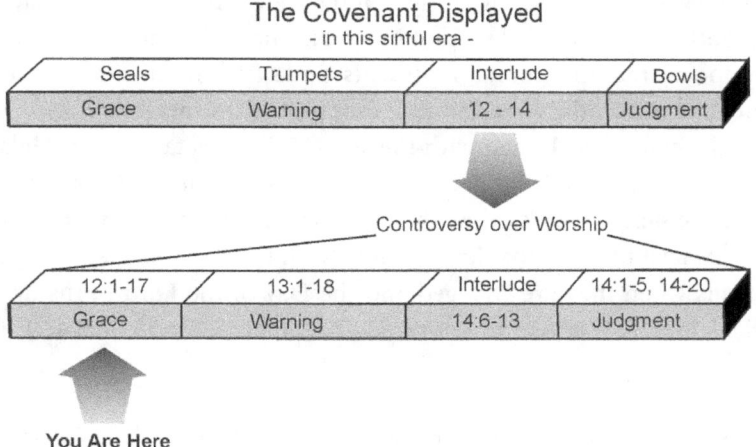

You Are Here

Identifying the **woman** is pretty easy. After all, she's part of a pattern. In chapter 17, we'll see a **harlot**. Harlotry is one of the most common symbols for idolatry in the Old Testament. Since this is the opposite of faithfulness, the **woman** represents God's saints. Right now, some of you will be shouting, "Wait a minute! It's Mary." And in a sense you're right. Let's look.

In verse 2, **the woman is pregnant and in labor.** Then in verse 5 her **male child is caught up to heaven.** If we take this literal*istic*ally, the woman is Mary and the child is Jesus. In a minute we'll see that the child really is Jesus. But the woman *isn't* Mary. In verse 6, *after* Jesus' ascension, the **woman flees into the wilderness.** We have no record that Mary did this. And God doesn't ask us to draw conclusions without evidence.[1]

The **woman** spends **one thousand two hundred and sixty days in the wilderness.** This is exactly the same length of time, expressed with exactly the same Greek words as the length of the church's **sackcloth and ashes ministry** in 11:3. It's the same period called **forty-two months** in 11:2 and 13:5, again in identical Greek. Finally, it's the period called **a time, times, and half a time** in 12:14, quoting the exact Greek of Daniel 12:7. None of these periods have anything to do with Mary, but all of them are intimately involved with the period the church preaches the gospel under persecution. Since these passages all use identical substantive language, the woman has to represent the church.[2]

But the New Testament church *didn't* give birth to Jesus. He was born over thirty years before the "church" got started at Pentecost, and His mother was a faithful servant of God in the Old Testament tradition. That means that the woman represents God's faithful in all ages.[3] At the same time, since Mary was faithful, she's part of the imagery.

The church is **clothed with the sun** (12:1). This takes us to Malachi 4:2, where Jesus is called the "Sun of Righteousness" and to Galatians 3:27 where the saints have "clothed themselves with Christ." But we can't stop there. Malachi tells us that Jesus comes "with healing" for the saints. This happens when they are changed and the Day of the Lord burns up the wicked, leaving "neither root nor branch" (1 Cor 15:51–55, Mal 4:1). This

---

1. Some of you will think about the time Jesus spent in Egypt as a baby. But scripture only tells us that he was there until Herod died. We don't have hard dates for his birth, so there is no way for us to verify this as 1,260 days in the wilderness, so we can't use it. Of course, Egypt wasn't a wilderness, since it had a thriving civilization. This is *symbolic*, not literalistic.

2. I hate using technical language here, but it's important. "Substantive language" refers to words or phrases that carry significant meaning. These phrases are substantive and aren't found anywhere else in scripture. That makes it a lead-pipe cinch that they're talking about the same thing.

3. Once again, the saints of the Old Testament are together with the saints of the New Testament. There's no difference between Jew and Gentile in God's plan.

is typical Old Testament language of God's promise to His covenant-keeping remnant. So with the first bit of symbolism, God introduces grace.

The **crown of twelve stars** and the **moon under her feet** draw us to Joseph's dream in Genesis 37. He saw the sun, moon, and stars bowing down to him. These represented his father, mother, and brothers. His brothers didn't like Joseph telling them about the dream, and sold him into slavery. After a long and involved story, Joseph ended up saving Egypt and his family from a seven-year famine. Joseph's comment at the end of this story is instructive. "God sent me before you to preserve life" (Gen 45:5).

This is the message of grace. Again. God wants to rescue every life He can. All we have to do is to come to Him. We'll be preserved in spiritual Egypt until the last person responds (11:8). Then He'll rescue us "by great judgments" (Exod 6:6; 7:4).[4]

Joseph was a type of Christ.[5] He was the savior of his family, just as Christ is the savior of His family. The stars/brothers that bowed down to him became the tribes of Israel, and here they are stars in the chaste woman's crown. Ancient Israel lives on in the church of the apostles.

> And another sign appeared in heaven. Behold! A great red dragon with seven heads and ten horns, and on his heads were seven diadems. (12:3)

Behold! tells us we're looking at another important part of the vision. God combines the four beasts in Daniel 7 to create the **dragon** (**Satan**—12:9). They are a lion, bear, four-headed leopard, and a terrifying beast with ten horns. That makes **seven heads and ten horns**. **On his heads were seven diadems**—king's crowns. These *aren't* the victors' crowns the saints wear. This beast is all about power, not victory over sin.

Daniel's vision covered all of human history from the time of Babylon until Christ's return. Combining these symbols means that this beast represents all of human government over all that time. But in 12:9 the dragon is called **the Devil and Satan**, not human government. This puts the emphasis on Satan's influence on human governments.

---

4. It's possible to misunderstand my last comment to mean that no one who trusts in God will die. I'm reminded of the story of Lazarus where Jesus says, "I am the resurrection and the life; he who believes in Me shall live even if he dies, and everyone who lives and believes in Me shall never die" (John 11:25–26). His point is that saints die like everyone else, but after the resurrection they will live forever with God.

5. Remember, a type is an acted-out prophecy.

The name **Devil** (12:9) literally means "Slanderer." Satan started out as the highest angel, but he rebelled and slandered God.[6] **With his tail, the dragon swept away a third of the stars of heaven and threw them to the earth** (12:4). His lies convinced a third of the angels—**stars of heaven**—to join his rebellion.[7]

The one thing Satan couldn't allow was a Savior. As long as everyone sinned, he'd win. So when Mary delivered Jesus, Satan tried **to devour her child** by enticing Herod to kill Jesus (Matt 2:16–18). But our Savior survived to give His life for us on the Cross. **He was caught up to God and to His throne,** and **will rule the nations with a rod of iron** (12:5, c.f. 2:27, Ps 2:9).

After Jesus **ascended,** He sent the Holy Spirit to guide the church (Acts 2). Three thousand were saved at Pentecost, the first public display of grace in the apostolic era (Acts 2:41).

And the woman fled into the wilderness where she had a place prepared by God, so that there she might be nourished for one thousand two hundred and sixty days. (12:6)

Persecution started in Jerusalem almost as soon as the apostles started preaching (Acts 4:5–22). Shortly it spread to other parts of the Roman Empire. For about three centuries, Christians suffered as madmen like Nero tried to wipe them out. Each persecution brought more people to Christ. Then the persecutors would lose interest.

Christianity became legal when Constantine issued the Edict of Milan in 313 AD. He made Christianity the official religion of Rome, and in 325 he convened the Council of Nicaea to try to unify Christianity under a single set of key beliefs.

The effort to unify the empire wasn't very successful. Various heresies made trouble. Edicts were issued, and wars were fought to protect orthodoxy. Eventually power became centered in the church of Rome. During the **1,260 days** (years), the organized church was the home to every form of depravity and corruption.[8] It was so bad that in 1510 Martin Luther

---

6. See chapter 1 of this book.

7. We note that the stars are angels for a couple reasons. First, they are "of heaven," and Revelation contrasts saints/holy ones/heaven dwellers with the wicked/earth dwellers. Next, Daniel 12:3 says that those who lead people to righteousness will "shine brightly like the stars forever and ever."

8. This is a restatement of Daniel 7:25 and 12:7. In Daniel 7:25 it's a period where God permits an evil power to have expanded authority. It's not the length of a kingdom, so we

said, "If there be a Hell, Rome is built on it!" The official church refused to allow any differences of opinion, and killed any "heretics" it could catch. Satan's minions worked hard to stamp out the true followers of Christ. The armies of Rome **poured after** the true church (12:15). But the **earth helped the church** by being too big to let Rome catch everyone (12:16).

MARVELOUS SYMBOLISM

I have to pause for a moment with this delicious language. The **serpent** sent **water like a river out of its mouth after the woman** trying to kill her. But Satan's **River** of Death dries up when **the earth opens its mouth to swallow it up**. In the end, Satan's intentions will come back to haunt him, since he and his people will be killed by **the sword from Jesus' mouth** (19:15–21). The law of *lex talionis* will give them back what they gave.

On the other hand, God provides a River of Life for his bride in the New Jerusalem (22:1–2, John 4:14). Men are to live by the words out of God's mouth (Matt 4:4, c.f. Deut 8:3). His word is true food (John 6:63). The saints are **nourished** by the word of God's mouth in the **wilderness**.

God's words don't return without doing what He intends (Isa 55:11). But Satan's own people screw up his attempts to destroy God's people! He's the ruler of this world (John 12:31; 14:30), but his rebellious spirit fills the wicked so completely that they won't even follow *his* wishes. His troops are in such disarray that their attacks on God's people simply disappear into the ground. This reminds us of one of God's promises.

> We know that God causes all things to work together for good to those who love God, to those who are called according to *His* purpose. (Rom 8:28)

God won't allow Satan to win the war. His saints are **nourished** as they continue to spread the message of grace (12:6, 14). They are a "voice crying **in the wilderness**" like John the Baptist. They prepare the way for the Reformation (c.f. Isa 40:3, Matt 3:3).

---

can't find (and shouldn't expect to find) temporal landmarks for it. See chapter 8 of my *Primer on the Book of Daniel* for a detailed explanation. See Appendix B for a discussion of the Year/Day principle.

THE STORY CONTINUES...

There was war in heaven (12:7). Before the cross, Satan had access to heaven, because until the Cross it was possible that Jesus would fail in His mission. But when Jesus died, Satan's last small hope ended. **The accuser of the brethren** was **thrown down to the earth** (12:9, 12), fighting a losing war (12:10). He was **full of wrath**, and brought **woe to those who live on the earth** (12:12). His **wrath** targets *his own people.*

God won't let him loose on the saints. Now this doesn't mean that they won't have troubles. As God's people, we'll always be the target of Satan's **war** (12:17, Mark 10:29–30). But it does mean there are limits. God will always give us strength to get through (1 Cor 10:13). We'll always be able to **keep the commandments of God and hold to the testimony of Jesus** (12:17). We used to be on Satan's side, but since we've tasted God's grace and became part of the heavenly community Satan doesn't deceive us anymore. The only people he can dupe are the wicked. And they get it in spades.

If you're wondering why I'm spending so much time on this, I'll give you a sneak peek. In chapter 20 God gives us the most detailed view of the millennium. Interpreters argue about what this period means. The key in verse 3, where Satan is **unable to deceive the nations**. Lots of theologians get lost there because they don't see the patterns in the book. We've set up the first part of that pattern here. We'll finish it there.

God's people, those **who dwell in heaven**, have **overcome Satan because of the blood of the Lamb and because of the word of their testimony, and they did not love their life even to death** (12:11). Jesus gave the saints the victory. Grace wins the war, not anything we can do. His people praise Him even in death, and they receive eternal life. It is truly cause for **rejoicing** (12:12).

16

The Controversy over Worship, Part II

THE "BEAST COMPUTER" IS already at work in The Hague! Don't let yourself take the mark of the beast! They're going to put a microchip under your skin! Nobody can buy anything without it! And on . . . and on . . . and on . . .

Revelation 13 has probably led to more outrageous ideas and breathless sermons than any other part of the Bible.[1] Everybody seems to "know" just what's going to happen. And if you don't see it their way, you're a heretic—or worse. There are so many *different* ideas that seem to have a grain of truth that it seems impossible to sort it all out. So what can we do? Will the Bible straighten this mess out for us? Can the Bible interpret itself *here*?

The easy answer is, "Of course!" But because there's so much insanity out there, we have to be disciplined in our approach.[2] We have to trace symbols back to their sources. Then we have to carefully follow the sequence in the vision. If we do this, answers will come. But if we use the daily newspaper for our prophetic bookmarks, we'll end up a loooong way from the story God wants us to hear.

---

1. Except maybe Armageddon.

2. If you think *I'm* being over-the-top in my description, just search for "Mark of the Beast" or "Number of the Beast" on the internet.

126 A PRIMER ON THE BOOK OF REVELATION

The Covenant Displayed
- in this sinful era -

Seals	Trumpets	Interlude	Bowls
Grace	Warning	12 - 14	Judgment

Controversy over Worship

12:1-17	13:1-18	Interlude	14:1-5, 14-20
Grace	Warning	14:6-13	Judgment

You Are Here

The map is our first stop. Every interlude so far has been a recap of the series it's in. Since this is part of the interlude in the Seals, Trumpets, and Bowls, it's part of their recap. Chapter 12 was a recap of the Seals. So chapter 13 will be a recap of the Trumpets—a warning of judgment to come.

> And I saw a beast coming up out of the sea, having **ten horns and seven heads**, and on his horns *were* ten diadems, and on his heads *were* blasphemous names. And the beast which I saw was like a leopard, and his feet were like *those* of a bear, and his mouth like the mouth of a lion. (13:1–2)

If this looks like an instant replay of the **dragon** in 12:3, you've been paying attention in class. Just like the **dragon**, the **beast** has **ten horns and seven heads**. That means it comes from the *same* Old Testament source, Daniel 7. It also means that it has the *same* basic meaning—human government from the time of Babylon on. Just as important, it means that the **beast** *isn't* a single person or organization.[3]

Beast	Heads	Horns	Daniel text
Lion	1	0	7:4
Bear	1	0	7:5
Leopard	4	0	7:6
Frightening	1	10	7:7
Total	7	10	

---

3. . . . or computer, or Roman emperors, or President Bush or . . .

This time there are **ten diadems** instead of seven. This round number points us to the horns.[4] They represent the era described in Daniel 7:7–8; 19–25 after the fall of pagan Rome in 476 AD.[5] Next we see another one of those delicious parodies. All of the **heads** have **blasphemous names**. The High Priest in the Temple wore a turban with a gold plate engraved "Holiness to the Lord" (Exod 28:36–37). **Blasphemous names** are the exact opposite, showing that man's kingdoms owe their allegiance to Satan. God may be sovereign, controlling the course of history, but Satan is the ruler of this earth (John 12:31; 16:11), with **power over every tribe and people and tongue and nation** (13:7). And this isn't the only parody in chapter 13.

The *entire career of the beast* is a burlesque of God's warning of judgment in the seven Trumpets. Here we see Satan pulling the strings of nations, trying to make everyone think resistance is futile. In the final version of his lie in Eden, Satan cries, "**You'll die if you don't worship the beast!**" (13:15, c.f. Gen 3:4). He has power over **those who dwell on the earth** (13:8, 12, 14), but he can't control **those who dwell in heaven** (13:6). All he can do is **blaspheme God's tabernacle**, the saints. And this brings us to another wonderful image.

During the exodus, God refused to be separated from His people, so He had the Israelites build a tabernacle for Him to live in, right in the middle of the camp (Exod 25:8). Next, when Jesus came, He "tabernacled" with men (John 1:14, lit. Greek). After He ascended, He sent the Holy Spirit so that He lives in us making us God's tabernacle (Gal 2:20). Not only that, we are "in heaven" (Heb 12:22, Rev 13:6). What a wonderful picture!

Anyone who trusts in Christ will be protected from any real harm that Satan might try to inflict. Even if Satan is able to **overcome** a saint, his eternal life is secure (13:7, John 11:25–26). He may be able to "kill the body, but after that can do no more" (Luke 12:4). God will replace

---

4. In Daniel 1:20, Daniel and his friends are "ten times smarter" than the other kids in Babylon U. Now, if your kid can walk, talk, and chew gum, it's almost impossible for anyone to be "ten times smarter." The idiom really means "a lot" smarter. We can confirm this by looking in Daniel 7, where the "ten horns" of the fourth beast are "ten kingdoms" that come up after pagan Rome falls in 476 AD. Of course, there were more than ten, and the number varied over time. If we take the idiom to mean "a lot" of kingdoms, then it matches the picture perfectly.

5. We'll discuss why this *isn't* the same time described in 17:12–13 when we get there.

that cursed body with an immortal, incorruptible one (1 Cor 15:50–55). Satan's "victory" is an illusion.

John *saw* one of his heads as if it had been slain, and his fatal wound was healed (12:3). One of the *heads* was **wounded** so badly that it nearly killed *the Beast*. John doesn't say, but the **head** probably does die. Then **the Beast** (not the **head**!) recovers from the **wound**. Let's put this together.

The beast represents human government from Babylon on.[6] Babylon fell to Medo-Persia, which fell to Greece, which fell to Rome. So far, there aren't any gaps. It didn't take long for this situation to change.

Emperor Constantine made Christianity the official state religion around 320. In 380, Valentinian II declared that Trinitarian orthodoxy was true Christianity, and hinted that the state might use force against anyone who disagreed. In 445, Emperors Valentinian III and Theodosius II imposed an Edict supporting "the prince of the episcopal crown." No one was allowed to "attempt to carry out anything contrary to the ancient custom without the authority of that venerable man the Pope of the Eternal City. But let whatever the authority of the Apostolic See decrees or shall decree, be accepted as law by all." Local Governors were supposed to enforce the Edict.

In 476 the western half of the Empire fell to the Heruli under Odoacer, but no single government took over.[7] As the prophet Daniel said of the Roman empire, "It will become a divided kingdom" (Dan 2:41, lit. Aramaic). With no Emperor of the West, Imperial support for the Roman Church now had to come from Constantinople.

In 496 Clovis I of the Franks converted to Catholicism and became a protector of the papacy. In 507 he defeated the Visigoths at the Battle of Vouillé. For this Emperor Anastasius awarded him the title Patricius and Consul of the Roman Empire. In 511 he called the First Council of Orléans, which solidified the link between the throne and the Church of Rome. This meant that the Roman Catholic Church wasn't just the top dog in religion; it was the alpha male in *everything*.

---

6. You might ask why God started with Babylon. After all, Satan didn't start with Babylon. The vision recasts Daniel's vision of the four beasts (Dan 7), so it begins where Daniel's vision begins. If there had been an earlier set of symbols that would work, God might have used them. But Daniel's vision is the first one that provides symbols adequate for the apocalypse.

7. His name is also spelled Odovacar. He started as a leader of *foederati*, non-Roman military units in Roman service. Later he led the revolt that overthrew Roman authority in the Italian peninsula. This is generally dated to September 13, 476.

Once the Roman Church became the center of political life, all the crowned heads of Europe looked to Rome for legitimacy. The **deadly wound** inflicted in 476 had been healed. But the **beast** didn't look the same.[8] Human government was centered, not in a "political" entity, but in a "religious" body. No, it didn't deal with day-to-day political rule. But all the governments served at its pleasure. It got its way, but made the others do the dirty work. **All the earth was amazed and followed after the beast** (13:3).[9] **They worshiped the beast** (13:4).

At this point we have to remind ourselves that "worship" literally means "to bow down or prostrate before." It is expresses complete dependence on someone in authority. So if a person holds a human government as the highest authority, he's "worshiping" it. The flip side of this is that if a human government is your highest authority, God *isn't*. You've made humans into gods, and are an idol worshiper.

The **beast was given a mouth speaking arrogant words and blasphemies** (13:5). This brings us right back to Daniel 7:8, where the "little horn" does the same thing. It even does it for **forty-two months**, the same period that the **two witnesses** prophesy (11:2–3) and the church is **nourished in the wilderness** (12:6, 14). All these are the *same* period, since they use the same language, quoted from the same sources (Dan 7:25; 12:7). They are describing the same events—the persecution of true Christianity during the Dark Ages.

"time, times, and half a time"	Dan 7:25; 12:7, Rev 12:14
"forty-two months"	Rev 11:2; 13:5
"1,260 days"	Rev 11:3; 12:6

All who dwell on the earth worship the beast; everyone whose name has *not* been written in the book of life (13:8).[10] Only the wicked follow Satan's lieutenants.

---

8. Daniel notes that this kingdom is "different from all the others" (Dan 7:19).

9. Sharp students of history will raise their hands here, complaining that the Papacy didn't exert absolute control. And they're right. The Church was in the center of the political storm, sometimes on top, and sometimes being pushed around. But when push came to shove, all the kings came to Rome for the Pope's blessing. In one famous example, Pope Gregory VII made Henry IV of Germany stand barefoot in the snow for days like a common penitent before admitting him to an audience (January 25–28, 1077).

10. This verse is a classic example for students. It defines the term "earth-dwellers." First, it describes what they do, and then it tells us who they are. We don't need to go to a dictionary or commentary. Everything we need to understand the term is in the verse

> If anyone has an ear, let him hear. (13:9)

We heard this call seven times in the seven messages to the churches. Each time it reminds us of the call to Israel in the *Shema*, "Hear O Israel!" (Deut 6:4). That call continues. "Yahweh is our God, Yahweh is One!"[11] God calls out to true Israel, the saints of all ages, to listen to Him.

> If anyone is destined for captivity, to captivity he goes; if anyone kills with the sword, with the sword he must be killed. Here is the perseverance and the faith of the saints. (13:10)

God quotes Jeremiah 15:2, declaring that destiny of the wicked has been fixed. A false prophet (Jer 14:15) or a wicked person (Jer 14:20-15:1) has no hope. Only those who trust in God will survive. Anyone who rejects God will be destroyed (Jer 15:6). God will rescue His people on the Day of the Lord when He destroys the wicked.

THE LAMB-LIKE BEAST

And I saw (new scene!), after **the deadly wound was healed**, an **earth beast** with **two horns like a lamb, but a voice like a dragon** (13:11-12). Once again, God shows us how Satan tries to hide his true nature. He deceives many by appearing like a pure Lamb of God (cf. 5:6). "Come join us! We have the keys of salvation!" False religion snares the unwary. But **the dragon** Satan can't successfully disguise his voice. His people preach a different gospel (cf. Gal 1:8-9).

The **land beast exercised all the authority of the sea beast in his presence** (13:12). This gives us another perspective on Papal Rome at the center of the political world. The Pope claimed to be the holy voice of God on earth. At the same time, he led the most evil and corrupt power imaginable.[12] Rome convicted "heretics," and then handed them over to the civil government for execution. Forgiveness of sin was sold for a price. Even the "Holy See" was bought and sold. All **earth-dwellers**—the wicked!—were forced to **worship the sea beast**.

---

itself. Of course, verse 6 does the same thing, defining God's tabernacle as the "heaven-dwellers," the saints.

11. Modern Jews have substituted *Adonai* for *Yahweh*, since the name of God is too sacred to speak.

12. I'm using "he" to speak of the long line of Popes during this most corrupt era.

The **land beast performed great signs** that **deceived the earth-dwellers** (13:13–14). The "miracles" attributed to various "saints" fill many books. **Fire from heaven** reminds us that counterfeits look just as real as the fire Elijah called down from heaven (2 Kings 1:10–15).[13] Even Pharaoh's magicians were able to duplicate some of Moses and Aaron's miracles.

Next, the **land beast** makes an **image to the sea beast** (13:14) that carries out the **death sentence** against **those who do not worship the beast** (13:15). As we saw just a moment ago, this is a perfect picture of civil authorities executing heretics convicted by papal courts.

The **sea beast, land beast,** and **image to the beast** make up a false trinity, yet *another* parody of God's truth. The Father, Son, and Holy Spirit are so unified that they make up the One True God. The false trinity is also unified, but works to undermine and overthrow the One True God.

THE MARK AND THE NUMBER

The **number of the Beast** is so famous that it seems to be everywhere. A Google search on "**666**" yields over a fifteen million hits, with lots of cult-style applications, often in hard rock music. On one website, a mathematician calls the number **666** "cool," and shows dozens of its mathematical properties.[14] A brief look at the "theological" sites shows enough wildly varied theories of its meaning to drive you crazy. So we have to invoke the first rule of interpretation again—the Bible interprets itself.

> And he causes all, the small and the great, and the rich and the poor, and the free men and the slaves, to be given a mark on their right hand, or on their forehead, and he provides that no one should be able to buy or to sell, except the one who has the mark, either the name of the beast or the number of his name. Here is wisdom. Let him who has understanding calculate the number of the beast, for the number is that of a man; and his number is six hundred and sixty-six. (13:16–18)

The **land beast makes everyone receive a mark on their right hand or on their forehead.** Let's get one thing straight right here. This isn't a physical mark. That idea is *literalism*, and denies the symbolism in the

---

13. It wasn't literal for the two witnesses, and it's not literal here.
14. http://www.cadaeic.net/666.htm. Accessed 6/29/2009.

book. This is an echo of a command God gave the ancient Israelites. It's so important that we should give it a detailed look.

> Hear, O Israel! Yahweh is our God, Yahweh is one! And you shall love Yahweh your God with all your heart and with all your soul and with all your might. And these words, which I am commanding you today, shall be on your heart; and you shall teach them diligently to your sons and shall talk of them when you sit in your house and when you walk by the way and when you lie down and when you rise up. And you shall bind them as a sign on your hand and they shall be as frontals on your forehead. And you shall write them on the doorposts of your house and on your gates. (Deut 6:4–10)

This begins with the *Shema*—literally, "Hear"—the most important statement of Hebrew faith. There's only one God for man. Of course, if there's only one true God, then there's only one God to be worshiped.

Next, God commands Israel to keep "these words . . . on your heart." Fidelity to God isn't simply obedience; it's a matter of the heart. To emphasize this, the *Shema* is to be written on the doorposts and gates while being bound "as a sign on your hand" and "as frontals on your forehead." Ancient Hebrews did write the words on their houses and wore phylacteries.[15] This isn't wrong, because it would tend to make you think about the verses, but it wasn't God's intention. His real point was for you to make Him the center of what you do every day. Of course, that's true worship.

The **mark of the beast** is a pale imitation of binding God's words on your hand or forehead. It shows that **earth-dwellers** put men above God. It's not about microchips or tattoos. It's about what you do and who you worship. And make no mistake about it; even "atheists" worship someone: Man. Of course, if they ally themselves with man's governments and man's religions, their daily lives—**buying and selling**—won't be affected.

> Here is wisdom. Let him who has understanding calculate the number of the beast, for the number is that of a man; and his number is six hundred and sixty-six. (13:18)

The first part of this reminds us that when man thinks he's smart, he's really not (Isa 29:14). Man doesn't discover wisdom, God reveals it (Job 28:12–13). Yet God tells **him who has understanding** to **calculate the number**. I can just hear God sneer, "You think you're so smart? Figure it

---

15. Phylacteries are small leather boxes worn on the forehead. They contain a slip of paper with a passage from Torah written on it. See Exodus 13:16 and Matthew 23:5.

out!" And right then, for anyone who recognizes his own limitations, God says, "Here's the number. As always, I Am the revealer of knowledge."

Literally translated, the verse says, "**It's man's number.**" This fits perfectly with what we've been saying all along. Man puts himself in God's place, and then worships himself. Every step of the way, he threatens God's people. But God shows us that we shouldn't waste our time on man's threats. We should fear Him who can destroy body and soul in Hell (Matt 10:28).

The reference to **calculation** takes us outside the Bible for the first time, but it doesn't take us outside Bible times. In ancient Greek society, one use of "calculation" was to figure out the numerical value of words. We call this gematria, from the same root for the word "geometry."

Greek didn't have separate characters for numbers, so each letter had a number value. When certain names or words were added up, the number value was considered to have secret spiritual importance.[16] In this case, **666** was a very important number in pagan religion.[17] It's the sum of the magic square of the sun, one of the most important pagan deities. It's the gematria value of Syene (ΣΥΗΝΗ), a city in southern Egypt that was thought to be a place of celestial alignment where the divine secrets of the sun god were displayed on earth.[18]

Pagan religion opposes the true God, and the numbers derived in pagan religion are another sign of man's rebellion. Even though these numbers are "secret," God understands them. Man thinks he's the final authority, but God isn't fooled.

Just to put the final nail in the coffin, God has included an implicit joke in this passage. The entire chapter is about "the Great Beast." And even though those exact words *aren't* in the chapter, the gematria value of *to mega therion* is—do I even need to say it—666!

Man may warn that everyone must fall in line, but God laughs at such pride. In the end, God wins, and His people win with Him. Man's warning of judgment is a puny shout against the only real power in the universe. Satan's backing is worthless.

---

16. If you want to see a more technical discussion of the number of the Beast, check out Appendix A.

17. For a relatively complete exploration of the number in pagan religion, check out *Jesus Christ, Sun of God*, by David Fideler (Wheaton: Quest Books, 1993).

18. Syene, present-day Aswan, is on the tropic of Cancer, so at noon on the summer solstice the sun casts no shadows around buildings or down wells.

The symbolism and story of the false trinity had its first application in a time long past. This could make modern men sneer that it has nothing to do with us now. But this would be far from true. The fundamentals of the war between Christ and Satan haven't changed. Men haven't changed. We're all corrupt and rebellious. We've heard Satan's call to worship him by putting everything ahead of God, but his warning of judgment is a phony. It's God we must fear and worship.

17

The Controversy over Worship, Part III

THE TRUMPETS HAVE ECHOED into silence. It's time for judgment. But before we look at Revelation 14, we have to look at the four kinds of judgment in the Bible.

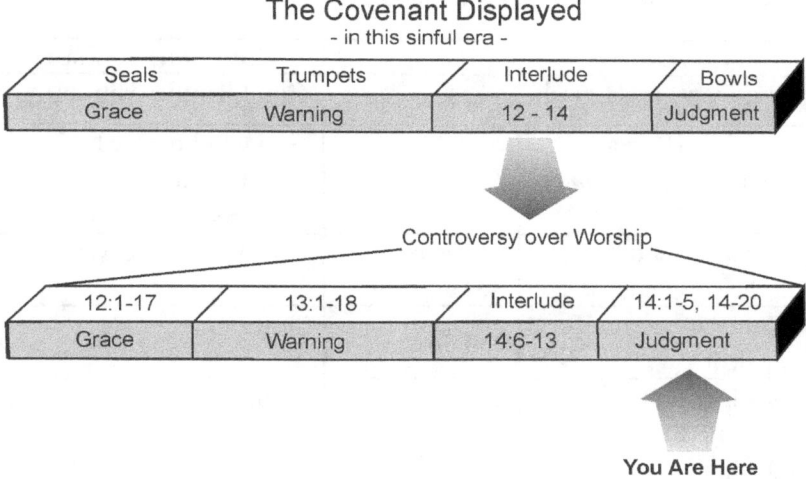

The most important kind of judgment is the *atonement*. In it, God vindicates the saints according to *His* righteousness, cleansing them from sin (cf. Psalm 35:24–28, Lev 16:30). We've already seen it in the seventh Seal, Trumpet, and Bowl.

The second variety is the least familiar. Its modern equivalent is a *slander suit*. Someone has spread malicious lies about you, and you ask the court for relief. The most direct example in scripture is the parable of the Unjust Judge in Luke 18:1–8. We'll see this again when we study the millennium.[1]

In the third type, evildoers face God's *covenant lawsuit*. The Bible has a number of these. My favorite is in the story of David and Bathsheba. God's prophet Nathan accuses David of murdering Uriah the Hittite to get Bathsheba (2 Sam 12). This story has all the usual courtroom drama. Nathan is the voice of God. He tells David of the good things God has done for him. Then he accuses David of the crime. David becomes a witness against himself. When he admits his guilt, God stays the death sentence, substituting calamities that will trouble David for the rest of his life.

The steps of the covenant lawsuit parallel the covenant we explored in the Message to the Church. They perfectly match the steps in a modern trial. All we have to do is substitute "Plaintiff" (civil court) or "the State" (criminal court) for God, and rest plays out the same. God uses an orderly process to show the guilt of the wicked.

Covenant		Covenant Lawsuit
God Identifies Himself	*Preamble*	God Identifies Himself
God tells His good deeds for Israel (*bona fides*)	*Prolog*	God tells how He has honored the covenant (His good deeds for Israel)
God lays out the terms of the covenant	*Indictments/ Stipulations*	God accuses the wicked
Witnesses solemnify the deal	*Witnesses*	Testimony
Blessings for compliance and Cursings for rebellion	*Consequences/ Verdict*	"Guilty" or "Innocent"

We should note that there's another way God identifies the wicked. They haven't asked Him to atone for their sins! Either you're cleansed in the atonement, or you've condemned yourself (John 3:18). And this brings us to the last kind of judgment.

We're all familiar with how God freed Israel from captivity in Egypt "by great judgments" (Exod 6:6; 7:4). In technical language, those were *execution of judgment*. That is, the Egyptians were guilty of denying Yahweh's authority (Exod 5:2). Once God established their guilt, He could *execute*

---

1. This theme also occurs in the Psalms. See Psalms 43, 54, 72, etc.

the penalty for that guilt. It's the same as our modern courts. Once the jury brings in the guilty verdict, the defendant heads for the slammer.

Execution of judgment is nothing more than the result of a trial. In Egypt, we saw the guilt played out. In the Trumpets, the wicked did not repent (9:20–21). Since the wicked haven't asked for forgiveness, they stand condemned by their own (in)actions. God could freely punish them for their rebellion, but He hasn't brought them into court yet. So He executes a preliminary judgment against them. The final judgment has to wait for the covenant lawsuit.

Biblical Judgments	
Atonement	Cleanses the Saints
Slander Suit	Lawsuit against false accusations
Covenant Lawsuit	God accuses wicked of breaking the covenant
Execution of Judgment	Verdict of the Court is carried out

> And I looked, and behold, a white cloud, and sitting on the cloud *was* one like a son of man, having a golden crown on His head, and a sharp sickle in His hand. (14:14)

John looks up and sees Jesus, but He's not on a throne. Instead, He's on a white cloud. He left this earth on a white cloud to receive title to His kingdom (Acts 1:9–11, cf. Dan 7:13–14). Now it's time for Him to come back and take physical possession of it. He's wearing a stephanos, the golden crown of victory He won for us on the cross. In His hand is a sharp sickle, a symbol of the harvest.

> And another angel came out of the temple, crying out with a loud voice to Him who sat on the cloud, "Put in your sickle and reap, because the hour to reap has come, because the harvest of the earth is ripe." And He who sat on the cloud swung His sickle over the earth; and the earth was reaped. (14:15–16)

We're workers in the field of God's harvest of the earth (Matt 9:37–38).[2] At the end comes the harvest of saints from the whole world (cf. 7:9). The wheat and weeds have grown together. It's time to gather them—the saints to God (John 14:1–3, 1 Thes 4:13–17) and the wicked to destruction.

---

2. The Greek word used in this verse (*kosmos*) indicates that the harvest covers the entire earth.

> And another angel, the one who has power over fire, came out from the altar; and he called with a loud voice to him who had the sharp sickle, saying, "Put in your sharp sickle, and gather the clusters from the vine of the earth, because her grapes are ripe." And the angel swung his sickle to the earth, and gathered *the clusters from* the vine of the earth, and threw them into the great wine press of the wrath of God. And the wine press was trodden outside the city, and blood came out from the wine press, up to the horses' bridles, for a distance of two hundred miles. (14:18–20)

The wicked in the sixth Seal (6:15–17) were right to be afraid of God's wrath (Heb 10:28–31). Now their blood covers an area like the sacred temple district in Ezekiel 45:1-6. But once again we have to be careful about being too literalistic. If we do the math, it's about twice as much blood as in all the people who ever lived. So it probably represents God's promise to repay double for wickedness (18:6).

God will do everything in His own time (Acts 1:7). But when that time comes, it comes with a thundering finality. As the **strong angel** in 10 said, "When it's over, it's over!" The trials God's people endure will finally end when Jesus takes them home with him. At the same time, the wicked will be destroyed. No one will be left alive on the earth.

18

Three Angels

ONE RECAP REMAINS. It's the simplest and most direct statement of the themes from the first half of the apocalypse. If the rest of the book wasn't there, this central message would still come through loud and clear.

> And I looked, and behold, the Lamb was standing on Mount Zion, and with Him one hundred and forty-four thousand, having His name and the name of His Father written on their foreheads. (14:1)

Christ's "kingdom of priests"—His "holy nation" is assembled (Exod 19:6). The **144,000** saints **from every nation and tribe and people and tongue** (7:9) have **Jesus' name and the name of the Father written on their foreheads**. The High Priest had "Holy to the Lord" on his turban. Now *everyone* has God's holy name written directly on them. They belong to God—*forever*.

The **144,000 are blameless** (14:5). They've been saved and have been changed from corruptible to incorruptible, mortal to immortal (cf. 1 Cor 15:51–55). Like the cherubim in Ezekiel 1, they **follow the Lamb wherever He goes** (14:4). **He has purchased them from among men as first fruits to God and the Lamb.**

This is a good time to remind ourselves not to get too liter*alistic*. If we go too far, the **144,000** are like my daughter's poodle—they follow God around. But that's not what God wants us to understand. In Micah 6:8 the gospel command is, "Love justice, do mercy, and walk humbly with your God." We know God wasn't walking around on the earth like a man during Micah's day, so walking with God has to mean following His direction.[1] That's what the **144,000** do. They are true saints, keeping God's commandments (c.f. John 14:15; 23). They "neither turn to the right nor to the left" (c.f. Deut 5:12, Ezek 1:12).

---

1. "Walking with God" is an idiom that uses the "path" metaphor to describe our life.

The **144,000 have not been defiled with women. They are virgins** (KJV, NET). This *obviously* means that they're sexually pure, unmarried men! But while "virgin" *is* one meaning of *parthenos*, that translation forgets that a married man can also be *parthenos*. He just has to be faithful to his wife. Adultery will defile him, but sex with his wife won't. And that points us to the way John uses language.

In 17:1 **the harlot**, a defiled woman, is God's enemy. The wicked defile themselves by practicing idolatry with her (17:2). On the other hand, the **144,000** are **chaste** (NAS) or **pure** (NIV). They have not "played the harlot" of idolatry (cf. Exod 34:15, Judg 2:7).[2] They follow God. Purity isn't about marital status. It's about devotion to God.

John **hears a voice from heaven like the sound of many waters and like the sound of loud thunder and like harpists** (14:2). This is God's voice from 10:3. The **144,000** answer by singing a **new praise song** to God **no one else could learn** (14:3). This joyful scene reminds us of Jesus' coronation. The **elders, living creatures,** and **144,000** all sang with joy when their king arrived. Here they joyfully respond to their salvation. They've answered the call of grace, and give God the glory for His gracious gift.

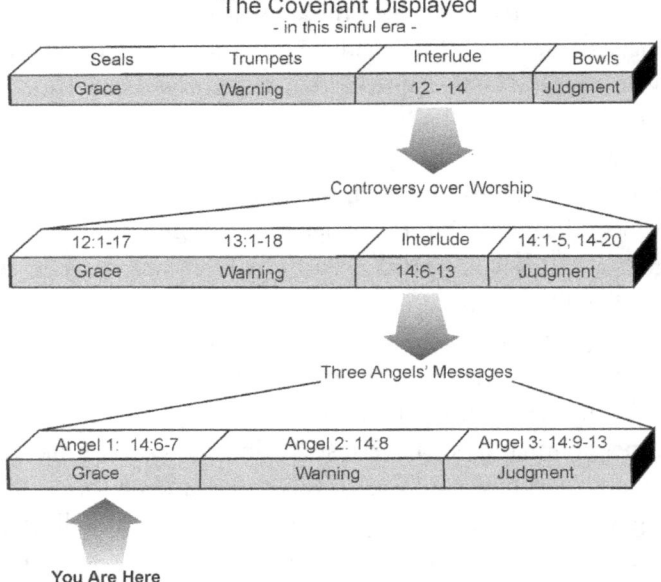

---

2. "Harlotry" is the most common metaphor for idolatry in the Old Testament. The expression "played the harlot" occurs 22 times and "play the harlot" 19 times in the NAS. Other forms of the idea are too numerous to count.

THE FIRST ANGEL

> And I saw another angel flying in midheaven, having an eternal gospel to preach to those who live on the earth, and to every nation and tribe and tongue and people; and he said with a loud voice, "Fear God, and give Him glory, because the hour of His judgment has come; and worship Him who made the heaven and the earth and sea and springs of waters." (14:6–7)

The first angel announces judgment, which is good news for the saints. This means that the judgment is the Atonement. Thus, the First Angel's Message repeats the call of grace. We heard it in the Seals. Then we heard it in the sealing of the saints. It was repeated again in Revelation 12. And this is the final, Readers' Digest Condensed Version. Fear God and give Him glory!

Anyone who truly worships God will be saved. But there's a time limit. The hour of God's judgment is coming. And right now I can hear the shouting. The Bible says this is past, and you've put it in the future. That's wrong! And by now you know my next line. "Hang in there for a moment! I'm not really crazy." We need to look at the Greek.

The verb "to come" here is in the "aorist tense." Greek "tenses" aren't like English tenses that generally describe the *time* of action in the past, present, or future. Instead, they generally describe *"aspect."* The aorist aspect is often described as "punctiliar," meaning "all-at-once." Its main impact is to say that the action happens and is completed as a unit. It's not particularly concerned with *when* it happens. While most of the time its action in the past, there are plenty of times it looks to the future. You just can't tell by looking at the verb.[3]

Generally the aorist is translated into English as a simple past tense, the way the original quotation has it. But that misses the point of John's message. As a simple past, it says the judgment's already over, and that's just not true. The Day of Atonement comes at the end of the drama of

---

3. For those of you who are really technically inclined, the description I just gave isn't adequate. There are forms of the aorist that don't quite match this description. One is the "constative aorist." It speaks of successive actions over a length of time. They are the same action, repeated, so that the writer can see them as a single "block" action. Two examples are the aorist of *sozo* in Acts 15:11 and 1 Corinthians 15:2. In both of these cases, the writer says that we "are saved" by grace. But every person is receives salvation at a different time, so this usage looks at a large number of fundamentally identical events as a single completed event.

sin, not part way through it. If we let the aorist work, the sentence really says that the Day of Atonement is coming. When it comes, it will be an "all-at-once" event. God's people will be clean, and God will give them immortality (cf. Lev 16:30, 1 Cor 15:51–55). It will be done and over, with nothing else to do.

There's a flip side to this. Obviously, if you don't answer the call of grace, you won't get immortality. So there's a hint of warning here. You need to get right with God, so that when the Atonement comes, you will be ready. But the main focus is, "Come to Me. I will give you life. I made everything, and I can save you."[4]

THE SECOND ANGEL

And another angel, a second one, followed, saying, "Fallen, fallen is Babylon the great, she who has made all the nations drink of the wine of the passion of her immorality." (14:8)

The verb is fallen is aorist. And just like "has come" in verse 7, if we take it literally, it says God has already destroyed idolatry, but that just isn't true (cf. 1 Cor 15:23–25).[5] God's really saying that in the end He *will* defeat all His enemies. It's an ironclad guarantee. The aorist emphasizes that this will happen all at once, with a resounding crash.

Once more God warns that anyone who doesn't turn from idolatry to Him will be lost. This is the final recap of the Trumpets, the Strong Angel, the two witnesses, and the Mark of the Beast. One more recap remains.

THE THIRD ANGEL

And another angel, a third one, followed them, saying with a loud voice, "If anyone worships the beast and his image, and

---

4. "Worship Him who made heaven and earth and the sea and springs of waters" is a reference to Exodus 20:11, where God commands Israel to "remember" the Sabbath day since He created it to bless them. This language strongly suggests that the seventh-day Sabbath remains a central feature of God's plan for man throughout time.

5. A number of interpreters let the past tense translation stand. They take it as a "prophetic perfect tense," where the prophet sees the future so clearly that he speaks of it as if it had already happened. One classic example of the prophetic perfect tense is Isaiah 53, where the prophet describes Jesus' suffering and death in the past tense (in Hebrew, so there's no confusion with the aorist). But, since there is a perfectly natural reading with the aorist that does *not* involve the prophetic perfect, it should be preferred.

receives a mark on his forehead or upon his hand, he also will drink of the wine of the wrath of God, which is mixed in full strength in the cup of His anger; and he will be tormented with fire and brimstone in the presence of the holy angels and in the presence of the Lamb. And the smoke of their torment goes up forever and ever; and they have no rest day and night, those who worship the beast and his image, and whoever receives the mark of his name." (14:9–11)

In a way, this is the final warning, but it's really a recap of the Bowls. After all, in the Bowls, God gives the wicked **blood to drink** (16:6) because **they deserve it**. It's His **wrath** (16:1), which is **mixed in full strength in the cup of His anger**. The wicked call for **the rocks to fall on them and hide them from the wrath of the Lamb** (6:16). But it doesn't work. They suffer the fate of Sodom and Gomorrah, when **fire and brimstone** fall on them. And right here we stumble over yet *another* key interpretive problem.

The smoke of their torment goes up forever and ever; and they have no rest day and night. This *obviously* means that the wicked are tormented forever and ever in Hell-fire. But we must be careful, since that's *not* what the text says! It says that the smoke rises forever and ever. It doesn't say anything about how long the fire burns.

This is a *visual*. John sees a column of smoke starting from the ground. It rises up, and up, and up, and up . . . It keeps rising until it goes completely out of sight. And that's what the idiom means. The smoke rises out of sight. John's not talking about how long the fire burns. He's talking about how *far* the smoke rises. Time simply isn't part of the picture. For that matter, fire isn't even mentioned.

This picture would be very familiar to any observant Jew. In Exodus 14:24–25 God used the smoke of His presence to torment Pharaoh and his army right before He destroyed them in the Red Sea. The pillar of smoke rose up to heaven—it rose forever and ever.

The wicked will be destroyed like Pharaoh was. God will "redeem His saints with an outstretched arm and with great judgments" (c.f. Exod 6:6). God redeemed ancient Israel from bondage in physical Egypt. He'll redeem end-time Israel from bondage in spiritual Egypt. He'll destroy His enemies in order to free His people.

> **Here is the perseverance of the saints who keep the commandments of God and their faith in Jesus. (14:12)**

The saints in the fifth Seal (6:9–11) had to patiently wait for God to act in His own time (c.f. 2 Pet 3:8–9). Their patience will be rewarded. If we keep ourselves fixed on the firm foundation of Jesus, we'll have nothing to fear. Our enemies may be able to "kill the body, but after that have no more that they can do" (Luke 12:4).

> And as for me, I know that my Redeemer lives, and at the last He will take His stand on the earth. Even after my skin is destroyed, yet from my flesh I shall see God; whom I myself shall behold, and whom my eyes shall see and not another." (Job 19:25–27)

19

Millennium!

BEFORE WE WALTZ INTO another controversial area, let's briefly review where we've been. The message to the church (chapters 1–3) was the *Covenant Described*. It used formal covenant structure explain what God wants from us. Next, the *Inauguration of the Worthy King* in chapters 4 and 5 began the *Covenant Displayed*. Chapters 6 through 16 tell us about the *Covenant in this Age*, with the call of grace, warning of judgment, and judgment. Of course, there were all those recaps.

The three main series—the Seals, Trumpets, and Bowls—all end at the heavenly Day of Atonement and the earthly Day of the Lord. When those Days are over, all the saints are in heaven and the wicked on earth have all been killed.[1] Now, if everybody on earth is dead, it's pretty obvious that the story of redemption has entered a new chapter.

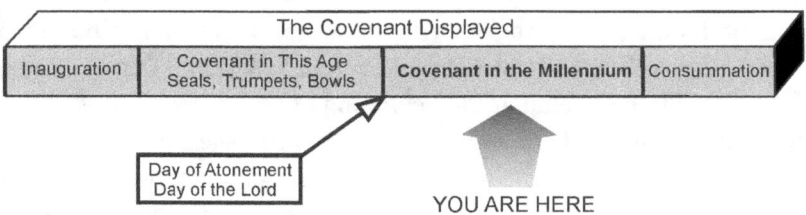

From the title, you've guessed we're going to talk about the millennium. Like we've done before, we'll skip a couple of chapters. This time we're going directly to chapter 20 because it's a lot clearer than chapters 17—19. They're also about the millennium, but please bear with me. Like every time before, everything become clear when we let the Bible speak for itself.

---

1. If anyone has any questions here, they should go back to our discussion of Matthew 24:36–42 on pages 103–4.

THE BOTTOMLESS PIT

The scene opens with an **angel coming down with a great chain and the key to the abyss** (20:1). Some translations call it the **bottomless pit**. That gives us a better visual, but the Greek tells us what's really going on.

The Bible uses *abussos* 45 times.[2] Sometimes it means a long way underground, such as Genesis 7:11, where "the fountains of the *great deep* burst open" in the flood." We've also seen it describe Satan's home, which is also figuratively underground (Rev 9:1, 2, 11). The best picture may be in Genesis 1:2 where the earth before creation is *abussos*.[3] For the moment, let's file away the fact that there weren't any people on the earth then, either.

If Satan rules the **abyss**, and it's on (or under) the earth, that means that when the **angel from heaven takes the dragon, the serpent of old, who is the devil and Satan and binds him for a thousand years in the abyss** (20:1-3), Satan's going to be stuck on earth.[4] And because there won't be any people on earth, he **can't deceive the nations any longer** (20:3). Right here theologians make everything muddy. I'm going to take a minute to talk about how they approach the millennium so you'll understand what all the fuss is about.

"... MILLENNIALISM"

We hear about "a-millennialism," "post-millennialism," and "pre-millennialism." Each position has strong defenders, and they make "scriptural" arguments for their favored beliefs. Amillennialists say that Jesus "bound the strong man" with His ministry (Satan, cf. Matt 12:28-29). That *must* mean that the binding of Satan at the beginning of the millennium is already done, so the **thousand years** symbolizes the church age. Postmillennialists take statements like "the kingdom of God has come upon you" to mean that the millennial kingdom is already present during Christ's ministry (Luke 11:20). Dispensational premillennialists take the period literal*isti*cally. They combine **reigned with Christ a thousand years** (20:4) with the symbolic temple in Ezekiel 40-47 to get a thousand-year kingdom on

---

2. I'm including the Septuagint.

3. This is a Greek translation for *tohu wabohu*, a Hebrew expression that means "unformed and unfilled."

4. Do you think it's possible that God used four titles here because He *really* wants us to know who's being chained in the abyss?

earth. To say the least, the arguments are large and involved. Reading the debate is almost guaranteed to confuse you.

"NOT DECEIVE THE NATIONS"

As we look at this section, we have to remember a couple key facts. First, the Bible does interpret itself. Second, we have to let simple statements tell us what the complicated ones mean. So let's start with **Satan not deceiving the nations**. If we don't understand these words, we can't understand the passage. There are three key words here: **Satan**, **deceive**, and **the nations**.

We all know who **Satan** is. **Deceive** shouldn't be hard, either. The Greek word literally means, "to wander." Since we're supposed to "walk with our God," sinners "wander away" (cf. Micah 6:8). So **deceive** means Satan tells lies to get people to wander away from God. That's not so hard! It's the obvious meaning of the text, to which my granddaughter Sarah would say, "Well, Duh!" The **nations** are the wicked people who lived around Israel in Old Testament times. They're the **earth-dwellers**.

When we put the three terms together, **chaining Satan in the abyss** takes away his ability to tempt people. There's no way he can make anyone wander away from God. *Any other reading of this passage tries to avoid the plain language of scripture.* Trying to make this say anything else is pushing theology into scripture, rather than getting our theology from scripture. We should always let God tell us what to believe.[5]

Some interpreters try to fit puzzle pieces together in prophecy. They haven't figured out that prophecy is all about God's plan of redemption. He has to solve the sin problem *forever*. When these guys get busy solving Rubik's Cube, they discover that some things just don't fit with *their* plans. The plain language of scripture won't work with the way they've figured things out, so they find ways to get around direct statements. They think they've found a way to make scripture say something that it doesn't say. This solves a problem that exists *in their minds*, so they *can't* understand what God needs to do. They haven't understood the problem behind sin, so they can't figure out *why* there will be a millennium.

---

5. Obviously, a lot of theologians will argue with such a strong statement. But I've read their papers, and anyone who disagrees with what we've just discovered simply refuses to accept the biblical fact that "the nations" is the general term for the wicked people around Israel. They lean on less clear ideas like the ones I listed earlier and try to make them overrule the clear meaning of "the nations."

Our job is to listen to God. We've taken the time to listen to His revelation about how sin began. We're listening to how He's going to resolve the problem. Satan got a chance to demonstrate his case on earth. Now we get to see how God answers that demonstration.

Satan isn't literally tied up or **sealed** in anything. The **chain** isn't literal; it's a chain of circumstance. He's trapped on earth. Since there's nobody left alive on earth, he's got nobody to tempt. We'll continue after I step off my soapbox.

JUDGMENT

While Satan's stuck on earth, **those who had been beheaded because of the testimony of Jesus and the word of God** *and* **those who had not worshiped the beast or his image and had not received his mark on their forehead** are **seated on thrones** in heaven (20:4). This *merism*—"martyrs" and "faithful"—represents all the possible descriptions of all the saints.[6]

Judgment was given to the saints. This Greek word can mean to pass laws, but God's already done that. It can mean to identify who's saved or lost, but God's done that, too. The only thing left for God's **kingdom of priests** is "to sit as a court" (20:6; 1:6, cf. Jer 26:8–11). Jesus told the disciples they'd be seated on thrones, judging Israel (Matt 19:28, Luke 22:30). This would happen "in the regeneration when the Son of Man will sit on His glorious throne." That's right here, in the millennium, and this is the *only* scripture that actually describes it. The Day of Atonement is over. The wicked all died on the Day of the Lord, and can't appear in court to defend a covenant lawsuit.

There's only one case left. The **Devil**—literally, "the slanderer"—is about to have his day in court. He started the whole sin problem in the first place, so God has to bring him into the dock. If Satan can prove that his "slanders" are actually true, then he'll win. In a sense this means that God's actually on trial.

---

6. A merism is a figure of speech where a few parts are used to imply a single large thing. For the technically minded, there's a legitimate alternate reading possible here. The *kai* between the two descriptions can be taken as "epexegetical." Read that way the description becomes: "those who had been beheaded because of the testimony of Jesus and the word of God, *that is*, those who had not worshiped the beast or his image and had not received his mark on their forehead." The result's essentially the same. This list includes all the saints.

God has to prove that He's been absolutely true, faithful, and righteous in every action. The court can't convict Satan unless *every* act by God was perfect and holy.[7] The verdict comes. **Hallelujah! Salvation and glory and power belong to our God; because His judgments are true and righteous** (19:1–2).[8]

They came to life and reigned with Christ for a thousand years. They are **blessed and holy. The second death has no power over them** (20:6). In every commentary I've studied, **reigning** gets glossed over. Adam and Eve had "dominion" over everything in Eden (Gen 1:28). The rabbis translated this into Greek with *katakurieuō* to carry the impact of delegated authority. But in 20:4 the saints have *basileuō*, the power to rule by inherent right. They don't answer to anyone. They have overcome through Jesus' blood, and now truly have dominion (cf. Dan 7:22; 27).[9]

When we sit as the court, God submits Himself to us. Bringing the slander suit against Satan forces God to lay himself completely bare, with every act open to *our* judgment. Even though God is the plaintiff, if we find any single event where Satan is correct, we have to find against God. His holiness will be destroyed forever, and sin will never be abolished. What amazing condescension! The Creator completely and totally submits Himself to His creation. Only when the verdict of **Holy, Holy, Holy!** is shouted out can God resume His place as sovereign over all. And even then, He will be sovereign *because we give Him our consent*.

If God didn't do this, sin could never be banished. There would always be doubts, and another rebel could always come. If God was "not holy" just once, He can't ever again be holy. He'd be "not holy" forever, just as we remain sinners in this life. We become victors by being weak, allowing God to do it all for us, and God triumphs in the end by being completely surrendered to *our* will![10] Once our verdict is announced, every righteous

---

7. Romans 3:4 prays that God "will be proved right in what He said, and will win His case in court" (NLT, cf. Ps 51:4). It's worth noting that almost every English translation treats God as if He's on trial here.

8. I can see your look of confusion here. When we get to the parallels in 17–20 you'll see what's going on.

9. This can open up a can of worms. My basic intent is to point out that the saints are sovereign in this courtroom scene. I'm not intending to suggest that they become gods in a way similar to the Mormon doctrine.

10. Your sharp eyes have noticed that we "reign with Christ." If Christ is God, how can He be co-regent with us if God is effectively on trial? Think about the Trinity. Although God is "one," God exists as three persons, the Father, Son, and Holy Spirit in a complex unity, something like a marriage. Jesus was human for about 33 years, and lived by faith

being in the universe will be immunized against sin. Paul says that now we see things like a reflection in a poor mirror, but in the end, we "will know everything completely, just as God now knows me completely" (1 Cor 13:12 NLT). We walk by faith, not by sight, but in the end we will see God face to face (2 Cor 5:7).

This trial will show that God has been, as advertised, completely faithful and righteous in every way. It will also show everyone the stark face of evil. We will all love God fully and completely. Our ability to choose won't be gone, but our knowledge will turn rebellion into a dead option. The universe will be safe from sin.

THE SECOND RESURRECTION

God is very orderly. He hasn't shown the wicked their guilt, and He's not going to destroy anyone without them understanding their guilt. So, **the wicked dead come to life after the thousand years** (20:5). The **second resurrection** is only for them. Once they come back to life, **Satan is released from his prison** (20:7). No, nobody came to open a cellblock door. With the wicked alive on earth, the chain of circumstances that kept Satan bottled up will be broken. He'll have people to tempt! **The nations**—the wicked, remember?—will be **in the four corners of the earth** (20:8). He will gather **Gog and Magog together for the war** (20:8).

Gog and Magog takes us to Ezekiel 38–39 where God tells "Gog of the land of Magog, the prince of Rosh, Meshech and Tubal" that he will "put hooks in his jaws" (Ezek 38:3). Then "after many days" (the millennium) he'll be summoned and will devise an evil plan to attack Israel (vv. 8–12 ff). Twice God goes on to symbolically tell how He'll destroy Gog and his army. This is exactly what happens in Revelation 20. The wicked army **surrounds the camp of the saints** (20:9), but **fire comes down from heaven and devours them** (cf. Ezek 39:6).

We have to be careful here. Fire from heaven destroyed Sodom and Gomorrah (Gen 19:24). But if the wicked are destroyed immediately, they'd have to be resurrected *again* to face the **Great White Throne**. And that doesn't make a lot of sense, so it seems best to suggest that **fire from heaven** is just a symbolic description of God ultimately destroying them.

---

as we do. The Father and Holy Spirit reigned from heaven without the Son for that time. Since the trial involves *all* of God's activities and decisions, it treats Jesus as man this time. As the second Adam, Jesus is our representative in heaven, and properly one of us during the trial (1 Cor 15:45).

The Devil, the beast, and the false prophet are thrown into the lake of fire (20:9).

Even the **lake of fire** might be symbolic, but it's hard to be sure. We *do* know it represents something very important. The wicked committed adultery with Satan. Ordinary adulterers were stoned to death (John 8:4–5). But if a priest's daughter was caught in adultery, she had to be burned to death *outside the camp* where the **lake of fire** is (20:9–10, Lev 21:9).[11] Since all are called to be God's kingdom of priests, the **lake of fire** is the proper end for anyone who persists in rebellion.

This brings us to a very difficult item. **The devil, beast and false prophet** are **tormented forever and ever**. If this is literally true, then the **lake of fire** will be on the earth forever. It would be a twisted tourist attraction in the middle of a **world made new** (21:5). That doesn't sound so good.

One possibility is to be literal*istic*, and suggests that Satan will never finish paying the price for all the sins he caused. This idea *is* attractive, and torment forever definitely fits our human desire for revenge. But the torment of the **beast** and **false prophet** is obviously symbolic, since they aren't real people. So maybe Satan's is symbolic, too.

The expression "forever and ever" comes from Old Testament passages like Psalm 145:1, where David declares that he "will bless Your name forever and ever."[12] It's pretty clear David is dead, so he isn't praising God's name right now (Ps 115:17, Acts 2:29). The best way to read David's expression is that he will praise God's name "throughout." That is, as long as he can, he'll praise God.[13]

If we apply this to Satan's torment, it seems that the expression means it will last a long time, but it will end. He'll be tormented as long as he can be tormented, but at the end, he *will* die. Now this may seem odd to some of you, but think about it. If Satan, the author of evil, is alive forever, God has a new problem.

The wages of sin is *death* (Rom 6:23).[14] If Satan doesn't die, he doesn't receive the penalty for his sin, and God's a liar! Do we really want to be-

---

11. See Mishna tractate Sanhedrin 9:1 b.
12. The Greek of the LXX uses the same wording here as in Revelation.
13. This is a very short version of a much longer study of the Hebrew expression.
14. This is another one of those places where lots of theologians dance around the plain meaning of words. The most common variation is that "death" *really* means "spiritual death," or separation from God. But those theologians forget that since God is the

lieve that after the millennial trial, God's suddenly going to change and not punish sin the way He said He would? That would start the heavenly questions all over again! Is God really as holy and faithful as He seemed to be when we looked at the records? The bottom line is that Satan has to die, just as God said (Ezek 28:8, 10). That means his torment in the lake of fire has to end sometime. **Forever and ever** must mean "throughout."

Once Satan has organized **the nations**, they **surround the camp of the saints and the beloved city** (20:9). This is Satan's last hurrah. He has told them that God's people are undefended (Ezek 38:10).[15] Why does this happen? Maybe God wants us to have a demonstration more powerful than evidence in court. Maybe if Aunt Elizabeth comes up with a pitchfork in her hand and fire in her eye it will be even more convincing than the movies we saw in the trial.[16]

Now we see **the dead are standing in front of a Great White Throne** (20:11). The **books are opened, and they are judged** based on **their deeds that were written in the books** (20:12). Hallelujah! I don't have to be judged on all my past sins, since Jesus covers them with His blood. I'm written in the **book of life**, and Jesus' righteousness is mine (20:12).

Of course, if you're being judged on your actions, you aren't covered by Jesus' blood, and that means that only the wicked **stand in front of the throne**. We are **reigning with Jesus *on* His throne**. The wicked all end up **in the lake of fire** (20:15). And, Praise God, **death and Hades are thrown into the lake of fire** (20:14). The final victory has been won (cf. 1 Cor 15:25–26).

---

one who gives us life and sustains us, if we are *completely* separated from God, we are *completely* separated from the source of life, and will . . . die! It seems that there's no way around it. You die or . . . you die.

15. It's obvious here that the saints have been returned to earth, otherwise this vision would be nonsense. We'll see that in the parallel vision in Revelation 19.

16. I'm being figurative here. If we're judges, and we get to see the evidence, we'll see historical scenes. In effect, we'll see movies of the past. If your aunt's name is Elizabeth, please forgive me. I picked a name out of the air.

The Millennium

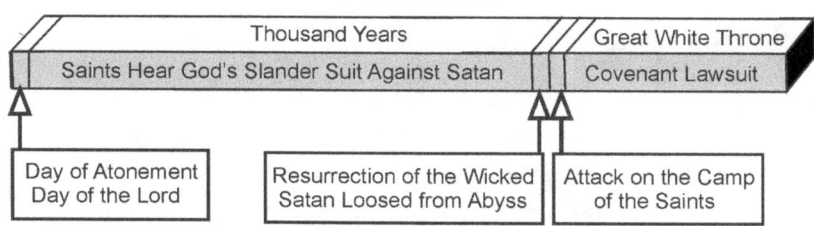

I saw a new heaven and a new earth (21:1). It's time to celebrate! Sin has been totally abolished and **the first heaven and the first sinful earth have passed away**. It's time to **make everything new** (21:5).

God's tent isn't a long way away from us anymore, it's **with us** (21:3).[17] This Ancient Near Eastern image is incredibly rich. God's tent is His home in the center of His land. It's the place where He's the gracious host. We're right there, enjoying fellowship in person (1 Cor 13:12). We see what He's doing and we share in His feast. We're **sons of God** (21:7, cf. Luke 20:36, Gal 3:26) and will dwell in the house of the Lord forever (Ps 23:6).

The wicked mourned as they were destroyed, but God's people won't have to cry again because **no one will ever die again** (21:4). **God will wipe away every tear from our eyes** (21:4).

The drama of sin is over. **It is done** (21:6, cf. 16:17)! God is **the Alpha and the Omega, the beginning and the end.**[18] **He will give to anyone who thirsts from the spring of the water of life without cost.** God's gift is just that—a gift. Shortly He'll fill in more details (21:9).

---

17. "Tent" is a literal translation for *skēnē*, the word commonly translated "tabernacle."

18. These merisms are short for "I'm everything."

20

The Harlot Rides the Beast

Millennium, Part II

By now, that subtitle isn't a shock. You're probably saying, "There he goes again!" and you're right. We're going on a Bible discovery trip. We're not going to let anybody's ideas about what Revelation means stand in the way of what God says in the book. So, let's have a little fun being detectives.

The most important questions are usually, "Who?", "What?", "When?", "Where?", and "Why?" I tell my class these are the "newspaper questions." Any good reporter figures these facts out to be able to tell the story well. The "Who?" and "What?" are pretty easy.

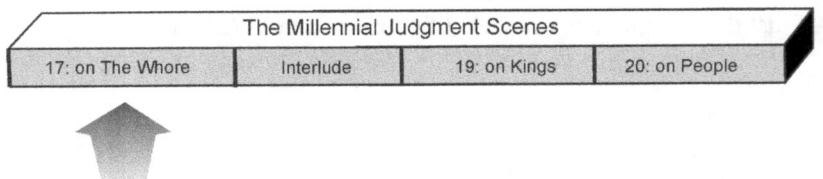

YOU ARE HERE

An **angel** took John to **see the judgment of the great harlot who sits on peoples and multitudes and nations and tongues** (17:1, 15). He saw **a woman in a wilderness, sitting on a scarlet beast, full of blasphemous names, having seven heads and ten horns** (17:3). There's more, but we'll get to that in a minute.

The **beast** should be familiar by now. It represents man's governments by combining the four beasts from Daniel 7. It had **blasphemous names on its horns** in chapter 13. This emphasized the evil in man's governments, but the real power behind the throne was Satan, **the beast from** the abyss (17:8, 11:7-8). Now **the beast is full of blasphemous names** (17:3). It's Satan again, but this time he's not camouflaged.

The beast was, is not, and is to come (17:8). Since the beast symbolizes human governments, John's looking at a time when human governments "**are not.**" This means there isn't anyone alive on earth to have a government.[1] In other words, it's during the millennium. When Jesus returned for the saints, He killed every wicked person. Nobody was left behind. This is the **great chain** of circumstances that **bound Satan in the abyss** (20:3, cf. Jer 4:23-31).

The **harlot** embodies spiritual adultery of all times by all people, so it's no surprise **the kings of the earth committed immorality with her** (17:2). She has **purple and scarlet** royal robes and all sorts of **gold, precious stones and pearls** (17:4). It's almost as if to say, **I am a queen, and will never mourn** (18:7, cf. Isa 47:5-7). She even has the name of the queen from Isaiah, **Babylon** (17:5). **She is the mother of harlots and of the abominations of the earth** (17:5), and is **drunk with the blood of the witnesses of Jesus** that she has killed (17:6, c.f. 16:6).[2] Like Isaiah's queen, she's about to be condemned.

The **harlot "rides the beast"** by **reigning over the kings of the earth** (17:18). What better way could God say that apostate religion and civil power are really tight with each other? Examples are everywhere. In the fourth century, Sylvester, the bishop of Rome, cozied up to Emperor Constantine to promote the spread of "Christianity." Today various religious groups try to make the government carry out their version of "God's plan."

The seven heads are seven mountains . . . and are seven kings. Five have fallen, one is, and the other has not yet come (17:9-10). This imagery comes straight out of Daniel 2 where God's kingdom is a mountain. The **seven heads** are **seven kingdoms**.[3]

The beast comes from Daniel 7, so we should start counting where Daniel's prophecies started. The first kingdom was Babylon, then Medo-Persia and Greece. The fourth and fifth stages were Rome in its unified and fragmented stages.[4] But Daniel's prophecies don't go past the return

1. I have to thank my late father for his clear thinking that led to this analysis.

2. It's tempting to notice the charge Stephen levels against the Jews in Acts 7:52. They persecuted the prophets and killed Jesus. This is almost the same charge God aims against apostasy in general here in Revelation.

3. Daniel uses "king" and "kingdom" interchangeably in his interpretation of Nebuchadnezzar's dream in Daniel 2.

4. Shameless commercial plug. If you have questions about this, read my *Primer on the Book of Daniel*.

of Christ for the saints (Dan 12:1–3), so he doesn't have any symbols for the millennium and beyond.

DANIEL'S BEASTS		
DANIEL 7	**KINGS**	**REV 17**
Lion	1	Babylon
Bear	2	Medo-Persia
Leopard	3	Greece
Terrifying Beast	4	Rome
Horns	5	Fragmented Rome
	6	King of the Abyss
	7	King after Millennium

The sixth king "**is**" at the time John sees the vision. We've already figured out this is Satan, the king of the abyss. That fits, since this scene is in **a wilderness** (17:3). Now the fun starts. One more king is **to come**. He will rule over **all those who dwell on the earth, whose name has not been written in the book of life** (17:8). They are **ten kings . . . who have authority with the beast for an hour** (17:12). If this looks familiar, that's because we saw it in chapter 20. Let's look at the parallels.

REV 17	**REV 20**
Beast "is not" in "wilderness" (3, 8).	Satan is locked in the abyss for millennium (2–3).
Beast "to come" out of the abyss (8).	Satan is released from the abyss after millennium (3, 7).
	Court hears God's slander suit against Satan (4).
	The wicked come to life after the millennium (5).
The wicked "wonder after the beast (8), and "give their kingdom to the beast (17).	Satan deceives "the nations" (8).
The wicked "ten kings" join with the beast to "make war against the lamb" (12–14) and the saints (14).	"The nations" join Satan and attack the camp of the saints (8–9)
The Lamb overcomes the attackers (14).	Jesus destroys the attackers (9)
The Harlot is burned with fire (16).	Satan and wicked thrown in the lake of fire (10)

Can there be any doubt that these two chapters are telling the same story? The difference between them is that chapter 20 focuses on individuals while chapter 17 focuses on general apostasy. And when we get to chapter 19, we'll see the same story, this time focusing on rulers. Three lenses: three different camera angles.

When Christ comes for the saints, He kills all the wicked. The earth becomes desolate for a thousand years, with only Satan and his angels around.[5] After the millennium ends, the wicked are raised. They **wonder after the beast** (17:8, cf. 13:3 KJV), **give their power and authority to him** (17:13), and one last time **wage war against the Lamb** (17:14). After **the Lamb overcomes them** (17:14), they become enraged and **burn the harlot with fire** (17:16). They can't win against God, so in symbol God shows how they turn on anyone who led them into rebellion. "Repent" isn't in their vocabulary. Their course can't be reversed. All they can do is get angry when they see their fate.

The **harlot** that would be queen can't overcome her evil nature. All her attempts at royalty are pure vanity. In the end Jesus triumphs **because He is Lord of Lords and King of Kings** (17:14).

---

5. Let's not get too picky about whether a "thousand years" is exact or not. There are good arguments in both directions, and it really doesn't matter whether God's referring to a long age or a counted length of time. It's long in either case.

21

One Called Faithful and True

HERE HE GOES AGAIN! Yes, I hear it. I've skipped back over chapter 18 and ten verses of chapter 19. But by now, you've probably figured out that I've got a pretty good reason for this scriptural hopscotch. You're going to see another set of millennium parallels as God tells this story one more time from one more angle.

I saw heaven opened; and behold, a white horse, and He who sat upon it *is* called Faithful and True; and in righteousness He judges and wages war (19:11). This time He's not the horseman **overcoming and to overcome**, He's the conquering king. His eyes *are* a flame of fire, and upon His head *are* many diadems; and He has a name written *upon Him* which no one knows except Himself. And *He is* clothed with a robe dipped in blood; and His name is called The Word of God (19:12-13).

Jesus has replaced His overcomer's crown (*stephanos*) with a king's crown (*diadema*). **Armies from heaven, Who have put on fine linen, white *and* clean, follow Him on white horses** (19:14). God's saints are wearing priestly robes, following Jesus back to earth (Exod 28).[1] The Greek of these verses uses the "middle voice" emphasizing everyone has put on his own robe. In Jesus' case, He comes in judgment to enforce the negative side of the covenant, and He's worthy to do that because He died on the Cross (5:9). This means that the blood on His robe is His own, shed on the Cross. The saints who follow have put on His righteousness (cf. Rom 13:14).

The saints don't have any fighting to do, because the battle belongs to the Lord (1 Sam 17:47). **From Jesus' mouth comes a sharp sword, so that with it He may smite the nations; and He will rule them with a rod of iron** (19:15, cf. Ps 2:9). The wicked **nations** don't stand a chance since

---

1. Remember, when discussing Revelation 20, I said that the return of the saints to earth was implied. Here it is in black and white.

Jesus "**erects a booth**" over the saints (7:15, Ps 18:2). The attack against the saints fails (17:14; 20:9).

Jesus **kills the wicked with the sword from His mouth** (19:21). Then their bodies lay on the earth like dung, unburied, which is a great curse (Jer 8:2; 14:16). **Birds feast on the flesh of the bodies of kings, commanders, horses, and all men (19:17–18). Then the beast and the false prophet are thrown into the lake of fire which burns with brimstone (19:20).**

Rev 17	Rev 19	Rev 20
Beast "is not" in "wilderness" (3, 8).		Satan is locked in the abyss for millennium (2-3).
Beast "is to come" out of the abyss (8).		Satan is released from the abyss after millennium (3, 7).
		Court hears God's slander suit against Satan (4).
		Wicked come to life after the millennium (5).
	Saints return with Jesus to the earth (14).	
The wicked "wonder after the beast (8), and "give their kingdom to the beast (17).	The beast and false prophet deceive those with the mark of the beast (20).	Satan deceives "the nations" (8).
The wicked "ten kings" join with the beast to "make war against the lamb" (12–14) and the saints (14).	The (ten) kings of the earth make war on Jesus (19).	"The nations" join Satan and attack the camp of the saints (8–9).
The Lamb overcomes the attackers (14).	Jesus makes war on the (ten) kings of the earth (15, 21).	Jesus destroys the attackers (9).
The Harlot is burned with fire (16).	The beast and false prophet are thrown into the lake of fire (20).	Satan and the wicked are thrown in the lake of fire (10).

With all these parallels between chapters 17, 19, and 20, I don't think there can be any doubt that they're all the *same* story. They're just told from different angles. The focus in 17 is on God's judgment against spiritual adultery, personified as the **harlot** (17:1). In 19, it's on God's judgment against **kings** (19:18). Finally, in 20, God looks at individual people (20:12–15).

It's possible to nitpick and say that the stories can't be the same since they have detail differences. But that's literal*ism*, and ignores the fact that these are *symbolic presentations*. It's obvious that you can't have all those dead bodies laying around for birds to eat if they've really been thrown in the lake of fire (19:17–18, 20:15). And that's not the point.

Each description brings into view a specific set of symbols for a specific purpose. **Fire from heaven** (20:9) reminds us of God's judgment on Sodom and Gomorrah (Gen 19:24–25). Dead bodies that aren't buried emphasize the rebellion brings a curse. And the **lake of fire** emphasizes the final penalty for adultery by the daughter of a priest (Lev 21:9). Jesus is our high priest, and spiritual adultery "profanes our father." We could go on with an exhausting discussion of symbols and sources, but we really don't need to. These three chapters have repeated the message that the ultimate fate of all rebels is death.

We live in a sinful world. We need lots of guidance to help us so we can wear those **white robes** and golden *stephanoi*. We also need to know how the story turns out for God, so we can know that sin won't ever rise again. In these chapters, God has given us *enough* information. We don't need lots of details for the millennium and beyond like we need them for here and now. In a sense, my wife's license plate frame says it all: "I know the future. God wins."

22

Two Choirs

The Millennium Interlude

THE CONTROVERSY OVER WORSHIP was an interlude in the story of covenant in this sinful age. The story of covenant in the millennial age has an interlude, too. It looks like this.

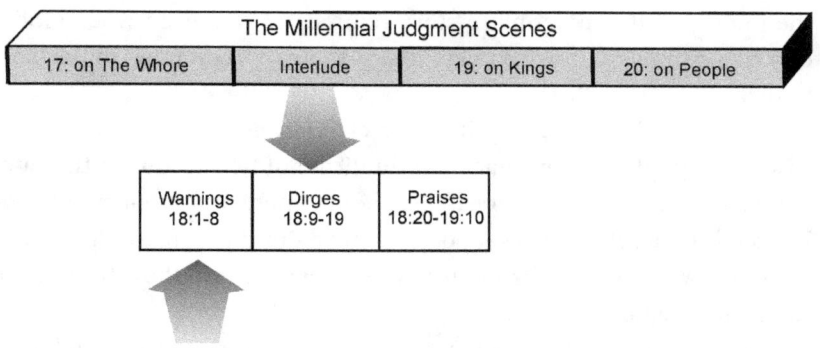

YOU ARE HERE

A powerful angel comes down from heaven and cries with a mighty voice, "Fallen, fallen is Babylon the Great!" She has become a dwelling place of demons and a prison of every unclean spirit, and a prison of every unclean and hateful bird (18:1–2). I couldn't make up all the bad stuff she's into.

- The nations have drunk of the wine of the passion of her immorality.
  Just turn on the radio or TV.

- **The kings of the earth have committed adultery with her.**
  Sex, money, and power make the world go around.
- **The merchants of the earth have become rich by the wealth of her sensuality.**
  Buzz makes the cash register ring.

Another voice from heaven calls for God's people to **come out of her** (18:4–5). Anyone who doesn't repent and come to God will **receive her plagues**, since **God has remembered her iniquities** (18:5). And this raises a problem. How can the saints "come out of Babylon" during the millennium if they're in heaven and the wicked are all dead on earth? I've screwed it up again!

Actually, I haven't messed anything up. It's just our old friend, the aorist tense. When this scene opens, God hasn't forgotten that the book is for the church in this sinful age. He uses the aorist tense for **is fallen** to emphasize that evil will definitely be destroyed. When this happens, anyone who wants to survive had better be on God's side. Otherwise, the plagues on the wicked in the seven Bowls will be their problem. This warning in the middle of the millennium story reminds us that even when God is describing things that will happen "then," there's a "right now" importance in them.

For the saints, revenge will be sweet.[1] They are to **pay her back even as she has paid, and give back the duplicate of her deeds. To the same degree that she glorified herself, give her torment and mourning** (18:6–7).[2] But how are the saints supposed to hand out this penalty? Jesus rules with the **sword out of His mouth** (19:15). **He** destroys the attack on the camp, not the saints (20:9).

Remember that the saints are the court that reviews God's righteous acts (20:4). This means that the final destruction of the wicked can't come until the saints sign off on it. They give the final OK for God's vengeance on wickedness. Then the idolatrous daughter of a priest **will be burned with fire** (18:8).

---

1. In know, we aren't supposed to seek revenge. But this will happen after we've been transformed (1 Cor 15:51–55), so we'll be dishing out righteous judgment.

2. Most translations say, "Pay her double." Commentators on the Greek generally agree that this refers back to a Hebrew idiom related to the principle of *lex talionis*, the law of just retribution, or "an eye for an eye" (Exod 21:24). "Double" would contradict both this principle and "Pay her back as she has paid." Since the Greek word can suggest a duplicate, this is a better translation.

As the **harlot burns** (18:9), **the kings** (18:9), **merchants** (18:10), **shipmasters, passengers, and sailors** (18:17) all cry out, **Woe! In one hour God has laid Babylon waste** (18:19). Everyone who joined with Babylon cries out **"What city is like the great city?"** (18:18).[3] **They throw dust on their heads and weep and mourn** like the ancients did when all was lost (Josh 7:6, 1 Sam 4:12, etc.). Their special privileges are gone forever.

Right after the dirge we hear the call to **Rejoice! Heaven, and saints, and apostles, and prophets are to celebrate God's judgment against Babylon** (18:20). Then an angel throws a stone like a great millstone into the sea and declares that Babylon is history (18:21).[4] The people of Babylon, the wicked **musicians, craftsmen, millers, and merchants** will be destroyed (18:22–23). The wickedness that **killed prophets and saints** (18:24) will end with great **violence** (18:21).

A great multitude in heaven answers the call to **Rejoice!** (19:1). They celebrate **God's true and righteous judgments against the great harlot who corrupted the earth. God has avenged the blood of His servants** who cried out in the fifth Seal (19:2, 6:9–11). And right here we need to appreciate just what the saints are saying.

Glory and honor and power belong to God *because* His judgments are true and righteous (19:1–2). This is a verdict. The court that sat in 20:4 has made its decision. God has been found true in every deed because none of Satan's slanders were true (Rom 3:4). Because every act has been thoroughly examined, the saints can shout **Hallelujah!** (19:1, 3). The wicked daughter of a priest burns outside the camp in the **lake of fire, and her smoke rises up forever and ever** (19:3).[5] As the chorus sings, **the twenty-four elders and the four living creatures fell down and worshiped God with "Amen, Hallelujah!"** (19:4).[6] **Praises continue from all God's**

---

3. This dirge is basically lifted from Ezekiel 27. While some details differ, the similarity is striking. Ezekiel uses Tyre as a type of the end-time Babylon. Just as Tyre was destroyed utterly, Babylon will be completely wiped out.

4. This echoes Jeremiah 51:61–64, where a stone weighs the prophecy scroll down so that it sinks in the river, never to rise again.

5. Let's remember the last couple of times we went through this visual image. The focus is on how far the smoke rises, not how long it takes the fire to burn. God traveled with ancient Israel in a pillar of cloud that rose up to heaven. Visually, it rose "forever and ever." This pillar of smoke repeats the original one.

6. Once again, let's not forget what we figured out in Revelation 4–5. The elders and living creatures are symbolic representations of Israel. So one more time, the church and Israel are blended into one picture, showing that they are identical.

servants so loud they would drown out many waterfalls and mighty thunder. Hallelujah, for the Lord God Almighty reigns! (19:5-6).

If this wasn't dramatic enough, the **rejoicing** builds into anticipation of the **marriage supper of the Lamb** (19:7-9). What a marvelous day is coming! God is Israel's bridegroom (Isa 61:10, Matt 25:1-13). Everyone who puts himself in Jesus' hands will come into an intimate union with the almighty. No, this isn't a banquet that ends (cf. Matt 22:2-4). This is literal membership in the household of Abraham and Jesus (Matt 8:11).

A guest in a Middle Eastern household was protected as long as he was under his host's roof. But as members of God's house, we aren't guests. Our Father permanently watches over us. He will use *lex talionis* against our tormentors. And when He's done, the wicked will cease to exist. Nobody can be harmed ever again.[7]

Every righteous person will have become completely convicted of God's righteousness. Their faith was proved right in the millennial trial. They love God completely and without reservation. Yes, they are still free to choose to rebel. But sin will never rise again, because they've all been immunized against it. Sin will be just as dead as the wicked people who didn't give it up.

It's time for the final scene.

---

7. I know this may sound different from what you're used to. See Appendix D for more details.

23

The New Jerusalem

> *... all who remain will worship the King, the Lord of hosts, and celebrate the Feast of Booths.*
>
> (Zech 14:16)

WE'RE ALMOST DONE WITH our trip through Revelation. Before we finish, let's look back at some key typology. If we know where we've been, it will be easier to see where we're going.

When Jesus died, He was our Passover sacrifice (1 Cor 5:7, cf. Lev 23:5). The original Passover led to ancient Israel's delivery from physical Egypt. Jesus, our spiritual Passover, leads our delivery from spiritual Egypt (11:18). He rose as the first fruits from the dead (1 Cor 15:20; 23, cf. Lev 23:10). Finally, at Pentecost, three thousand were added to the church in the spring harvest of souls (Acts 2:41, cf. Lev 23:15–16). Jesus' first advent fulfilled the spring feasts of Israel in order. This suggests that He will fulfill the fall festivals in order in His second advent.

Revelation starts its recap of the spring festivals with Passover in the **lamb standing as if slain** (5:6). Next, Jesus is the first fruits from the dead in 5:9. And 5:6 echoes Pentecost with **seven Spirits of God sent out into all the earth**. These three festivals are all blended in one scene.

Spring Festivals		
Calendar Type	Historical Fulfillment	Revelation Echo
Passover—Lev 23:5	The Cross—1 Cor 5:7	Throne Room—Rev 5:6
First fruits—Lev 23:10	The Resurrection—1 Cor 15:20	Throne Room—Rev 5:9
Pentecost—Lev 23:15	Pentecost—Acts 2	Throne Room—Rev 5:6

The fall festivals are Trumpets, Atonement, Booths, and the *Shemini Atzeret*.[1] The annual Feast of Trumpets warned the people to prepare themselves for the Day of Atonement ten days later. Seven Trumpets warn of the ultimate Day of Atonement. Next, the Day of Atonement appears in the seventh Seal, Trumpet, and all the Bowls. Judgment comes in favor of the saints, but anyone who rejects God dies on the Day of the Lord.

The Feast of Booths comes last. After the Israelites were delivered from Egypt, they built small shelters (booths) to protect themselves from the sun. These booths became a symbol of God's protection.[2] We see this protection in 20:9, where the wicked multitudes **surrounded the camp of the saints and the beloved city, and fire came down from heaven and devoured them**.[3]

Now we can look forward. For the Feast of Booths the people built temporary shelters and lived in them for seven days (Lev 23:39–43, Deut 16:16). On the *eighth* day, everybody came out of the booths and moved into their permanent homes. So far, every act in the drama has been moving toward a goal. Now we've arrived.

Fall Festivals		
Calendar Type	Historical Fulfillment	Revelation Fulfillment
Trumpets—Lev 23:24	None	Seven Trumpets
Atonement—Lev 23:27	None	7th Seal, Trumpet, and all Bowls
Booths—Lev 23:34	None	Rev 7:15; 17:14; 19:15; 20:9
Shemini Atzeret—Lev 23:36	None	New Jerusalem

And I saw a new heaven and a new earth; for the first heaven and the first earth passed away (21:1). The drama of sin has come full circle. Adam and Eve were created sinless and perfect. God put them in Eden, a perfect home on a perfect world. But they believed Satan and rebelled.

---

1. You won't find Shemini Atzeret in the Bible. It's Hebrew for "Eighth Assembly," and is the Great Sabbath of the Feast of Booths (Lev 23:36, 39).

2. Pss 17:8; 27:5; 31:20; 36:37; 57:1; 63:7; 91:1; Isa 4:6; Amos 9:11; Hos 14:7, etc.

3. This was promised in 7:15, which literally says he will erect a booth over them.

We've lived the rest of this drama for thousands of years. Finally, when every one of Satan's accusations has been answered, sin can be permanently abolished and God can put us back into the Garden, secure from ever sinning again.

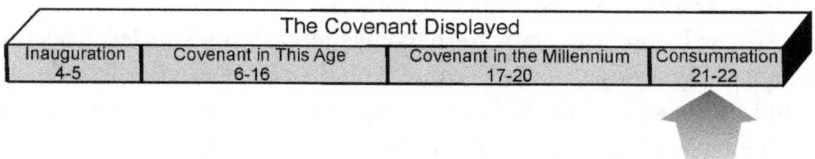

An angel said, **Come here, I will show you the bride, the wife of the lamb** (21:9). He hears one symbolic description and then sees something else, just like several times before. **The holy city, Jerusalem, came down out of heaven from God, made ready as a bride adorned for her husband** (21:2, 10). We know from 19:7–8 that the **bride of the Lamb** is the church—the saints of all ages—so the **holy city** isn't a physical structure at all. It's a symbolic description of the saints.

The physical size and shape of the city confirm this. It's **12,000 stadia long, wide, and high** (21:16).[4] If we put that city on the surface of the earth, it would rise 1,300 miles higher than the orbit of the space shuttle. Now, I'm not about to say that God *can't* build a city like that, but it doesn't make sense. After all, He's in the process of restoring the perfect world of Eden for us, and a physical city like that is completely out of place.[5]

That cube shape should tip us off to something really important. The inner compartment in Solomon's temple was a cube (2 Chron 3:8). It was overlaid with gold so that when the high priest entered, he effectively walked on a **street of gold** (21:21). The **Shekinah glory of God** filled the chamber with light so that **there was no night in it** (21:23, 25; 22:5). Its size is also important. Each side is twelve—the number of completeness in Israel—times ten—another number of completeness in Israel—times ten times ten stadia long. In other words, it's a perfect fit for Israel.

There was no temple in it, for the Lord God, the Almighty, and the Lamb are its temple (21:22). **The tabernacle of God is among men, and He shall dwell among them** (21:3, cf. Exod 25:8). **Those whose name is written in the Lamb's book of life** (21:27) **will see His face and His name will be on their foreheads** (22:4). What a prospect!

4. I used the original Greek measurements. These convert to about 1,500 miles.
5. We'll be talking about restoring Eden in a bit.

There's no way we can physically enter God's presence now. His glory would kill us (1 Tim 6:16, cf. Lev 16:17). In ancient Israel only the high priest could go in, and then only when he was shielded by a large cloud of incense on the Day of Atonement. His turban had "Holy to the Lord" on it (Exod 28:36–37), but **the Lord's name** will be directly on us.

Now, before you accuse me of going literalistic on you, let's back up a moment. By saying that **God's name is on the saints' foreheads**, we're not pointing out a bit of divine face painting. If you remember our discussion of the **mark of the Beast**, you'll realize that this is a symbolic way of saying that the saints have Jesus in their minds at all times. They belong fully and forever to God. And that leads us to another piece of symbolism.

He shall wipe away every tear from their eyes (21:4). This almost sounds like Jesus is running a Kleenex franchise in heaven. But what it really means is **there won't ever be any mourning, or crying, or pain**, because **the first things have passed away, and there is no more death** (21:4). **The curse is gone** (22:3). Wow! We don't have to worry any more. No kids will get leukemia. No crooks will shoot innocent bystanders. And no old folks will leave children without parents. Its *over*! God will **make *everything* new** (21:5).

The **twelve foundation stones have the names of the twelve apostles** (21:14). These precious stones remind us of the precious stones on the high priest's breastplate (21:19–20, cf. Exod 28:15–19). The church is blended completely with ancient Israel—again. The **twelve pearly gates have the names of the twelve tribes of the sons of Israel** (21:12). This time it's reversed—Israel is blended with the church.

Every saint of every age is part of the city. As the apostle Paul said, "There is neither Jew nor Greek, there is neither slave nor free man, there is neither male nor female; for you are all one in Christ Jesus" (Gal 3:28). Nobody gets any particular place based on who his parents were. And that makes me back up for a moment.

WE'RE ALL IN THIS TOGETHER

God's problem wasn't related to Jews, Greeks, or any other group of people. It was sin, rising in a perfect universe. Everybody who ever lived has sinned (Rom 3:23).[6] So when God redeems fallen humans, He isn't inter-

---

6. Except Jesus, of course.

ested in what your skin color is or where you lived or what your father did. He's only interested in whether you put your faith in Him.

The court that heard God's slander suit against Satan wasn't interested in any of those things, either. In fact, if God *had* bothered with that stuff, Satan would have a legitimate claim that God was playing favorites. Satan would win and God would lose. Sin could never be abolished.

God treats everyone the same. No one, regardless of heritage, has any special advantage. And Revelation shows that everyone is equal in His sight. We all suffer before redemption, and we all celebrate together in the end.

THE FEAST OF BOOTHS

The nations shall walk by its light, and the kings of the earth shall bring their glory into it (21:24). What a wonderful reversal! All through history, the "kings of the earth" have opposed God. Now they come to pay homage to God. Of course, by now, all the wicked are dead, so these kings are all righteous. And this fulfills Zechariah's prophecy that all who remain of the nations will go to Jerusalem to celebrate the feast of booths (Zech 14:16). God has brought the saints safely through the wilderness, and now they enter the **New Jerusalem**, their permanent home, just like they did each year in the *Shemini Atzeret* (cf. Lev 23:39–43).

The **Tree of Life** in the **New Jerusalem bears fruit for the healing of the nations** (22:2). The ancient hatred between the wicked Gentile nations and the Hebrews is gone. They're all one nation, the Jerusalem of God (cf. Heb 12:22, Gal 6:16). **The River of Life** runs through the city, like the river of Eden (22:1, Gen 2:10), fulfilling prophecies by Ezekiel and Joel (Ezek 47:1–12, Joel 3:18). The **fruit in every month** (22:2) sets the table for the **marriage supper of the Lamb** (19:9). The hills drip with sweet wine and flow with honey (Joel 3:18). The curse that forced man to till the ground for food is reversed (Gen 3:17–19). The garden provides food, just like in Eden (Gen 1:29–30). In Eden, Adam and Eve ruled by grant from God (Grk. *katakurieuo*). Now they **reign** by right **forever and ever** (Grk. *basileuo*, 22:5).

God has **made all things new**. The Eden that was "very good" (Gen 1:31) has been recreated for us to live in forever. Like Adam and Eve, we'll walk in the Garden with God (Gen 3:8).

24

That's a Wrap!

JOHN'S ANGELIC GUIDE IS ready to end the tour. **These words are faithful and true** (22:6). One more time, as if John didn't already get it, the angel emphasizes that this prophecy is one we need to **heed** (1:3; 22:7). Of course, this message is really aimed at the church, since the apostle doesn't have the same case of The Dumbs the rest of us have. God knows we're a hardheaded bunch, wanting to steer our own boats.

Because we're stubborn, we have to hear the message from almost every possible angle. So we heard the call of grace in the seven **Seals**, re-capped in the **144,000**, re-told in the story of the **chaste woman and the dragon**, and visited one more time in the **First Angel's Message**. The same pattern holds for the warning of judgment and the Day of the Lord. We've seen the story so many times from so many angles that we have no excuse (cf. Rom 1:20). So when this angel emphasizes the truth of the story, he's just repeating what the **faithful and true witness** told us (3:14).

Behold, I am coming quickly (22:7, 20). When Jesus returns, it will be **like a thief** in the night for anyone who is not prepared (3:3; 16:15, cf. Matt 24:43). God's saints will **heed the prophecy of this book** and will receive the blessed hope (Titus 2:13). They have **washed their robes and have the right to enter in through the gates into the city** (22:14). But the wicked **sorcerers, immoral persons, murderers, idolaters, and liars will not enter** (22:15). Their **place is in the lake of fire** (21:8).

The time is near (22:10). But God doesn't think our way. A thousand years is like a day to Him (2 Pet 3:8-9, Ps 90:4). He's not going to leave anyone behind who wants to repent, and until every person has made up his mind, God will wait.[1] But when it's over, He'll say **Let the one who**

---

1. This sort of near/far tension runs through all of scripture. Eve thought the Messiah had come when she gave birth to Seth (Gen 4:25). She was only 4,000 years too early.

does wrong, still do wrong; and let the one who is filthy, still be filthy; and let the one who is righteous, still practice righteousness; and let the one who is holy, still be holy (22:11, cf. Ezek 3:27, Dan 12:10).

A time is coming when the opportunity for decision will be over. Will you answer the call of grace? Will you hear the warning of judgment for the wicked? Or will you be lost in the judgment on the Day of the Lord, condemned by your choice to the lake of fire?

Revelation isn't about strange beasts and black helicopters. It's not about the nations of the world at war in the valley of Jezreel. It's about salvation. We need to hear and repeat its message. If we use our own cleverly designed fables (1 Tim 4:5, 2 Pet 1:18) to **add to or take away from the words of this book** (22:18–19, cf. Deut 4:2, 12:32, Prov 30:6). **God will send us plagues and take away our place in the holy city.**

The final choice isn't up to God. It's up to you. In that Great Gettin-up Morning, whose side will you be on?

ONE FINAL RECAP

In this book, I haven't tried to explain every symbol. That would be a huge job and would put you to sleep. I haven't even covered every verse. In this last chapter, I skipped over John trying to worship his angelic guide. What I've tried to do is cover the material that's at the core of the message. I'm quite sure I missed at least one of your favorite points.

Next, I'm also sure that I gored someone's sacred cow somewhere. Dispensationalists will be upset that I treated the book in a symbolic rather than a literalistic way. But that's what John tells us to do in 1:1! So I just tried to be faithful to scripture. Historicists may not like how I see the fifth and sixth trumpets in the future. Preterists will object to the focus on our future hope with Christ rather than the Roman destruction of Jerusalem in AD 70.

Fortunately, I don't have to satisfy men. My job is to read the message God gave for us in the Bible. To do that, I have to be very careful to respect what God said. At times that's tough, but I think you can see that I let scripture interpret scripture all the way through. And I tried to explain God's word in a way that most people can understand. *That* was my goal.

Now to Him who is able to keep you from stumbling, and to make you stand in the presence of His glory blameless with great joy, to the only God our Savior, through Jesus Christ our Lord, *be* glory, majesty, dominion and authority, before all time and now and forever. Amen. Jude 1:24–25

Appendix A

"666" in Perspective

A LOT OF PEOPLE claim they've solved the puzzle in Revelation 13:18.

> Here is wisdom. Let him who has understanding calculate the number of the beast, for the number is that of a man; and his number is six hundred and sixty-six.

Most people try to figure out this "Rubik's Cube" of prophecy by looking for a single person or office with the number "666." They take the "obvious" reference to gematria and find names or titles that add up to the number. One group says the Roman Caesar Nero was the beast. An alternate form of his name (Neron Caesar) is transliterated into Hebrew, where it adds up to 666.[1]

Another school suggests that the Pope's miter has the inscription "*Vicarius Filii Dei*". Using Latin gematria, this adds up to 666. These interpreters observe that the miter belongs to the office, not the person, and identify the papacy as the beast. While this seems to satisfy the longer view of apocalyptic prophecy, the Pope's miter never had such an inscription. Put bluntly, these all sound pretty fishy. If we want the right answer, we ought to find enough scriptural evidence to understand God's intention here.

GEMATRIA

The short description of gematria is "the numerical evaluation of words." It comes from ancient civilizations that had a written alphabet but no separate numerals. Letters did double duty as letters and numbers. Human

---

1. See the section on Nero below.

curiosity led people to add up the letters to get numeric values for names. But by themselves, numerical names are meaningless.

If we assume that names somehow come from the gods, then the value of a name could have spiritual meaning. If two names have the same numeric value, they should have the same spiritual value or importance. This is the ancient principle of *isopsephos* or "equal pebbles."[2] In practice, isopsephy relied on the original number value of a name of known spiritual importance. For example, the value of the Greek god "Hermes" is 353. If someone's name added up to 353, his spiritual value was great. In the same way, physical constants were assumed to come from the gods. Therefore, the mathematical relationships in musical notes, physical constants, and geometric relationships ought to yield spiritual secrets as well as physical information.

Gematria Character Values						
Hebrew				**Greek**			
Aleph	א – 1	Samek	ס – 60	Alpha	A – 1	Xi	Ξ – 60
Bet	ב – 2	Ayin	ע – 70	Beta	B – 2	Omicron	O – 70
Gimel	ג – 3	Pe	פ – 80	Gamma	Γ – 3	Pi	Π – 80
Daleth	ד – 4	Sade	צ – 90	Delta	Δ – 4	Qoppa*	Ϙ – 90
He	ה – 5	Qoph	ק – 100	Epsilon	E – 5	Rho	P – 100
Waw	ו – 6	Resh	ר – 200	Digamma*	F – 6	Sigma	Σ – 200
Zayin	ז – 7	Shin	ש – 300	Zeta	Z – 7	Tau	T – 300
Heth	ח – 8	Tav	ת – 400	Eta	H – 8	Upsilon	Y – 400
Teth	ט – 9	Final letters		Theta	Θ – 9	Phi	Φ – 500
Yod	י – 10	Kaph	ך – 500	Iota	I – 10	Chi	X – 600
Kaph	כ – 20	Mem	ם – 600	Kappa	K – 20	Psi	Ψ – 700
Lamed	ל – 30	Nun	ן – 700	Lambda	Λ – 30	Omega	Ω – 800
Mem	מ – 40	Pe	ף – 800	Mu	M – 40	Sampi*	ϡ – 900
Nun	נ – 50	Sade	ץ – 900	Nu	N – 50		
*Note: Digamma, Qoppa, and Sampi are archaic Greek characters used only to designate numbers, and weren't considered to be actual letters of the alphabet.						

2. This word comes from the use of small stones to teach arithmetic. Another word for pebbles, *kalkuli*, is the root of our word "calculate."

Gnosticism was one of the pagan religions that many early Christians converted from.[3] Gnostics believed they had special secret religious knowledge derived from their numerical investigations. When they joined the church, they brought those pagan methods. Justin Martyr, for example, said that since eight people were saved in the ark, this prefigured Christ's resurrection "on the eighth day."[4] This is Sunday, counting from the prior week.

Numerology was uniquely Greek, since Jews were forbidden to use divination (Deut 18:14). After Alexander the Great conquered Palestine in 332 BC, Greek became the language of commerce and law. When the Septuagint was translated, Greek became the language of the Bible. So it's not surprising that the Jews eventually picked up the practice. Philo Judaeus (ca. 30 BC–45 AD) was the first Jew known to apply gematria to interpretation of scripture. He lived in Egypt, so his Greek methods took a while to travel to Palestine. The earliest record of the rabbis using gematria is the second century AD. Jewish and Greek practices eventually combined to become the Jewish mysticism known as Qabalah.

Our first conclusion comes from this. The application of gematria to the Hebrew language in interpreting the Apocalypse is anachronistic.[5] John recorded his vision before 100 AD when gematria wasn't accepted in Judaism. Since John's readers would have been able to "hear and understand" his message, asking them to use a method of interpretation that they didn't know must be incorrect. Further, Aramaic was the language of ordinary Jews, so Hebrew would be an unlikely language for gematria when Revelation was written.

Our second conclusion is related to the first. The church fathers wrote in Greek, and the areas heavily evangelized were generally Greek speaking. In particular, the seven churches in Asia were Greek-speaking. Latin wasn't a language the church would have used frequently. This again suggests that John's intention relates to Greek, not Latin gematria. Finally, since gematria only applies to languages without separate numbering systems, modern languages such as English just don't qualify. It may be fun to play with proposed numerical equivalents to modern names, but it's

---

3. Technically, we probably should call this proto-Gnosticism, since parts of its belief system wouldn't mature until the second century AD.

4. Justin Martyr, *Dialogue with Trypho, a Jew*, chapter 138.

5. "Anachronistic" literally means "without time," and refers to the improper use of newer ideas and customs to interpret older writings.

not the right way to understand the number of the beast. We have to look in the Greek language and culture of John's day for the proper answer. And this agrees with Irenaeus that the "number of the name of the beast occurs according to the numeration *of the Greeks* be the letters in it . . ."[6]

A correct solution has to meet some other conditions. Any interpretation that focuses on geopolitical events rather than the war between God and Satan is incorrect since prophecy exists to reveal Christ (John 5:39; 13:19; 14:29, Amos 3:7). It has to be supported by substantial scriptural evidence, and can't be a coincidental match to one obvious feature. Simply picking a name or title that adds up to 666 won't cut it.

MORE BACKGROUND

A consideration of John's original audience forces us to look at other parts of John's writing. We begin with that most famous passage, John 1:1–3, 14 from the KJV.

> In the beginning was *the Word*, and *the Word* was with God, and *the Word* was God. The same was in the beginning with God. All things were made by him; and without him was not any thing made that was made . . . And *the Word* was made flesh, and dwelt among us, (and we beheld his glory, the glory as of the only begotten of the Father,) full of grace and truth.

There's a very large problem with this translation. While it's perfectly accurate, it ignores one fact. John isn't just calling Jesus the "Word." To Jews, "the Word" was a synonym for God, so they'd automatically identify Jesus as God.[7] At the same time, John's addressing Gnosticism. Gnostics believed that the highest deity was the "Logos." This Greek word means "word," giving us the translation we know so well. Unfortunately, this translation ignores John's thrust. The text reads as follows:

> In the beginning was *the Logos*, and *the Logos* was with God, and *the Logos* was God. The same was in the beginning with God. All things were made by him; and without him was not any thing made that was made . . . And *the Logos* was made flesh, and dwelt

---

6. Irenaeus, *Against Heresies*, Book 5, Chapter 30, emphasis added.

7. The rabbis translated the original Hebrew of the Old Testament into Aramaic, the common language of Jesus' day. Along the way, they added some commentary material, creating the Targumim. Many times they changed "Yahweh did . . ." into "the Word of the Lord did . . ."

among us, (and we beheld his glory, the glory as of the only begotten of the Father,) full of grace and truth.

Gnostics believed that the god of this world was really a material impostor called the Demiurge. The Logos—the true god—was a pure spirit being. He made lesser deities called "Aeons," who had some materiality. They made even lower deities until one of them made the Demiurge, who was mostly material. Therefore, when John said that the Logos was God, he attacked the fundamental Gnostic separation between the Logos and the Demiurge. He repeated this assault by saying that the Logos created the world, something the Gnostics said the Demiurge did.

John continued the attack in verse 14 where he said the Logos became a physical person and lived among men. This takes on a Gnostic belief known as "docetism" which says Jesus was an apparition without a physical body. John repeats his attack in 1 John 1:1.

> That which was from the beginning, which we have heard, which we have seen with our eyes, which we have looked upon, and our hands have handled, of the Word [Logos] of life.

The Logos and gematria were supposedly "secret" knowledge. Only the true spiritual Gnostic—*pneumatakos*—could learn it. This knowledge (Grk. "*gnosis*") gave the sect its name. Only *pneumatakoi* "knew" they were truly spirit beings created by the Logos and displaced into the material world, and only *pneumatakoi* "knew" the secrets of gematria and its associated mathematics. This conceit gave John his opportunity to present the truth of God.

In John 6, the feeding of the five thousand is a simple story that's full of spiritual lessons for everyone. But for *pneumatakoi*, it's a seismic shock. By his choice of words and details John presents a Gnostic gematria puzzle of phenomenal complexity. It includes so many secret elements of Gnostic spiritual mathematics that no Gnostic could avoid the fact that they were intended to be there.[8] The next blow comes in the story of the 153 fish in the unbroken net (John 21). Again John uses a complex gematria puzzle to present spiritual lessons.[9] He shocks the Gnostics with knowledge he isn't supposed to be able to have. Their concept of the Logos is a fraud

---

8. See Fideler, David, *Jesus Christ, Sun of God* (Wheaton, Ill: Quest, 1993), 109–119.
9. Ibid. 291–308.

and their "secret" knowledge isn't secret at all. The true God, who knows everything, has taken the foundation of Gnosticism and torn it apart.

SOLVING THE PROBLEM

Now we're ready to examine the number.

> Here is wisdom. Let him who has understanding calculate the number of the beast, for the number is that of a man; and his number is six hundred and sixty-six. (13:18)

God's about to hand down some "wisdom." Since wisdom is the proper use of knowledge, it requires knowledge (*gnosis*). Then He raises a challenge to those with "understanding." This can only be the Gnostics. He asks them to "calculate" the number. Curiously, the next thing He does is tell them what it is.

Let's get real here. There's no reason to tell anyone to calculate a number that you give them unless the act of calculation is important to them. Since the Gnostics were the only group that used calculation spiritually, this statement is pointed straight at them. They're supposed to use their secret skills to derive the number of the beast. Then God delivers His final blow. The number is 666, one of the most important of the Gnostic numerical secrets.[10]

The most obvious feature of 666 in Gnosticism is that it's the sum of the magic square of the sun, a six by six square of numbers. This square is a mystical representation of the "power" of the sun, the highest celestial deity in the Greek pantheon. Through various manipulations, the number 888 also arises from the square. This is the gematria value of ΙΗΣΟΥΣ, Greek for "Jesus." Thus, Jesus is the "Spiritual Sun" or "Solar Logos." By geometric manipulation of these two numbers, ΙΗΣΟΥΣ becomes closely related to 666 by way of 769, the value of ΠΥΘΙΟΣ, the name of Apollo at Delphi, the Greek god of harmony. Thus, Jesus becomes the Harmony of the Sun. 666 is also the gematria value of Syene (ΣΥΗΝΗ), a city on the Nile in Egypt.[11] It was on the Tropic of Cancer so that at noon on the summer solstice the sun stood directly over the city, shining directly to the bottom of wells, and cast no shadow around buildings.[12] This led to

---

10. For a more complete discussion, see Fideler (above) and Barry, Kieren, *The Greek Qabalah* (York Beach, ME: Samuel Weiser, 1999), for detail.

11. This is modern Aswan.

12. This was the key fact that allowed Eratosthenes to calculate the circumference of

the belief that Syene was a place of celestial alignment—a harmonic nodal point where the laws of heaven are reflected on earth. It was a center of sun worship.

If this hasn't driven you totally crazy, you'll see that there's a unifying theme in all these illustrations—sun worship. And since Ezekiel's imagery runs all through the Apocalypse, that's where we should look. God took the prophet on a tour of the Temple to show him the various Jewish abominations (Ezek 8). He sees idol worship (vv. 5–12) and women weeping for Tammuz (v. 14). But the greatest abomination is sun worship (vv. 16–18). In order to do this, the people have to turn their backs on the temple and God.

A few more equivalents should be considered. θεοσ ειμι επι γαινσ—"I am a god on earth"—equals 666. This is the claim of Satan when he rebelled against God (Isa 14:14). It's also the implicit claim of Satan represented by the mark of the beast. Ἡ φρεν—"the heart"—equals 666. This reminds us of, "The heart is more deceitful than all else and is desperately sick; who can understand it?" (Jer 17:9). This points us again to those who rely on themselves for wisdom. And finally, το μεγα θεριον—"the Great Beast"—equals 666!

To whom does this number apply? John says that it's "the number of a man." It's easy to take the English language and say it's a specific person as in "one man." That's why people try to find a single person or office the number fits, like Nero or the Papacy. But the indefinite article "a" doesn't have to mean "one" man.[13] We can understand John's statement better this way:

> "It is the number of man (as opposed to the number of God)."

Unlike most common interpretations, this fits John's audience. God's using 666 to represent man's knowledge in contrast with His knowledge. Those who receive the mark and number of the beast ally themselves with man. Those who have the seal of God rely on God. At the end of time, there won't be any bystanders. Everyone will be either for God or against Him. No abstentions will be allowed. Gnosticism, which relies on man's knowledge, is the prototype of antichrist because of its reliance on man, not God.

---

the earth around 240 BC.

13. If we check our grammar, the definite article "the" would do a better job of pointing to "one" man than the indefinite article.

> And He said to them, "Rightly did Isaiah prophesy of you hypocrites, as it is written, 'This people honors Me with their lips, But their heart is far away from Me. 'But in vain do they worship Me, Teaching as doctrines the precepts of men.' "Neglecting the commandment of God, you hold to the tradition of men." He was also saying to them, "You nicely set aside the commandment of God in order to keep your tradition. (Mark 7:6–9)

Men constantly try to demonstrate their own brilliance. But nothing comes close to God's truth.

> Oh, the depth of the riches both of the wisdom and knowledge of God! How unsearchable are His judgments and unfathomable His ways! (Rom 11:33)

> The wisdom of this world is foolishness before God. (1 Cor 3:19)

We need to totally rely on God. We must reject any understanding of scripture that doesn't reveal Him. God's purpose in the apocalypse is to highlight His war with Satan. A spotlight on man's self-reliance versus dependence on God clearly is part of that emphasis. But geopolitical fortune telling draws our view away from God. Revelation 13 points out that we'll all decide for or against God. By using a specific example directed at the beliefs of John's day, God shows us that being sealed saints means to be totally dependent on God's knowledge, rejecting the "knowledge" of men. Anyone who relies on himself is headed for destruction.

DOUBLE APPLICATION

We shouldn't arbitrarily exclude a secondary "double application" of 666. Interpretations like Nero don't reveal Christ because they're primarily geopolitical fortune telling. On the other hand, a person or office identified by gematria that does illuminate the cosmic controversy could constitute a legitimate second application.

We found some common threads in the gematria of John's day. Foremost of these is sun worship. While most Sunday worshipers will deny that this constitutes sun worship, the history of the change from Sabbath to Sunday shows that the application of solar imagery led to the switch. The Roman Catholic Church proudly claims it made this change on its own authority. Thus we may properly say the Roman Church matches some of the specifications of the beast. Since it's part of the beast, it's not wrong to include it in the picture of the beast.

The term "I am another God on earth" is a specific match for another of the claims of the Papacy. It not only makes this claim in nearly those exact words, it claims the authority to change divine law in its catechism. Again, this matches the beast revealed by gematria. But we should emphasize that the imagery of the beast includes man's governments over all time since Babylon, so the Papacy is only part of the picture.

666 = NERO?

A number of commentators say that the beast in Revelation 13:18 is the Roman Emperor Nero. This seems plausible at first glance, since Nero was the first Roman Emperor to severely persecute the Christian church. It's also possible that he's the one who sentenced John to exile on Patmos. But we need more than a casual similarity to the person in the apocalypse.

The identification of Nero depends on several points.[14]

1. The book of Revelation was written before the destruction of Jerusalem, during the time of Nero, who reigned from AD 54–68.

2. The first governmental persecution of the church occurred under Nero, who was an incredibly vile and contemptible man.

3. The Hebrew equivalent of "Nero Caesar" is "Nrwn Qsr" (pronounced Neron Kaiser). The Hebrew letters were nun/resh/waw/nun qoph/samek/resh (נרון קסר). When these letters are added up according to the table above, they total 666. A variant of the name, Nrw Qsr, (נרו קסר) equals 616, which is the number of the beast found in some ancient textual variants.

4. Nero was emperor of Rome, whose capital city is built on seven hills. These are supposed to be the seven mountains of Revelation 17:9.

5. The beast "was, is not, and is to come" (17:8). If Revelation was written just after the death of Nero, this could suggest that Nero "was" the beast in individual identity, but during the chaos that followed his death was no longer. But since the Roman Empire recovered soon after, the beast was reborn in corporate form.

6. The persecution by Nero lasted 42 months (13:5).

---

14. In this discussion, we'll be following the arguments presented by Kenneth L. Gentry Th.D., in his book *The Beast of Revelation* (Powder Springs, GA: American Vision, 2002).

A number of other detailed arguments have been presented, but these will be enough for us.

DATE OF WRITING

The first argument is about the date of Revelation. If the commonly accepted AD 94 date for Revelation is correct, to describe someone who had been dead for about thirty years as future would be nonsense. But there's only one clear statement that can date the book to the last decade of the first century. Gentry argues it's mistranslated, and the correct translation supports an early date. Several ancient authors explicitly date John's exile during Nero's persecution.

Next, the apocalypse seems to talk about the temple with its various courtyards as if they are presently standing (cf. Rev 11). Since the temple was destroyed in August of AD 70, this suggests an early date for the book. This is similar to a major argument for a date for Hebrews. The proposed early date of Revelation has too much support to be easily rejected.

FIRST PERSECUTION

The historical evidence is clear. Nero was the first Emperor to systematically persecute the church. When Rome burned on July 19, AD 64, Nero was accused of being behind the fire. To deflect criticism, he accused the Christians of setting the fire. In November, he embarked on one of the most depraved and cruel courses of persecution imaginable, including the famous acts of feeding Christians to lions and using them as human torches. Gentry's approach seems to fit.

GEMATRIA

Nero's name, when transliterated into Hebrew, appears to be Nrwn Qsr (נרונ קסר). The sum of the number values of those Hebrew letters is 666. But this transliteration is improper. It ignores the fact that the last nun in Nrwn would be written as a final nun (נרון קסר), giving a gematria value of 1136, not 666. It also ignores the fact that there are *three* Hebrew letters that could be used for the "s" sound—samek, sade, and sin (a form of shin). Sade and sin can increase the number to 1196 or 1376. But the book of Revelation was written in Greek to Gentiles in an era when Hebrew wasn't in common use. So conversion into Hebrew isn't in view. When John chose to bring the Hebrew language into view, he did so explicitly, as in the names "Har-Megidon" (16:16) and "Abbadon" (9:11).

Next, the ancient church father Irenaeus states, "Now since this is so, and since this number is found in all the good and ancient copies, and since those who have seen John face to face testify, and reason teaches us that the number of the name of the beast occurs according to the numeration of the Greeks be the letters in it . . ."[15] Notice that he states that the method is *according to the numeration of the Greeks*, and has the reported blessing of the author of the apocalypse. This confirms what I just said. The number is supposed to be calculated in Greek, not in Hebrew. It should also be reiterated that Jews didn't commonly use gematria until over a century later. The Greek value of Nero's name isn't 666 in any of his various titles and assumed names. Therefore, Nero isn't the beast.

Some older manuscripts have 616 as the number. The Greek of this variant is substantially different from the Greek of 666, so it doesn't seem possible that it appeared by accident. When transliterated into Hebrew, the alternate form *Nrw Qsr* (נרו קסר) has the value 616. The fact that both forms in Hebrew match ancient manuscript forms supposedly identifies Nero as the beast.

But as we noted, Hebrew transliteration isn't proper. The method must apply to the name in its native form, and no Greek form of Nero adds up to 616. The testimony of Irenaeus cited above tells us one other key fact. The oldest manuscripts in his day *did not have the alternate form*. At some point after Irenaeus, but before the oldest manuscripts we have today, someone changed the wording in the passage in his copy for unstated purposes. Because of the way that biblical manuscripts have been preserved, we now have old manuscripts with both wordings.

SEVEN HILLS/MOUNTAINS

Many commentators have accepted the idea that the seven hills of Rome are the seven mountains of 17:9. But the next verse says the mountains are "kings." Those who pay attention to that verse then go through the sequence of Roman Emperors to identify Nero as the sixth. That means that five before him have "fallen;" he is the sixth; and a seventh hasn't

---

15. Irenaeus, op cit. It's worth noting that Irenaeus is the author of the statement that Gentry re-translates to avoid the late date for Revelation.

come yet. But there were many emperors in Rome before it fell, not seven. Nero fails again.

Gentry tries to get around this problem by counting emperors up to Nero, making Galba the seventh, and the stable continuing empire under Vespasian as the eighth. But in his own book he points out that the sequence is Nero, Otho, Vitellius, and Vespasian. If the imagery means anything, Vespasian's number ten, not number eight. This again contradicts the Nero thesis.

The Bible has to be used as its own interpreter. "Mountains" in prophecy is a symbol for kingdoms, and Revelation explicitly says that's what it means here.[16] Thus, the idea of choosing a single evil person as the beast is flawed. We should be looking for kingdoms that make up the beast.

"WAS, IS NOT, AND IS TO COME"

We've talked about this earlier. The key concept for understanding 17:8 is that the beast kingdom is described by the angel at a moment *when it does not exist*. It had existed, and will exist again. For interpretive help we must look back to the book of Daniel.

The vision of the statue in Daniel 2 tells of an unbroken succession of kingdoms. Each one is followed by another. At the end of time, God's kingdom takes over and blows man's kingdoms away like dust. None of them ever come back. This vision ends when Jesus returns for His saints.

Revelation 20 tells of a thousand years *after* Jesus returns. At the end of this period, Satan will be allowed to "tempt the nations." In other words, at the second resurrection, the wicked will again populate the earth, and Satan will be their leader. Kingdoms that had gone away will come back. This is the *only* time envisioned in prophecy that conquered kingdoms are seen a second time. Since Nero is long gone, we can disregard him as a candidate for the identity of the beast.

42 MONTHS OF PERSECUTION

Nero's persecution supposedly lasted 42 months. It began in November of 64 AD and ended when he committed suicide on June 9, 68 AD. Using

---

16. See also Pss 2:6*; 30:7; 48:1; 68:15, Isa 2:2–3; 11:9*; 25:6–7; 56:7; 65:25*, Jer 51:24–25*, Ezek 20:40; 28:14, 16*, Dan 2:44; 11:45. Passages with asterixes are particularly important.

either the Julian or Gregorian calendar, this is 42 months. But by Jewish inclusive counting, it's 43 months. But even this method is faulty since it doesn't take John's Jewish calendar into account.

The Jewish luni-solar calendar is different from the Julian and Gregorian calendars. Each month started when a qualified observer saw the new moon. Since a lunar month is 29.5 days long, Nero's persecution lasted a bit over 44 lunar months. And since it didn't start or end on the first day of a month, Jewish inclusive counting would count it as 45 months. Divine prophecies are accurate. Nero is again excluded.

We've got to pursue the 42-month idea a bit further. The definition of 42 months for beastly persecution in 13:5 is an echo of the same prediction in 11:2. 11:3 restates it as 1,260 days. This exactness completely denies Nero a place in this prophecy. The period is repeated in 12:6, and it's "a time, times, and half a time" in 12:14. The Greek of this statement exactly quotes from Daniel 7:25 in the Septuagint. And this brings us to a key fact.

This 3½ year period comes from the career of the little horn of Daniel 7. That player arises among ten horns on the head of the Roman beast. If we're counting emperors, this means Nero has to be at least number eleven. Since he was number six, he's disqualified again. Three others were torn up by the roots because of the little horn (Dan 7:8, 20, 24). This again disqualifies Nero, since he didn't cause the deaths of the three preceding emperors. Finally, the proper identification of the horns in Daniel 7 is that they represent *kingdoms*, not *kings*. Nero's completely out of the picture.

TIME OF THE BOOK OF REVELATION

John says his revelation came while he was imprisoned on the Isle of Patmos (Rev 1:9). Several ancient witnesses place John on Patmos during the time Nero persecuted the church. They go on to say that the apocalypse was sent to the churches after he was released after Nero's death.

It's fairly clear that the apocalypse was intended to bring hope to the persecuted church. 13:8 puts the trials caused by the beast in John's future, since "all who dwell on the earth *will* worship" him. That raises a question. How is the book of Revelation supposed to encourage the church during the *future* persecution by "the beast/Nero" when the church didn't receive the apocalypse until *after* "the beast/Nero" was dead? This again eliminates Nero.

JOHN'S TESTIMONY

Gentry paraphrases Irenaeus. "It is not important for us to know the name of the Beast (or Antichrist), which was hidden in the number 666. Were it important, why did John not tell us? After all, he lived almost to our own era, and spoke with some men that I have known."

It's hard to overemphasize this important statement. John the Revelator didn't think it was important to tell anyone that Nero was the beast, even after Nero was long gone. This strongly suggests one of three things. Either: (1) Nero wasn't the beast, (2) John didn't know who the beast was, or (3) John didn't identify the beast as a single person.

As the recipient of the Revelation, it seems likely that John would know who or what the beast was. Of course, as we have shown, Nero wasn't the beast. John, a Hebrew steeped in Old Testament imagery, wouldn't miss the fact that the beast is a combination of man's kingdoms, based on Daniel 7. Thus, the idea that the beast is a single person doesn't work. John probably didn't think he needed to tell anyone who the beast was, since he expected them to see the same thing he did. Irenaeus reaches an incorrect conclusion about John's silence because he doesn't consider the third possibility.

SUMMARY

It may seem attractive to identify Nero as the beast. But a detailed evaluation disqualifies him at every turn. The beast is a combination of man's kingdoms beginning with Babylon. *To mega therion*, "the great beast," totals 666. And with this, God has a good laugh at "wise" man's expense.

Appendix B

The Year/Day Principle

THE YEAR FOR A day principle isn't obvious in prophecy. We can't import modern ideas into the Bible, so the year/day principle has to be a legitimate part of the original sense of scripture if we're going to use it. The fact that it was popular during the Reformation is irrelevant.[1]

> For I have assigned you a number of days corresponding to the years of their iniquity, three hundred and ninety days; thus you shall bear the iniquity of the house of Israel. When you have completed these, you shall lie down a second time, but on your right side, and bear the iniquity of the house of Judah; I have assigned it to you for forty days, a day for each year. (Ezek 4:5–6)

> According to the number of days which you spied out the land, forty days, for every day you shall bear your guilt a year, even forty years, and you shall know My opposition. (Num 14:34)

These are the only two texts that directly equate years and days in English. Let's be blunt. By itself, this is pretty flimsy. The first text changes literal years into days, and seems opposite to the idea we're evaluating. The second merely lists a literal punishment, and is difficult to stretch into a year of time for a day of prophecy.

But these aren't quite as weak as they might seem. In both cases the thought in the Hebrew is "according to the number of days . . . a day for a year." In each case the "day" is symbolic of the literal year. In Numbers, the 40 days of spying are symbolic of years of wandering, while in Ezekiel, the days of lying down are symbolic of years of literal iniquity.

---

1. The first recorded use of year/day principle was in 380 by Tychonius. It became more popular in the ninth century, and many of the Protestant Reformers used it.

There's much more to recommend the idea. Daniel and his three friends are to supposed to appear before Nebuchadnezzar after three years of training (Dan 1:5) but Daniel says it's "at the end of the days" (1:18). In 2:28 he tells Nebuchadnezzar that God is revealing what will happen "in the end of the days" (lit. Aramaic). Nebuchadnezzar was insane for seven years (Dan 4:25), but Daniel says he regained his sanity "at the end of the days" (Dan 4:34, lit. Aramaic). Nebuchadnezzar reigned for many years, but his reign was referred to as "days" in 5:11.

Gabriel tells Daniel that the vision of the ram and goat "pertains to the time of the end" (Dan 8:17). Later on, when Daniel has trouble understanding the it:

> "And the vision of the evenings and mornings which has been told is true. But keep the vision secret, for it pertains to many days in the future." (Dan 8:26)

Gabriel equates the "time of the end" with "many days" in the future. Gabriel said it this way because he knew Daniel would understand it. We'd think of it as many years in the future.

> "As for you, go your way till the end. You will rest, and then at the end of the days you will rise to receive your allotted inheritance." (Dan 12:13, NIV)

Daniel will receive his inheritance "at the end of the days," when the Messiah returns for His people.

In Daniel's chapter 10 prayer he says he was in mourning for three "weeks of days" (Dan 10:2, lit. Hebrew). The Hebrew word for "week" always means a literal seven-day week outside Daniel. The only reason Daniel would say "weeks of days" is to distinguish it from "weeks of years."

In Daniel 9 it's clear that "weeks" means "weeks of years."[2] The first "seven weeks" of Daniel 9:25 are too short to rebuild Jerusalem if they're forty-nine literal days, even though Nehemiah did repair its walls in fifty-two days (Neh 6:15). The strengthening of the covenant in Daniel 9:26 would be ludicrous if it only lasted seven days. Only a year/day understanding allows the prophecy to make sense.

The seventh-day weekly Sabbath is clearly defined in Exodus.

> . . . but the seventh day is a sabbath of the Lord your God . . . (Ex 20:10a)

---

2. "Week" is used seven times in Daniel 9.

Sabbaths also come every seven years. They're patterned after the weekly Sabbath.

> Six years you shall sow your field, and six years you shall prune your vineyard and gather in its crop, but during the seventh year the land shall have a sabbath rest, a sabbath to the Lord; you shall not sow your field nor prune your vineyard. (Lev 25:3–4)

The Jews' failure to keep land Sabbaths is one reason God sent them into captivity in Babylon.

> And those who had escaped from the sword he carried away to Babylon; and they were servants to him and to his sons until the rule of the kingdom of Persia, to fulfill the word of the Lord by the mouth of Jeremiah, until the land had enjoyed its sabbaths. All the days of its desolation it kept sabbath until seventy years were complete. (2 Chron 36:20–21)

Other Old Testament writers use the same kind of year/day equivalence. Exodus 13:10 says that the Passover will be kept "from days to days" (lit. Hebrew). The same word for "day" is used many times in a similar annual context. First Samuel 1:21 literally calls a yearly sacrifice a "daily" sacrifice. First Samuel 2:19 tells how Samuel's mother brought him a coat each year—"from days to days." This happens again in Judges 11:40.

First Samuel 27:7 uses "days and four months" (lit. Hebrew) to specify a span of a year and four months. Numbers 9:22 uses "two days, or a month, or days" to mean "two days, or a month, or a year." First Kings 1:1 is commonly translated that King David was "advanced in years" (NIV), but literally says that he was "advanced in the days."

This thought pattern seems to have its origin in the genealogy of Genesis 5. There we repeatedly see the statement that "the days of (x) were (y) years." Clearly, days and years were in many ways interchangeable in the Hebrew mind. We need to put ourselves in their shoes when we read prophecy. Fortunately, we have the opportunity to do just that.

The Book of Jubilees is a non-canonical work written around the time of the Maccabees in the second century BC. It describes Noah's age at his death as "19 jubilees, 2 weeks and 5 years." A jubilee is 49 years, so the total would be 936 years and 2 weeks if we take it literalistically. But we know that Noah was 950 years old when he died (Gen 9:29). If the 2 weeks are "weeks of years" then we get the correct total. Clearly, the Jews used the year/day principle.

In classical prophecy, very specific time spans are given and fulfilled. Man's wickedness was limited to 120 years before the flood (Gen 6:3). Abraham's descendents would be oppressed in Egypt for 400 years (Gen 15:13). The Babylonian captivity would last 70 years (Jer 25:11). Every time, the prophecy and fulfillment are quite explicit.

Apocalyptic prophecy is different. It focuses on the time of the end and uses symbolic language that describes various players non-literally. It uses non-standard terms for time. Daniel 7:25 and 12:7 talk about "a time, two times, and a dividing of time." Daniel 8:14 uses 2,300 "evening/morning." Daniel 9:24 identifies "seventy weeks." These prophetic time periods are not the normal way that literal time would be expressed. Not one of them uses the normal word for "year." The players in the prophecies are symbolic, and consistency requires that the times in symbolic prophecy are symbolic, too.

In Revelation, there's a 10-day period of tribulation (Rev 2:10) and a 3½ day period (Rev 11:9, 11). Taking these as literal borders on lunacy. Why would God bother telling us about such short periods in a prophecy that has the entire sweep of human history in view? It just doesn't fit. Revelation 11:2 and 13:5 tell about "forty two months," which 11:3 converts to "1,260 days," both of which are the same "time, times, and a dividing of time" Revelation 12:14 quotes from Daniel 7:25 and 12:7.[3]

Apocalyptic prophecy shows the war between God and Satan. The various stages of the battle take a long time to play out. A literalistic understanding of the time periods just isn't long enough for the players to fulfill their roles. A larger, symbolic understanding is required.

How long are the time periods? They can generally be translated into days, months, and years. Taken literalistically, they don't make much sense. But if we take the Hebrew year/day thought pattern into account, we can see a year of literal time in place of a day of prophetic time. When we do this, we have time periods that are consistent with the apocalyptic perspective.

Why would God use this roundabout way of describing time? While the symbolic language matches the style of the prophecy, it can also include additional meaning. Daniel's 8:14's use of "evening/morning" calls into view the morning and evening sacrifices and draws attention to the Temple. His use of "weeks" in 9:24 reminds us about the weekly Sabbath,

---

3. Revelation 12:14 is an exact quotation of the LXX of Daniel 12:7.

and reminds the readers that the 70 years of exile was due to failure to keep the covenant with its weekly and annual Sabbaths. The "seven weeks" in 9:25 recalls the Jubilee, which came every "seven weeks of years" (Lev 25:8–10).

In short, the year/day principle is a basic Hebrew thought pattern. It was impressed on them repeatedly by the sabbatical and Jubilee cycles. We see it in multiple ordinary uses throughout the Old Testament. Far from being a modern invention, it is a natural part of biblical history, and its application to apocalyptic prophecy is also natural.

Appendix C

The Structure of the Book of Revelation

MOST THEOLOGIANS DIVIDE THE book of Revelation into two parts: the epistle in the first three chapters and the apocalypse in chapters 4–22. Beyond that, all that remains is disagreement. In this book I've presented my view of how the Apocalypse is organized. Because I've presented the schema piecemeal, I'll lay out the structure here with minimal commentary. The most basic divisions are:

- Prolog
- Epistle
- Apocalypse
- Epilog

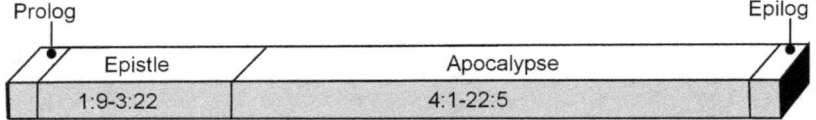

As with most epistles in the New Testament, it begins and ends with an apostolic prolog and epilog. These book-end the message.

Our first interpretive key is the voice like a trumpet. This brings God's voice at Sinai to view, and tells us that the covenant is the subject. The epistle is straightforward, with an introduction in the temple and seven letters to seven churches. Since all follow formal covenant structure, the epistle is the *Covenant Described*.

The difficulty comes when we get to the Apocalypse proper. But again, the voice like a trumpet tells us the subject is covenant, and the literary form tells us this is the *Covenant Displayed*.

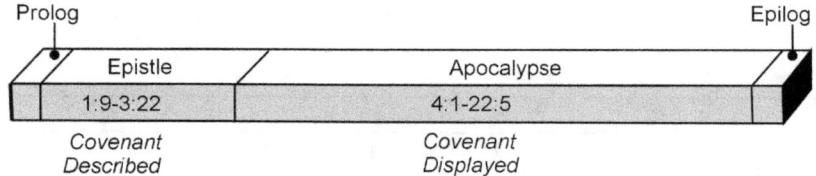

The *Covenant Displayed* follows a conventional chiastic pattern.

A: Inauguration of the Worthy King
  B: Covenant in this age
  B': Covenant in the millennium
A': Consummation of the Worthy King

If we note that the Day of Atonement ends this age, then logically we may present the chiasm as:

A: Inauguration of the Worthy King
  B: Covenant in this age
    C: Day of Atonement
  B': Covenant in the millennium
A': Consummation of the Worthy King

This makes Atonement the focal center of the apocalypse.

The story of covenant is built around the typological application of the temple services and festival calendars. Thus, the temple appears frequently, and the calendar provides structure.

Jesus antitypically fulfilled the spring festivals in His first advent. He died as our Passover (1 Cor 5:7), rose as First Fruits from the dead (1 Cor 15:20), and brought in the spring harvest of souls at Pentecost (Acts 2:41). Passover and Pentecost are part of the throne room scene in 5:6.

SPRING FESTIVALS		
CALENDAR TYPE	HISTORICAL FULFILLMENT	REVELATION ECHO
Passover—Lev 23:5	The Cross—1 Cor 5:7	Throne Room—Rev 5:6
First fruits—Lev 23:10	The Resurrection—1 Cor 15:20	Throne Room—Rev 5:9
Pentecost—Lev 23:15	Pentecost—Acts 2	Throne Room—Rev 5:6

The fall festivals are fulfilled in Christ's second advent. The Feast of Trumpets is the warning of judgment, fulfilled in the seven Trumpets. It leads to the Day of Atonement when God's people are cleansed. This closes the story of this sinful era, and includes the Day of the Lord, where the wicked are destroyed. Finally, the Feast of Booths completes the story as the New Jerusalem fulfills the imagery of the *Shemini Atzeret* after the millennial age.

FALL FESTIVALS		
CALENDAR TYPE	HISTORICAL FULFILLMENT	REVELATION FULFILLMENT
Trumpets—Lev 23:24	None	Seven Trumpets
Atonement—Lev 23:27	None	7th Seal, Trumpet, and all Bowls
Booths—Lev 23:34	None	Rev 7:15; 17:14; 19:15; 20:9
Shemini Atzeret—Lev 23:36	None	New Jerusalem

Typical of apocalypses, Revelation has a number of recapitulations. This prevents a linear understanding of the book. Further, it's organized thematically, presenting even more difficulty for a chronological schema.

- Seven Seals—The call of grace.
- Seven Trumpets—Warning of judgment to come
- Seven Bowls—Judgment in the great Day of the Lord

The seven Seals present the call of grace in theme, but not in linear array. They are recapped by the 144,000/Sealing of the Saints.

The Seven Seals

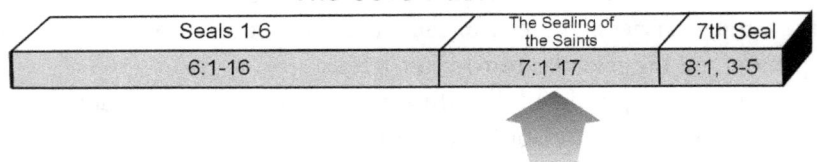

Recapitulation

The trumpets do the same, but with two recapitulations—the Strong Angel/Seven Thunders and the Measuring of the Temple/Two Witnesses.

The Seven Trumpets

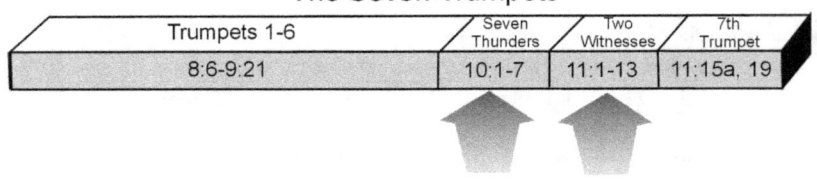

Recap 1   Recap 2

Finally, the Bowls have a recap—Armageddon.

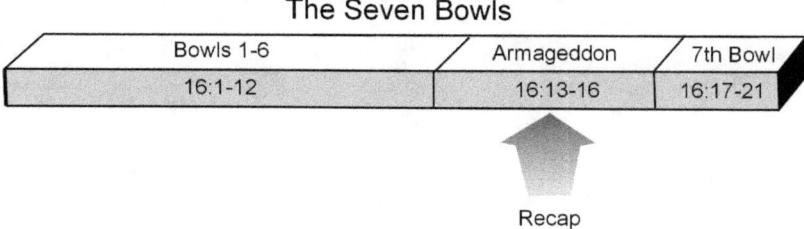

This pattern continues when we consider the three series as a single large series. There's a recap between the Trumpets and Bowls known as the Controversy Over Worship. It recaps all three series. Then, within that recap is another—the Three Angels' Messages. They again recap the Seals, Trumpets, and Bowls.

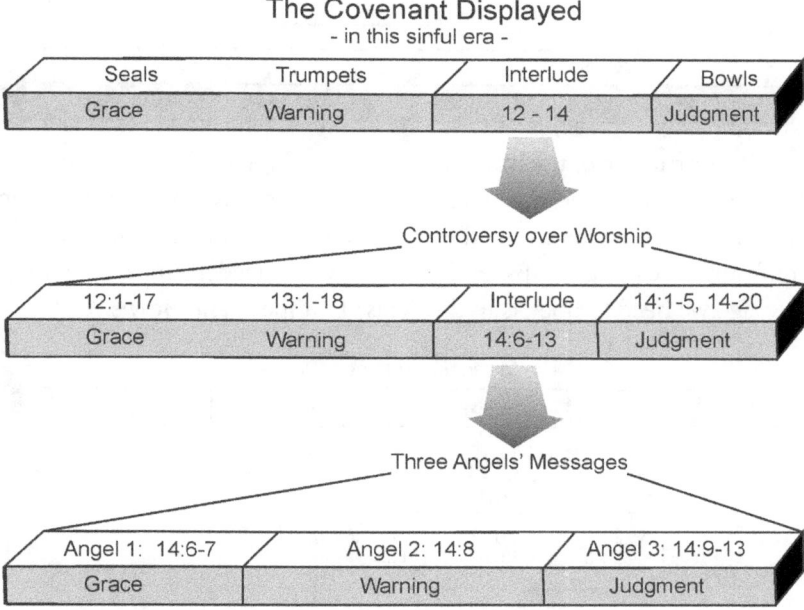

The structural connections between the Seals, Trumpets, and Bowls wrap up this part of the book. The seventh Seal is 8:1–5. Inside this scene (v. 2) is a "look-ahead." It's a brief note that the Trumpets are coming. In the seventh Trumpet, we see another look-ahead in 11:15b–18. This points us to the reward of the saints in the Atonement and the Day of the Lord in the Bowls. But in the seventh Bowl, there's no look-ahead. This tells us that the story of covenant in this sinful era ends with the Bowls.

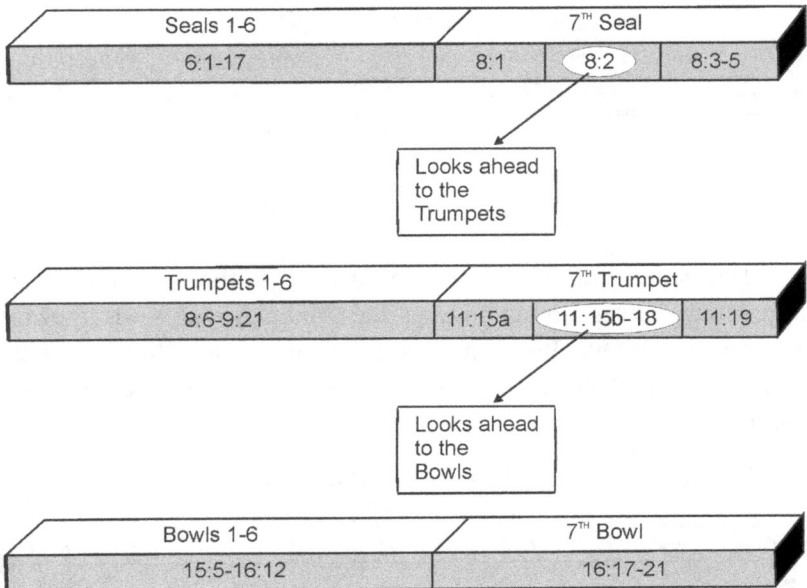

The structure of the millennial chapters is relatively straightforward. There are again three major elements separated by an interlude. Each presents a distinct focus on the purpose of the millennium. But there aren't any cascading recaps. Perhaps they aren't needed since the primary message we need to obey is in the Seals, Trumpets, and Bowls.

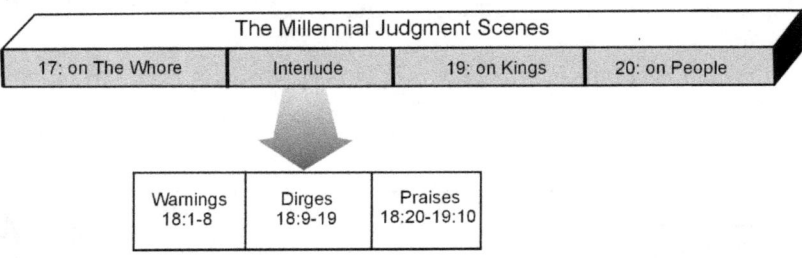

Finally, chapters 21–22 present the consummation of the Worthy King. This matches the introductory inauguration segment to complete the chiasm.

The Covenant Displayed			
Inauguration	Covenant in This Age	Covenant in the Millennium	Consummation
4-5	6-16	17-20	21-22

One academic item deserves a bit of attention. There has been a bit of debate about how many visions are in the book. Some insist there are seven, since seven is the number of perfection and appears a *lot* in it. But there are actually four. Alan Bandy points out that there's a key that identifies when a new vision starts—"in the Spirit." Each time a vision starts we see that phrase, and each time one ends there's a short "I will show you" segment that segues into the next vision.

VISION MARKERS	
"I WILL SHOW YOU"	"IN THE SPIRIT"
(none)	1:10—Seven Churches vision
4:1	4:2 —Covenant in this Age
17:1–2	17:3—Covenant in the Millennium
21:9	21:10—The New Jerusalem

I must make one final observation. In my studies, I haven't seen any author give a coherent explanation of *why* the Apocalypse is arranged the way it is. Many present lengthy discussions of some segment or other, but none have tackled the entire assembled book.[1] I believe that only through understanding this structure can the message truly come through.

I didn't set out to break new ground. But as I "put on my yarmulke" so that I began to think like an ancient Jew, a number of things became clear. I started asking, "Why?"[2] I couldn't be content just to ask, "What does this or that mean?"

I believe that the book is designed to present a repeated message: "Come out of her, my people!" It does it from so many angles that at least one will resonate with anyone willing to listen. Unfortunately, because so many fail to put on their yarmulke, confusion rules the day.

This book won't be the final word. As always, we build on the work of others. There's always more to learn. And our wonderful God wants us to know Him. Revelation is designed to help us see part of who He is.

---

1. Please don't take this as saying that none have proposed structures for the book. Several have proposed chiasms for the entire Apocalypse. But none I have found have tackled *why* the book should be arranged this way. They merely propose *what* they think they see.

2. As Athol Dickson notes in *The Gospel According to Moses: What My Jewish Friends Taught Me About Jesus* "Asking is not doubting. It is trusting." (Grand Rapids: Brazos, 2003), 19.

Appendix D

The Fate of the Wicked[1]

> "When I use a word," Humpty Dumpty said, in rather a scornful tone,
> it means just what I choose it to mean—neither more nor less."
> "The question is," said Alice, "whether you can make words
> mean so many different things." "The question is," said Humpty Dumpty,
> "which is to be master—that's all."
>
> –LEWIS CARROLL,
> THROUGH THE LOOKING GLASS

EVANGELICALS HAVE LONG PRIDED themselves on basing their beliefs on Scripture alone. In fact, however, we may argue *sola scriptura* when disproving the unbiblical beliefs of other denominations, yet when it comes to our own dearly held views, we are not above ignoring biblical evidence that contradicts us. Should Evangelicals ever argue from tradition rather than Scripture, though? Should Evangelicals base their teachings on ambiguous texts viewed by the light of traditional understandings, while ignoring clear texts that point to the opposite conclusion? Who among us would say yes?

It seems to me that like Humpty Dumpty, those arguing for the eternal torment of the wicked often assign arbitrary and contradictory meanings to words already perfectly clear in English, Hebrew, and

---

1. This appendix was written by Ed Christian, Assistant Professor of English & Bible, Kutztown University of Pennsylvania. This is, essentially, the text of the overhead transparencies used in a talk he gave on this topic at the 2001 annual meeting of the Evangelical Theological Society, held in Colorado Springs. It was originally published in *JATS*, 12:1 (Autumn 2001) 219–24. Copyright © 2001 by Ed Christian; used with permission.

Greek—words like "destroy," "consume," "dead," and "devoured."[2] It is true that these words, as used in Scripture, may refer to several areas of experience, and it is also true that they are often used metaphorically. However, *when metaphors are used, they always allude to the established meanings of words, not to their opposites.*

What follows is not a formal paper, but a collection of texts with a few words of commentary. My hope is that they will spark thought, discussion, and study.

WHAT DOES "ETERNAL" MEAN?

ETERNAL JUDGMENT *(krímatos aiōníou)*

Hebrews 6:2 "of the doctrine of baptisms, of laying on of hands, of resurrection of the dead, and of eternal judgment." [The period of judging or judgment is limited in duration, but the verdict will never be reversed, so the judgment is eternal.]

ETERNAL REDEMPTION *(aiōnían lútrōsin)*

Hebrews 9:12 "Not with the blood of goats and calves, but with His own blood He entered the Most Holy Place once for all having obtained eternal redemption." [Jesus redeemed us "once for all," but the effect of that redemption is eternal.]

ETERNAL SALVATION *(sōtērias aiōníou)*

Hebrews 5:9 "And having been perfected, He became the author of eternal salvation to all who obey Him." [Jesus saved us by a "once for all" act, called salvation, but the effect of that salvation is eternal.]

ETERNAL SIN *(aiōníou hamartēmatos)*

Mark 3:29 "but He who blasphemes against the Holy Spirit will never be forgiven, but is guilty of an eternal sin." [The sin occurs during a finite lifetime, but its effect is eternal.]

---

2. Rather than give instances that cause embarrassment to scholars, I will leave it to readers to consider what they've read and remember such instances. There have been many.

ETERNAL DESTRUCTION *(ólethron aiōníon)*

2 Thessalonians 1:9 "These shall be punished with everlasting destruction from the presence of the Lord and from the glory of His power." [Destroyed once, but the effect of that destruction is eternal.]

ETERNAL PUNISHMENT *(kólasin aiōníon / zōèn aiōníon)*

Matthew 25:46 "And these will go away into everlasting punishment, but the righteous into everlasting life." [Resurrection to life happens "in a twinkling of an eye," but the effect is eternal. Execution is an event completed only by death, and it has not occurred unless death results, but it is an eternal punishment because it is irreversible.]

ETERNAL FIRE *(puròs aiōníou)*

Jude 7 "as Sodom and Gomorrah, and the cities around them in a similar manner to these, having given themselves over to sexual immorality and gone after strange flesh, are set forth as an example [*deigma*, a specimen], suffering the vengeance of eternal fire." [The clear statement here is that Sodom and Gomorrah were destroyed by "eternal fire," yet that fire is not still burning. The effect of the fire is permanent, but the fire burned until the fuel was consumed, then went out. Genesis 19:24–29 tells us the cities were "destroyed," and 2 Peter 2:6 tells us they were turned to "ashes." We may think we know what Jesus means by "eternal fire" in Matthew 18:8 and 25:41, but the Bible provides its own answer.][3]

WHAT DO THE "WORMS AND UNQUENCHABLE FIRE" VERSES MEAN?

MARK 9:44, 46, 48

"Their worm does not die, and the fire is not quenched." Jesus is quoting Isaiah 66:24 "And they shall go forth and look upon the corpses [*peger*:

---

3. The word most frequently used with "eternal" is of course "life." It begins at the resurrection (1 Cor 15:42–43). The resurrection to life is a single event with eternal effects the Bible calls "eternal life." Similarly, "eternal destruction" is a single event with eternal effects the Bible calls "death" (Rom 6:23). "Eternal life" is lived in the presence of the "eternal glory" of the "eternal God" and the "eternal Spirit" because of God's "eternal purpose." It is interesting that when it refers to God, "eternal" has no implied beginning or end, but "eternal life" begins when we begin sharing in God's own eternality, so for us it is eternal in only one direction. Similarly, the "eternal covenant" was not always in place. Sometimes an "eternal" event has a clear beginning and end, with only the effect being eternal.

corpse/carcass] of the men who have transgressed against Me. For their worm does not die, and their fire is not quenched. They shall be an abhorrence to all flesh." [The correct understanding of Jesus' meaning must take into account the following points: 1) One is not a corpse until one is dead; 2) Maggots eat only dead flesh, but fire kills maggots; 3) Thus, this is a mixed metaphor, and literal fulfillment is impossible; 4) But, the metaphors point to an irreversible process of destruction following death.]

Ezekiel 20:47–48

"And say to the forest of the South, 'Hear the word of the LORD! Thus says the Lord GOD: 'Behold, I will kindle a fire in you, and it shall devour every green tree and every dry tree in you; the blazing flame shall not be quenched, and all faces from the south to the north shall be scorched by it. All flesh shall see that I, the LORD, have kindled it; it shall not be quenched.'" [This metaphorical language refers to the destruction of Jerusalem and Judah, using the image of "unquenchable fire" not to suggest an eternal process, but a process unstoppable until its end is reached.]

WHAT DOES IT MEAN TO "DIE"?

Genesis 7:21–23

"And all flesh died [*apéthane*] that moved on the earth: . . ."

John 11:26

"And whoever lives and believes in Me shall never die [*apothánē*]. Do you believe this?" [Logically, thus, those who do not believe will die at some time, becoming like those who died in the Flood. If they die, they are dead, and if they are dead, they are not alive, and if they are not alive, they cannot experience eternal torment. Death does not mean life.]

WHAT DOES "DEVOURED" MEAN?

2 Kings 1:12

"And fire of God came down from heaven and consumed [*wattōkal*[4]/ *katéphagen*] him and his fifty." [*kai katébē pûr èk toû oùranoû kai katéphagen aùtòn*]

---

4. From ʾākal, to "eat up" or "consume."

REVELATION 20:9

"They went up on the breadth of the earth and surrounded the camp of the saints and the beloved city. And fire came down from God out of heaven and devoured [*katéphagen*] them." [*kai katébē pûr èk toû oùranoû kai katéphagen aùtoús*] [If in Elijah's day God literally kills the wicked with fire from heaven, and if John then quotes this phrase exactly to indicate what he has seen in vision about the fate of the wicked, how can we say they will not be devoured to death?]

ISAIAH 24:6

"Therefore the curse has devoured [*édetai*, eaten] the earth, and those who dwell in it are desolate. Therefore the inhabitants of the earth are burned, and few men are left."

ISAIAH 26:11

". . . Yes, the fire of Your enemies [*hupenantíous*] shall devour [*édetai*, eat] them."

HEBREWS 10:27

". . . but a certain fearful expectation of judgment, and fiery indignation which will devour [*esthíein*, eat up] the adversaries [*hupenantíous*]." [What has been devoured or eaten up exists no longer. What has been devoured by fire can no longer be alive. *Esthiō* [and *edō* usually refer to eating food, and they are often used metaphorically, but they are not metaphors of something never eaten but remaining eternally uneaten, though eternally chewed.]

WHAT DOES "PERISH" OR "DESTROYED" MEAN?

MATTHEW 22:7

"But when the king heard about it, he was furious. And he sent out his armies, destroyed [*apōlesen*] those murderers, and burned up their city." [Jesus is not revealing that the murderers were tortured forever, but that they were killed. This is the primary meaning of the word.]

Appendix D

MATTHEW 26:52

"But Jesus said to him, 'Put your sword in its place, for all who take the sword will perish [*apolountai*] by the sword.'" ["Perish" here means death, not some never-ending flaying with a sword throughout eternity.]

LUKE 11:51

"from the blood of Abel to the blood of Zechariah who perished [*apoloménou*] between the altar and the temple. Yes, I say to you, it shall be required of this generation." [Was Zechariah still perishing in Jesus' day, or had he completed the process implied by the word and perished, as the text says?]

LUKE 13:3, 5

"I tell you, no; but unless you repent you will all likewise perish [*apoleísthe*]." [If the process of perishing cannot be completed, then Jesus is wrong about this.]

JOHN 3:16

"For God so loved the world that He gave His only begotten Son, that whoever believes in Him should not perish [*apólētai*] but have everlasting life." [If those who believe do not perish, then those who do not believe logically must perish. But if the wicked suffer everlasting torment in Hell, then they don't perish, and they also receive everlasting life. Thus, both the righteous and the wicked receive everlasting life—the difference is only in the nature of that life. If this were so, then Jesus would be wrong here.]

2 PETER 3:6

"by which the world that then existed perished [*apōleto*], being flooded with water." [That world died, along with the people in it, except for Noah and family.]

2 PETER 3:9

"The Lord is not slack concerning His promise, as some count slackness, but is longsuffering toward us, not willing that any should perish [*apolésthai*] but that all should come to repentance." [Those do not repent perish. If they cannot die, they cannot perish.]

Romans 6:23

"For the wages of sin is death [*thanatos*], but the free gift of God is eternal life in Christ Jesus our Lord." [The wages are not eternal suffering, but death. If we are not Humpty Dumpty, then death means death, not life.]

Luke 17:29

"but on the day that Lot went out of Sodom it rained fire and brimstone from heaven and destroyed [*apōlesen*] them all."

Matthew 10:29

"And do not fear those who kill the body but cannot kill the soul. But rather fear Him who is able to destroy [*apolésai*] both soul and body in hell." [If they live on in eternal torment, they have not been destroyed.]

HOW LONG DOES "STUBBLE" BURN?

Exodus 15:7 [Against Egypt]

"You sent forth Your wrath; It consumed them like stubble."

Obadiah 16, 18 [Against Edom]

"'And they shall be as though they had never been. . . . The house of Jacob shall be a fire, and the house of Joseph a flame; but the house of Esau shall be stubble; they [Jacob and Joseph] shall kindle them and devour them, and no survivor shall remain of the house of Esau,' for the LORD has spoken." [This is metaphorical, but it points to a process leading to swift and certain death. It points not to a never-ending process, but to a process that will reach a completion.]

Isaiah 47:14 [Against Babylon]

"Behold, they shall be as stubble, the fire shall burn them." [Experience shows us that stubble does not burn forever, but once burned, it cannot be restored, so the effect is permanent. The usage here is metaphorical.]

Nahum 1:9–10 [Day of the Lord]

"Affliction will not rise up a second time. For while tangled like thorns, and while drunken like drunkards, they shall be devoured like stubble fully dried." [Whether metaphorical or literal, the fire burns quickly. Note that the Old Testament prophets do not distinguish, in their "Day of the Lord" language, between the death of the wicked at Christ's coming, as seen in Revelation, and the punishment of the wicked in Rev 20. They know only the latter, and they see the burning as swift, with the effect permanent.]

WHAT ARE "ASHES"?

Malachi 4:1, 3 [Day of the Lord]

"'For behold, the day is coming, Burning like an oven, And all the proud, yes, all who do wickedly will be stubble. And the day which is coming shall burn them up," Says the LORD of hosts, "'That will leave them neither root nor branch. . . . You shall trample the wicked, for they shall be ashes under the soles of your feet on the day that I do this,' Says the LORD of hosts." [If the wicked burn in eternal conscious torment for all time, they cannot be ashes under the soles of the feet of the righteous at any time, much less "on the day" their burning begins. Even if the language is metaphorical, the metaphor points to death, not to eternal life apart from God.]

Ezekiel 28:18-19

"By the multitude of your iniquities, in the unrighteousness of your trade you profaned your sanctuaries. Therefore I have brought fire from the midst of you; it has consumed you, and I have turned you to ashes on the earth in the eyes of all who see you. All who know you among the peoples are appalled at you; you have become terrified and you will cease to be forever." [Some think this is speaking covertly of Satan. Whoever it may be speaking of, to "cease to be forever" cannot mean to be forever, even metaphorically. One cannot be "ashes" until one has "ceased to be." Ashes, formed during combustion, are what is left after something has been burned up.]

WHAT DOES "SLAY" MEAN?

Isa 65:15 [Day of the Lord]

"For the Lord GOD will slay you."

Isa 66:15–16 [Day of the Lord]

"For behold, the LORD will come with fire and with His chariots, like a whirlwind, to render His anger with fury, and His rebuke with flames of fire. For by fire and by His sword the LORD will judge all flesh; and the slain of the LORD shall be many."

Isa 66:24

"And they shall go forth and look upon the corpses of the men who have transgressed against Me. For their worm does not die, and their fire is not quenched. They shall be an abhorrence to all flesh." [One is not slain until one is no longer alive. If the wicked have been slain by the fire of God, they cannot still be alive. They are corpses. To say that "slain" here does not really mean "slain" but "not slain" is again to imitate Humpty Dumpty.]

WHAT DOES "END" MEAN?

Zephaniah 1:18 [Day of the Lord]

"Neither their silver nor their gold shall be able to deliver them in the day of the LORD's wrath; but the whole land shall be devoured by the fire of His jealousy, for He will make speedy riddance [NIV, "a sudden end"] of all those who dwell in the land."

Matthew 13:40

"As the weeds are pulled up and burned in the fire, so it will be at the end of the age." [There can be no "sudden end" of people who suffer eternal conscious torment for all eternity. Either the doctrine is wrong, or the Bible is wrong.]

Any fair discussion of the fate of the wicked should include these verses. Base your beliefs on the entire biblical witness, not a few proof texts. Establish the meaning of seemingly clear words by seeing how they are used elsewhere in Scripture. Do not twist the meanings of words so they fit beliefs. Let what is clear explain what is ambiguous. These are basic rules of sound interpretation, but they have been ignored too often in discussions of this topic.

www.ingramcontent.com/pod-product-compliance
Lightning Source LLC
Chambersburg PA
CBHW062027220426
43662CB00010B/1499